Contractor's Growth & Profit Guide

by

Michael C. Thomsett

Craftsman Book Company
6058 Corte del Cedro, Carlsbad, CA 92009

Library of Congress Cataloging-in-Publication Data

Thomsett, Michael C.
    Contractor's growth & profit guide / by Michael C. Thomsett.
        p.   cm.
    Includes index.
    ISBN 0-934041-34-2 :
    1. Construction industry—Management.   2. Contractors.   I. Title.
    II. Title: Contractor's growth & profit guide.
    HD9715.A2T495 1988
    692′.8′068—dc19   88-11078
                                                                    CIP

CONTENTS

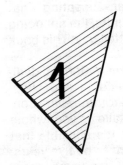

REASONS FOR PLANNING

Construction companies don't grow bigger and more profitable by accident — at least the construction companies I know about didn't. Construction is both a competitive and cyclical business. To make good money as a contractor, year after year, you've got to be very good at doing something that owners need and are willing to pay for. That doesn't happen by itself. Many builders never learn to do it. They're left to pick up the crumbs on the table, the work other, more profitable builders pass up, the small jobs that have more headaches than they're worth, the odds and ends that don't need special skills and yield slim profits at best.

If you're not content with work like that, keep reading. This book will explain how successful builders accumulate the skills, assets and knowledge needed to develop a prosperous, thriving construction business. I'm going to emphasize planning because your career and your future are too important to be left to chance. Anyone can go bumping along day after day, doing what needs to be done and barely getting by most of the time. Many builders are content to do that. And if you're content to drift with the current, year after year, accepting what comes your way until you're ready to call it quits, I'm not going to convince you otherwise. But there *is* a better way. This book will explain it.

Bidding jobs, hiring and firing, coordinating materials, dealing with owners, architects, inspectors, lenders and subs, handling problems, selling more work — the routine every construction contractor has to deal with — can take up your whole day . . . day after day and week after week. It's possible that you'll never take time to plan where you want to be five years, ten years or twenty years from now. Even if you know where you're going, do you know what skills, equipment, knowledge and financing will be required to get there? Where are you going to get the assets and abilities needed to handle the type of work you want?

The direction and prospects for your business aren't going to change very much without some type of plan. It may be as informal as a few notes on a scratch pad. Or it may be a fifty-page document in an engraved binder. Both can be valid plans. The thought that goes into a growth plan and what it says is more important than the quality of the paper it's printed on.

If you've never done any business planning before, don't be concerned. It's easy. I'll explain it step by step.

I'll admit that you could hire a consultant to prepare your plan — and spend hundreds or even thousands of dollars a day in consultant's fees. If you need the names of consultants who do work like this, write to me at the publisher's address.

But for most small construction companies, spending thousands of dollars on a business plan is foolish. It isn't needed. You've got better things to do with your money. And maybe, after spending thousands on consultants' fees, you wouldn't end up with a plan that did any good. I know a construction contractor who has a beautifully bound, detailed business plan. But the plan's gathering dust on a shelf — unused and forgotten except for the bitter remembrance of what it cost.

Even the best plan is a waste of time and money if it's never implemented. And it won't be unless you agree with it, understand what it requires, and are ready to make the changes that are necessary. That's why I believe that doing your own growth plan is better than hiring someone to do it for you. You're much more likely to follow your own recommendations than those of others, no matter how high their fees. And besides, you know your business and take a deeper interest in it than any hired consultant ever could.

Of course, drawing up a growth plan for a construction company isn't child's play. It isn't taught in high school. You've probably never done one before. That's why I'm going to start from the beginning and take it a step at a time.

Most business plans are directed at building sales volume. But that isn't always the only objective. Maybe you're satisfied with the current level of business but would like the company to be more profitable. Maybe profits and volume are satisfactory. What you really want is more time to go fishing. Even that's a valid reason to do some planning and make some changes. Whatever your reason, if you don't have a plan or aren't carrying out the plan you have, it's pretty unlikely that anything is going to change for the better — either now or in the future.

If you think a growth plan is a technical accounting report with a lot of big words, financial reports, earning forecasts, and complicated graphs, think again. A plan can be simple and to the point. In fact, it should be. The less complicated, the better. It's entirely possible to prepare a good, complete plan for a construction company in less than twenty pages. If you think that real growth plans have to be a hundred pages long and be written in language that only an accountant or lawyer could appreciate, stop reading. You'd do better hiring a Harvard MBA to prepare your growth plan.

Remember that the major reason for developing a growth plan is to help yourself. It's your blueprint for the future. It provides a goal and a schedule for getting there. It should be a flexible plan to accommodate the changes that are inevitable. As long as you're in charge of the plan, you'll have no problem adjusting it as goals change.

This book will guide you in creating a growth plan that you can use every day to improve profits and reach your goals. It covers everything you need to know, from how to analyze goals, to creating your own graphs and charts. There are case histories and examples to help you, including a complete growth plan, and a budget that you can use as a guideline for your own operation.

PLANNING GIVES YOU DIRECTION

When you started contracting on your own, you had a good idea of what you expected to accomplish. You took a risk in leaving the security of working for wages. You thought the potential rewards outweighed the risks. But are you getting what you wanted? Many construction contractors in their first year or two on their own will admit that they're working longer hours and earning less than they expected. If the rewards aren't as good as you hoped, a little growth planning could make a big difference in your future. With a plan, you can actually create profits where there weren't any before. But that's only part of the reason to plan ahead. Planning gives you control of your future. How? It forces you to take a good look at your operation, to analyze your goals, your capabilities and your markets. Then you make changes to find the opportunities that are available to every contractor in every community.

It's not unusual for contractors to take on work that they don't really want just to keep money coming in and crews busy. You've probably done it yourself. You get caught in a trap. The work begins to control you instead of you controlling the work. You end up with projects you should have skipped and making less money than if you had been working for someone else.

Having a plan gives you a road map of where you're going and a picture of how you're going to get there. Day by day you can check your progress, see when you're off track and take steps to get back on schedule. It gives everyone in your company the feeling that they're part of a well-managed, professional organization that's going somewhere — the type of company they should stake their future on.

CONTROLLING YOUR OPERATION

One of the first and most important steps in implementing a business plan will probably be controlling your operating expenses. That's no easy task. Expenses are hard to control. Overhead depends on the jobs you do and your volume of work. When work load goes up, overhead will probably go up with it. When jobs are scarce, it may be hard to shrink overhead as fast as volume drops, especially if you've borrowed money. Still, there are ways to anticipate most costs and control many expenses.

Here are some of the ways to control costs:

- Prepare and review cost and expense budgets.

- Make corrections when you find that an expense is running over budget.

- Break your expenses down into convenient units and identify what can be done to control each.

- Set a minimum profit that you will accept on each job, and then make sure that the jobs you bid meet that standard.

The Planning Cycle

The next step in controlling your operation is to set up basic operating standards. This is the core of your plan, the focus for your direction. There are three main elements of what I call the *planning cycle*: definition, time, and control.

9

Definition— The first element of any plan is to specify, or clearly define, what you want to achieve. This might mean setting a minimum profit per job, working toward a higher profit margin than you're earning now, expanding your operations, or reducing your general expenses.

Defining specific goals is the heart of business planning. When you define what you really want and expect, then you can analyze what changes are needed to reach those goals. This requires flexibility. Your business is always changing. You may have to adjust your operations or redefine your goals to suit those changing conditions.

Time— Set time limits for yourself. Knowing what you want in the future is the first step in planning. But knowing **what** is only part of a plan. The rest is **when** you expect to achieve the goal.

For example, you may want to improve your profit margin from 5 to 8 percent. You decide that by concentrating on more profitable types of jobs and reducing some of your variable expenses, you can do this within one year. If you plan and track your progress through the first three months, you should begin to see the results. But without specific time limits, you're less likely to begin today what has to be done tomorrow.

Control— With definitions and time limits, you have the seed of a successful plan. But you'll only see those profits grow and blossom if you're able to maintain control.

This means reviewing your progress, through budget comparisons, monitoring job costs, watching profits, and reducing expenses. The benefits come from making changes according to plan, not from the plan itself.

The planning cycle is summarized in Figure 1-1.

the planning cycle

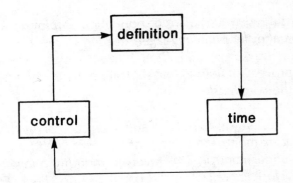

Figure 1-1

_____ **CASE HISTORY** _____

White and Adams Construction is a partnership. The firm specializes in building and renovating gas stations in a suburban area of a large Mid-Western city. They usually have about twenty people (including one office manager/bookkeeper) on the payroll. The owners, Mark White and Henry Adams, are now on their second business plan.

The first one was prepared by a consulting firm and cost $1,900. Unfortunately, it was money wasted. Mark hired the consultants and tried to make the plan work. Henry was too busy supervising company projects to spend much time with the consultants. He liked the plan they developed but really didn't understand how it was going to help their company. Several years after the first plan was prepared, Mark admitted that the money spent on the first plan hadn't been a good investment.

11

Mark decided to prepare another plan on his own. His first step was to list the things he wanted to change during the coming year. He summarized company goals as follows:

1) Reduce overhead expenses to 15 percent of gross billings.

2) Start a retirement plan for non-union employees (two partners and the office manager).

3) Improve cash flow so that short-term loans won't be needed in the coming slow season.

The next step was to put a deadline on each of the three goals. Mark set six months into the year as a time limit for getting expenses under control. This involved monthly budget reviews, and developing controls to keep expenses in check. For example, Mark set spending limits for most overhead categories. These limits were expressed as a percentage of gross revenue for each calendar quarter. As volume changed, overhead could change with it. But overhead would not continue to expand if contract revenue fell. Largely as a result of this budget, Mark and Henry had to postpone buying a new pickup truck that they had hoped to buy at the end of the model year.

They also agreed to meet with their accountant every three months for a tax planning session. The retirement plan was one way to reduce taxes and put away some profits for the future as well. Their accountant suggested that they conserve available cash by renting a backhoe when needed in the coming year instead of replacing the company hoe with a new one.

Mark's plan required that they end the high-volume summer season with a comfortable cash cushion that would see them through the slow winter months. They scheduled seasonal layoffs and decided to rent heavy equipment by the month instead of leasing it annually. That way, they wouldn't be paying for the equipment while it sat idle during the wet season.

Writing down and defining their goals was the first step. Mark had no trouble getting Henry to agree on these goals. It was the spending limits that would present the biggest problem. As long as money was available in the bank, Henry was accustomed to spending what he thought was required to get the job done. Several times during the following months Mark had to point out that Henry's spending plans would shatter the budget they had both agreed on.

Gradually Henry began to get the point. He learned to work within the budget and began to take pride in the savings he saw accumulating. Before the year was out, he had several opportunities to turn the tables on Mark, pointing out that Mark was suggesting that they spend money that wasn't in their budget!

At the end of the year, Mark and Henry agreed that the spending limits had added thousands of dollars to their profit margin — without requiring a major sacrifice. They could both cite several extra jobs they had won because their overhead was lower than most of the competition. Henry still wanted a new backhoe and complained that the work hours of their office manager/bookkeeper had to be cut back in December and January. But he admitted that having the extra work was good for the company.

CONTROLLING YOUR MARKET

Most growth plans focus on controlling costs. But building sales volume is usually just as important.

Many contractors make the mistake of taking a passive attitude toward selling. Every construction contractor should have a marketing plan that's suited to their community, their skills and their finances. Too many contractors wait for work to come to them. Instead of bidding what's available, seek out owners who need and can pay for your service. Share your experience and knowledge with them. Offer to assist in developing a plan that's both economical and adequate for their needs. If your suggestions and recommendations help shape the project, you're two steps ahead of the competition when it comes time to sign a contract.

Of course, you must approach your market realistically. It isn't practical to specialize in work that won't support your business. Evaluate your community to be sure it can support the volume of business you're planning. For example, if you're a general contractor specializing in residential construction, you should be working in a community that's growing and has progressive ordinances and regulations that favor continued growth. Is it likely that economic conditions or employment prospects could change in your community, making it hard for all builders to earn reasonable profits?

Planning for a Change

What about the future? Are you content with the business you have now, or do you want to move into a different market or type of operation in the next year or two? If you want to make changes, you'll need to include some marketing research in your plan. The following items should be covered in your research.

- Identify your market, both the area and the type of work.

- Decide on the level of profits possible in that market.

- Determine how much competition there is for your business.

- Consider how much you'll have to invest in new tools and equipment to compete in that market.

- What employees and subcontractors will you use?

- Estimate the total additional capital you'll need to make your transition.

- Create a plan for reaching your market.

The following example shows how one contractor created a business and marketing plan to help him through a transition from new home construction to home improvement contracting.

The contractor realized that housing starts in his area were declining and probably would continue to decline. He knew that the home improvement market was growing in his community. But it was a very competitive business and required skills he had never developed as a new home builder. He planned to make the transition into home improvement contracting over a two-year period:

First, he spoke with other contractors to get an idea of the demand for improvement work. He didn't make the mistake of by-passing his competition. By contacting them, he hoped they would be willing to refer some types of work his way, or even sub out some projects to him.

Next, he studied his mix of workers, equipment, and subcontractors, and decided that he wouldn't need to plan for a big change in labor force or purchase much new equipment. But he would need to contact subcontractors in the area who would handle small jobs in an occupied home.

He started spreading the word of his interest in improvement work. He let his many contacts and established customers know that he was taking on remodeling projects. He made a special effort to talk with contacts in home inspection services, real estate agents, lenders, and moving companies — the people who are familiar with changes in his community. This word-of-mouth approach resulted in several referrals and two good jobs in the first three months.

Reviewing Your Present Market

Even if you want to keep your business just as it is, you should include a study of your present market in your business plan. Be sure there's a continuing demand for your services. Plan alternatives in case that demand suddenly decreases. If you use your business plan to help get a loan, this is one of the points the loan officer will be most interested in. Be sure you can show a good demand for your services in the future.

Your local chamber of commerce or municipal government can probably supply information on population and business trends in the area. Other agencies may be able to provide you with statistics about the number of contractors opening businesses or going out of business. Your local newspaper probably publishes some of the information you need: the number and value of building permits issued, trends in selling prices in both new and existing homes, and loan rates at local savings institutions. The Yellow Pages of your telephone directory will list the names and numbers of most of your competitors.

If you're a contractor specializing in new home construction, collect information about the volume of sales in your community. How many new homes have been built? At what average prices? And what is the *swing* (difference between asking and selling price)? Interest rates can also tell you a lot about marketing trends. The lower the interest rates for mortgages and home improvement loans, the more activity there's likely to be in the market.

All of this information indicates the relative strength or weakness in the housing market. If homes are staying on the market an average of four months, and a year ago they were selling in thirty days, that's a sign of a weakening demand for new homes. If the swing is less than 5 percent, that's a sign of strong demand. And if interest rates are stable or decreasing, more people will be buying homes and financing improvements.

Commercial construction and renovation tends to be specialized work. Realtors or lenders that handle commercial projects will be good sources of information if you plan to deal with non-residential projects.

Components of Profitable Planning

When studying the potential of a new market (or even the one you're serving now), there are five major planning points that you should consider.

Marketing— If you want to pursue a line of work, you must decide how to reach that market. Will you advertise, depend on referrals, or use some other means of letting the customer know you're there?

Pick the marketing method most suited to your type of work. Who or where are your customers? What do they read or listen to? You must get the word out in the right places and at reasonable cost to be effective in reaching your potential customers.

Demand— There must be a demand for the service, or your investment of time and money will be wasted. For example, if a new line of work requires buying heavy equipment, will you be able to stay in that line long enough to recover your investment?

There are a lot of reasons cited for business failures, but in many cases the cause is quite simple. People start up businesses and offer services when the demand isn't strong enough to support their operation. Evaluating demand is a relatively easy job. If people are on a waiting list to buy homes when only the models are built, you know there's a demand for housing. If there's a high vacancy rate in commercial space, it's clear that there's a glut in that market.

Construction follows a business cycle; high demand today can evaporate by tomorrow. You have to anticipate these cycles correctly. No tree grows to the sky. When every contractor is busy and profits are good, you should be planning for the coming slump. When work is scarce, you should be laying a foundation for the next surge in construction activity. But not all construction is affected equally by the business cycle. Demand for new construction will be slow when interest rates are high. But the home improvement market may be extremely healthy. Owners improve their homes or add space rather than moving when interest rates are up.

Capital— Expanding or shifting to a new line of work usually requires capital. You may need to buy new equipment, pay salaries while you're building up your business (and income lags behind), or do extra advertising. Fixed overhead expense goes on even when your income doesn't. You'll have to plan cash reserves carefully.

Make sure you have the capital to finance a change before you commit yourself to it. You'll have to maintain your credit rating and manage your debts carefully during the transition. Don't try to do too much too soon.

Scheduling— Think of a new market as a project. Just as you schedule subcontractors to meet a completion deadline, you schedule your new market so it brings in profits within a set time.

Break your marketing plan down into steps. Create a time schedule for each step. Trying to reach your goal too quickly may drain your capital off too fast. It takes time for the word to get out, even with a direct advertising campaign. Be realistic about the time you commit to your move, and stick to it.

Control— Write down your expectations for your new market. If results start falling behind schedule, stop and take the time to figure out where it's going wrong. Stay in control of the situation.

Compare your actual results to your planned results, just as you would on a job. Follow your plan; stay on schedule and within budget, and you should reach your goal. Figure 1-2 summarizes the components of profitable planning.

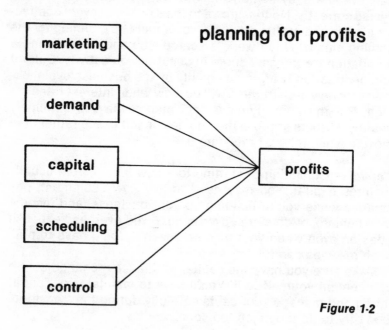

planning for profits

marketing

demand

capital → profits

scheduling

control

Figure 1-2

SETTING AN INCOME GOAL

When you evaluate your present and future markets, you'll also be predicting income. Estimating future income and expenses will help you anticipate the profits that are possible. If you're planning to enter a market that brings in just enough income to break even, staying in the existing market may be more attractive. As part of your plan, you should establish a minimum level of profit in percent and a minimum level of profit per sale. That means working toward quality volume and not just quantity. If there isn't a good potential for profit in a market, don't bother with it.

Of course, taking on any new type of work is likely to be less profitable for a while. But with a complete plan, you'll be able to survive the start-up period. Entering a new market requires an investment in the future. But be sure the profits will eventually be there.

The following guidelines will help you in setting goals for your future income:

• Establish a minimum profit base you consider acceptable, and apply that minimum to *all* the work you plan to perform.

• Evaluate jobs that fall below your standard to see where your forecasting went wrong. Correct problems in your job costing, such as poor estimates of expenses, or cost overruns. Make corrections by improved controls, better scheduling, and careful monitoring of jobs.

• Develop your break-even volume, and build from there. Break-even is the minimum amount you must earn to cover costs and pay expenses. It's the amount you must earn before you show a profit. When you figure your percentage of return on a job, keep in mind that a large portion of your overhead is fixed expense (such as phone bills and office salaries). These expenses go on even if little work is available. With small volume, fixed expenses probably eat deep into the profit on each job.

19

- Determine a reasonable growth rate for the company. Growth of 20 to 25 percent a year is a good expectation. Try not to exceed that figure. Why? This might seem to be strange advice in a book about increasing growth and profits. But more isn't always better. The fact is, when growth happens too fast, you can lose control. Here's what can happen when your business grows too fast:

1) You lose quality. As the volume increases, you may not be able to ensure that the work is up to your standards. It takes time to personally check all work on every job. Cutting corners usually means sacrificing quality.

2) Your jobs get off schedule. If you're trying to juggle more work than you can easily manage, you'll inevitably fall behind schedule. Delays cost you money. So more volume can actually mean lower profits.

3) You'll have cash flow problems. Payments on jobs are often delayed (especially if you're off schedule), but you must continue paying suppliers, wages and other expenses. You can easily outrun your capital if you're not careful.

When you've calculated the volume you need as a base (your break-even volume) and a reasonable top (your maximum growth level), you have a good range in which to set your goals for future income. This idea is summarized in Figure 1-3. As you can see, there's still room for flexibility. The key is staying in control.

Getting larger, and doubling or even tripling your present volume, is possible in time. But it should be on **your** terms. You want to be able to offer customers quality work and still maintain a healthy, stable cash flow.

PLANNING FOR YOURSELF

How much you want your business to grow is a personal decision. You can't depend on an accountant, planning consultant, or other outside expert to tell you how much volume

setting growth standards

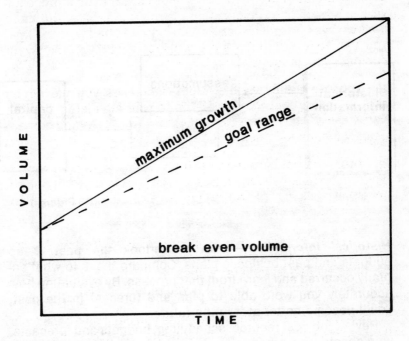

Figure 1-3

you can handle or how much profit you want. They can advise you, but in the end, it's up to you.

Experts can analyze historical information and tell you how you might avoid problems or attract opportunities. This advice can help you decide how to proceed. But deciding what direction to take is a personal choice. As a business owner, this is part of the freedom you enjoy, and part of the risk of running your own operation.

Useful Elements of Planning

You can plan for yourself with three sources you have now or can easily develop. These elements of planning are shown in Figure 1-4.

required elements

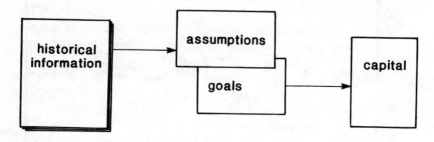

Figure 1-4

Historical information— Never overlook the past. Keep budgets and past business plans. Compare these to what actually occurred and learn from that process. By evaluating how accurately you were able to plan and forecast in the past, you'll become better at it in the future.

Review job cost records, scheduling, budgets and forecasts, worksheets, and other estimates you've developed. Also look at your financial statements. Use both types of records together. When your results are very different from what you expected, break it down. What was it you didn't anticipate? Will that recur next year? How can you improve accuracy?

You'll never be able to anticipate every possible problem. Planning isn't an exact science, and it's not intended to be. But you **can** look for major trends in your business, and prepare for the future in the best way possible.

Assumptions and goals— Setting goals is essential. There's an old saying, "If you don't know where you're going, any road will take you there." When you develop a plan for your business, you put goals in writing. If actual results differ from the plan, you can find out what went wrong.

Assumptions and goals should be flexible. Nothing is permanent, and your goals will change as your business grows.

Capital— Almost all plans work on paper. On paper we can all become millionaires working ten hours a week with very little effort at all. But, unfortunately, reality is a different matter. Growth takes money — for promotion and marketing, buying equipment, building a labor force, and financing work in progress.

Keep your business plan realistic by limiting it to the resources available to you. That means the money you have now, plus whatever portion of your profits you can afford to invest, and any financing you will be able to get. Your completed business plan should limit your expansion over a period of time. It should also indicate the amount of outside lending you can safely handle. Never borrow more money than you can afford to repay. Otherwise you defeat the purpose of the plan.

No plan is a good plan if it requires cash that you don't have.

PLANNING FOR LENDERS

Your plan should serve several purposes. Its main purpose should be for controlling operations and growth, ensuring acceptable profits, and watching marketing trends in your business. But the plan can also be useful when you want a loan.

Business plans are often prepared just for the purpose of borrowing money. By explaining the structure of your business and putting together financial statements and budgets, you can show why you need to borrow money and how it will be repaid. From the lender's point of view, it shows something even more important. Your plan shows that you've studied the future and are prepared to deal with it.

Lenders consider all borrowers risks. The big question to them is, will you be a good risk or a bad risk? Naturally, they want to loan money only to the good risks. And the best way to ensure that you fall into this group is by presenting a thorough business plan.

Modify Your Plan for the Lender

You may want to modify your plan slightly for the lender when you make a loan application. You'll have to go into more detail about how the funds will be used. But essentially, a solid, well-prepared business plan will work as well for your lenders' purposes as it does for your own.

Take these steps when preparing a plan for a lender:

1) Remember that the lender views you as a risk. Prepare your plan to clearly show the uses for the borrowed money. Demonstrate a repayment plan in your cash flow projections.

2) Be specific in your marketing plan. Show how borrowing the money will improve your profits and make your financial position stronger.

3) Make reasonable forecasts of income and growth. Bankers won't take you seriously if you're overly optimistic. If you claim you'll double or triple volume within one year, you'd better be able to back it up with numbers, and show how you arrived at those numbers.

4) Show a minimum percentage of net profit in your plan. Explain your break-even and ceiling volume, and pinpoint your goal range.

5) Be candid, even if you have losses or poor results to report. Don't try to hide the facts from the lender. But you don't have to dwell unnecessarily on the bad news either.

6) Lenders want to know how you'll use any new equipment that's in your plan. If you want a loan to buy new equipment, break down the hours of use, expected income per hour, and your budget for operation and maintenance. Carry these numbers out far enough into the future to prove that the investment will be profitable. Show that the income produced by the new equipment will be enough to repay the loan.

Prepare a financing policy— Your lender might also like to see a financing policy. This is something that isn't usually part of a business plan, but you can include it. A financing policy shows the limit you set for borrowing money. If you plan to use a short-term loan to get through a slow season, be prepared to show how this is saving money rather than depleting your net worth. If borrowing is part of an expansion plan, discuss the profits from new markets.

You need to establish a healthy balance between the net worth of your business and what you borrow. If your total net worth (assets less liabilities) is $200,000 and you're carrying $125,000 in loans, your working capital is 62.5 percent borrowed funds. Only 37.5 percent comes from your equity. These percentages make up what is called your **funded debt ratio**. It's important to know. Bankers use these figures to determine how healthy your business is. State your funded debt ratio in your finance policy. Set a limit on it, and and make it a policy that you'll never exceed that ratio.

How much funded debt is too much? That depends on the strength and volume of your business, your cash flow, and your profits. If you have a very high volume and a healthy level of profits, a funded debt ratio over 50 percent may be reasonable. But if your volume is low, you have marginal working capital, and low profits, the debt ratio should be lower. The higher the funded debt, the weaker your operation appears. This makes you a greater risk to the lenders.

For example, one builder with a gross volume of $480,000 per year earned a profit of about $75,000 for each of the past two years. He carries a funded debt ratio of 62 percent. This is healthy, considering these three factors: One, he's reporting profits even after paying interest. Two, the money is used to support a growing operation. And three, cash flow is healthy enough to carry the monthly payments.

Another builder grosses only $95,000 and earned a net profit of only $2,300 last year (after paying his own salary). Cash flow was shaky all year. It's obvious that a high funded debt ratio would be a disaster for this operation.

The **right** level of funded debt depends on volume and profits. Are those profits adequate to make repayments, absorb interest costs, and still yield what you consider an acceptable rate of return?

Bankers realize that a healthy company is more able to repay a loan. So the observation that banks lend money only to people who don't really need it is partially true. Lenders always want to reduce their risks, so the more financial strength you can show, the better.

Build Up Your Financial Strength

If your construction company wouldn't qualify for a loan now, start building your financial strength. This takes time, but could be one of the goals in your growth plan. Make higher profits a prime objective. Leave those profits in the business. That's how you build financial strength. With a stronger company, you'll have the flexibility to borrow the money you need.

If cash isn't available for the expansion you want, revise your plan. Some changes and growth are possible no matter how limited your finances. If you've been turned down for a loan, it's probably because you don't have the financial strength to be seen as a "good" risk.

Don't feel like the effort needed to apply for the loan was wasted. The advantage is that you can see your plan more objectively and from the lender's perspective. Any goal worth reaching is worth working for. Revise your plan and begin again. That's not necessarily bad news. It only means that you'll have to set goals within the limits of your capital. A well-prepared plan will help you do this.

2 FOLLOWING YOUR PLAN

Almost anyone can draft a simple, practical business plan. But doing that is a waste of time and effort unless you can *use* the plan to control costs and expenses, build the income you need, and reach your goals. And you need a system to keep track of progress toward meeting the goals you develop in your business plan.

A good business plan lays the groundwork for your financial success — *if* you refer to the plan regularly and follow the course you've set. That's not easy. But keeping your goals in mind will help the plan become reality.

MAKE YOUR PROGRESS VISIBLE

You've heard the old saying about a picture being worth a thousand words. That's true in managing your business, too.

Making charts and graphs can help you visualize your goals, and your rate of success in meeting those goals. Using visual aids helps you focus on the *process*. By focusing your attention, charts constantly remind you that your progress is a direct result of your actions. They show a concrete goal, a standard you've set for yourself, and give you a way to measure your progress toward that goal. That's the only way you can know if you're doing the job right.

All good employers let their employees know if their job performance is satisfactory. They praise and reward outstanding work. You deserve rewards and praise, too — but since you're the boss, only you can give it. How do you give this kind of positive feedback to yourself? It's simple. Compare your performance against the standards you've set. That's what the charts accomplish. And that's where planning can serve you best.

Many people who start their own businesses get discouraged because they have to deal with every problem that comes up. They take all the risks, but they don't get any encouragement or recognition for a job well done. To avoid that discouragement, give yourself tangible and conclusive proof that you are, in fact, succeeding.

Review Your Charts Regularly

A few simple charts will make it easy to see where you're going and if you're on schedule. In your planning routine, set these standards for yourself:

1) Draw up your financial goals in the form of charts. Keep these charts handy so you can review them regularly. Get into the habit of updating the charts at least monthly. Planning should be a natural part of your daily routine.

2) Compare your goals to actual results. Let's say you've plotted a graph with your sales goals expressed in dollars. Every week or month draw in your actual sales figures. Then compare actual and planned results. You might also chart your goal for number of jobs, expressed in time and volume, and the

the progress chart

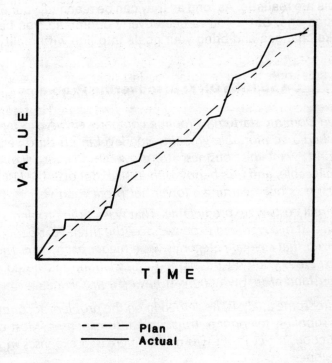

Figure 2-1

reduction you'd like to make in expenses, in either dollar amounts or percentages. Figure 2-1 shows a typical progress chart, with projected and actual results.

3) Spend at least fifteen minutes a day planning — while you're shaving or driving to work or whenever you can get a quiet quarter hour to yourself. Use the time to review your goals, your progress, and decide what steps you need to take to reconcile the two.

4) Revise your plan goals when necessary. If you discover you're not reaching a goal on schedule, review your assumptions and make some changes. Be willing to change so your goals are realistic. As long as they can be reached, your plan is a good one. But if you've been overly optimistic, you have to make changes and bring your goals into line with reality.

_____CASE HISTORY: Discovering Problems _____

Steve Dominic started his roofing company eight years ago. He reached a comfortable gross income level in his third year. He doesn't want his business to grow any larger. It's local, manageable, and he's happy with its size. But over the last three years, he's been earning a lower net profit each year.

Direct costs were predictable. That wasn't the problem. Steve looked at his overhead expenses over the three-year period and realized that several categories were higher each year. The rise in expenses couldn't be blamed on inflation, and he couldn't understand at first why he was having a problem.

After some analysis, he zeroed in on the problem accounts: office supplies, telephone, truck and auto expenses. Most of the reduction in net profit was due to increased expenses in these categories.

He immediately set a goal for himself and included it in his business plan. He would reduce all three accounts back to the percentage of gross income they had been three years ago. Here are the actions he took:

Office supplies— *He asked his office manager to get approval from him before spending more than $100. To get the best possible prices, he asked her to check with two or three suppliers before ordering. He also thought some of his workers were taking supplies home for their personal use. Steve had always taken a relaxed attitude about minor pilferage. But if* every tradesman took $5 worth of office supplies home every week, the loss would be in the thousands by year end.

The supplies had been kept on a shelf in a heavily traveled area between the office door and the warehouse. Everyone who worked for the company went by there every day. He decided to move supplies to a locked room on the other side of the office — but clearly visible out the office manager's window. She would usually see who was drawing supplies and would unlock the room at the beginning of the day.

Telephone expenses— First, Steve instructed his employees to take all incoming long distance calls, even if that meant telling someone else they'd call back. That cut down on "call-back" expenses. He also started a log of outgoing calls and compared these to the phone bill. If anyone was making personal calls, just having the log would discourage that practice.

Truck expenses— Steve also started a mileage log for all three company trucks. Supervisors used the trucks for going back and forth from the office to various job sites, but gas expenses seemed too high. By requiring employees to log their miles, he could check for excess mileage and compare expenses between different trucks.

It may have been coincidence, but the expenses Steve was watching seemed to level off or even fall after these changes were made. Profits went up, and Steve was satisfied. But the controls had to be monitored and exercised each month. Steve knew that just setting up new policies didn't solve the problem. He had to make sure the policies were followed. That took time and some pointed reminders. It probably took him four hours the first month to set up the policies and a few minutes each month following to make sure these policies were followed. But the total savings were over $1,200 each month. That's a pretty decent hourly rate.

PLOTTING YOUR SUCCESS

Start by drawing up a square or rectangular chart for each major goal you have. In Chapter 4, we'll explore goals and their relationship with underlying assumptions. In Chapter 6, we'll look at some major goals. For now, let's concentrate on how you actually plot and visualize the goals you've chosen. Assume you've stated as your goal: *To build a new line of business during the next twelve months, reaching a profitable volume of $8,000 per month by the end of the year.*

You've set standards for judging your success, and imposed a deadline for reaching it. But just having a schedule isn't enough. You want to see at a glance exactly how you're moving toward the goal. The best way is to keep a chart that shows monthly or weekly progress.

Down the left side, list volume levels. Along the bottom, list the weeks. Then draw one line for your goal, following the schedule you set for yourself. Use a broken line to show projected results and a solid line for the actual result. You could also use two different colors, such as a black line for the goal and a red line for actual sales.

As each week or month passes, enter the actual dollar value on the chart. For a plan as ambitious as yours, you might want to make four charts, one for each quarter of the year. If you want to reach a sales volume of $8,000 a month within a year, it's reasonable to set a goal of $2,000 a month by the end of the first three months. Figure 2-2 shows your first quarterly chart with the income goal plotted. It shows the goal and the actual results. As long as your actual income stays at or above the line, you're reaching that goal. If it falls below the line (or appears to be heading that way), it's time to take corrective action.

Charting Can Be Easy and Effective

Here are some practical tips for making your charting easy and effective:

- Make the chart small enough so it can fit on a single page of graph paper. A chart that's too large or too small isn't prac-

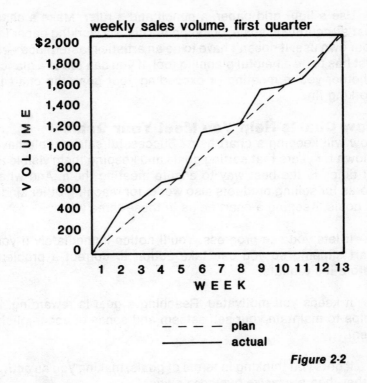

weekly sales volume, first quarter

WEEK

VOLUME

- - - - plan
——— actual

Figure 2-2

tical. Use sales increments that match the graph paper you're using. We might have to plot sales in increments of $200 or $500 instead of $100 by the second quarter in the sample graph.

- Try to set the horizontal and vertical points on the chart so that it's close to being a square. If your chart is too one-sided, it either won't fit on one page, or will distort what you're trying to report.

- Keep the distance between increments the same. Otherwise, results are distorted. For example, the time line should consist of either weeks, months or quarters. Don't mix these up. And your volume or other value points should be equally spaced.

• Use a light grid paper, a pencil and a ruler. Make a chart that's accurate in scale, but simple. This is a working paper for your own use. It doesn't have to be an artistic masterpiece — it just has to be a helpful planning tool. If you can tell at a glance whether you're meeting or exceeding your goal, the chart is working fine.

How Charts Help You Meet Your Goals

How will keeping a chart help? Successful salespeople have known for years that setting goals and keeping them visible at all times is the best way to ensure meeting them. And what works for selling products also works for reaching other kinds of goals. Keeping a chart helps in these three ways:

1) It lets you see progress. You'll notice immediately if you start slipping so you can take action to correct a problem before it's too late.

2) It keeps you motivated. Reaching a goal is rewarding. It helps to maintain your self-esteem and sense of accomplishment.

3) It gets you thinking in terms of goals, making you an *active* rather than a *passive* business owner.

You'll discover that you can create success by defining your goals and keeping those goals in mind. Success isn't going to happen by itself. You already know that hard work is the best way to achieve anything worthwhile. The charts are a tool that lets you measure the success of your hard work. Just as you check a job site to make sure the right materials are on hand, the workmanship meets your quality standards, and it's running on schedule, you must also constantly check your own business plan.

You can and do delegate responsibility to others. You send out crews to do the construction — you can't do it all yourself. But you also know that you have to keep a hand in it, even with the most dependable supervisor or foreman. That means checking the site, holding production meetings, and making sure the budget and schedule are being followed. The same is true in your business plan. And this is one area where you can't delegate. These are steps only you can take:

- Set up the plan.

- Monitor it constantly.

- Change it when necessary.

- Watch for unfavorable trends, and take action to correct them.

- Figure out the reasons for success, and take steps to continue favorable trends.

- Measure the final results to improve the process next time around.

__CASE HISTORY: Keeping Up with the Process __

Andy Wittaker put a lot of effort into writing a business plan for his general contracting operation. It included ideas for increasing sales over the coming year, holding expenses in check, and expanding operations into the next county. It was a complete and realistic plan with a goal of adding $50,000 to the company's after-tax profit.

For the first six months, Andy's plan was on target. He was ahead of his goal in every category, and it looked like this year would be his best one yet. Then the summer months came, bringing in a lot of new work. Andy was kept busy checking on jobs in progress, running the operation, and troubleshooting. He was putting in fourteen hours a day.

With the plan proceeding well, Andy stopped reviewing his plan and didn't have time to spend fifteen minutes planning each day. He fell behind. In August, he decided to update his charts and see where he stood. He was surprised to discover that expenses were running well above his target. Even though income figures were good, his net profit percentage was below what he expected. During that busy summer, he hadn't made any real progress toward his goals.

He began to put more emphasis on the controls he had devised as part of the plan, just as he'd been doing for the first six months. He realized he'd fallen for the oldest pitfall of all. When volume was heavy, controls were relaxed, and expenses rose. So those extra profits were eaten away.

By October, Andy's plan was back on the right course. But he had to revise his profit projection for the year downward because of the increased expenses during the summer. Those excessive expenses took more than $10,000 out of his expected profits for the year.

Taking Action

Without a plan, you have no way to measure progress. Your records may show that a certain expense is averaging $300 a month. But that doesn't reveal anything about the trend in expense — either up or down. With a plan, you can judge everything against the standard you create. Expenses may be higher or lower than your target. A variance either way will tell you that some action must be taken.

Here are the two key words: *goal* and *actual*. The goal is your standard — a minimum or maximum acceptable income or expense, for example. The "actual" can and should be compared to the goal every time you review the figures.

What can you do when actual results start falling behind your goal? That depends on the type of financial goal involved. For example, if your goal is to reduce general expenses, you set up controls to bring those expenses down to an acceptable level. And if the expenses continue to exceed the goal, you can take action by tightening up on those controls. That reduces expenses and keeps you on target.

With income, the process is much different. You can't force income to rise in the same direct way you can keep expenses down. You need to take a different type of action. The first step is to examine your assumptions. When you're not reaching a goal, always look back at the way you developed it in the first place. Is it realistic and practical? If not, you can't expect to reach it. For example, if building activity is slow in your area, it's not realistic to expect a significant increase in work. But once you've decided that reaching a particular goal is realistic, then you can make things happen.

That could mean increasing promotional efforts. With some types of business, you can get in touch with potential customers directly. One plumbing contractor increased his business by mailing advertisements to his past customers, reminding them that he was still there. It resulted in more than thirty calls in one week. At the same time, he also called several general contractors about subcontract work, and ended up with several commercial contracts over the coming year. Keeping in touch was effective in that case.

Another contractor specializing in home maintenance had dropped an ad in the local paper when his business increased. But a few months later, business was down because repeat calls weren't as high as he thought they would be. He started the ad again, and business gradually increased.

NATURAL PHASES IN TRACKING A GOAL

There is a natural sequence of phases in tracking a goal. You're going to experience this sequence any time you're keeping a chart. Take the time now to learn how to deal with it. Figure 2-3 shows a typical sequence. The steps are:

Start-up— As you establish your goal, it's likely that actual results will lag behind for the first few weeks or months. You can't expect instant results. Be especially aware of the timing in your start-up. Anticipate highs and lows in sales activity, and time your start during a busy period to get started off on the right foot.

chart phases

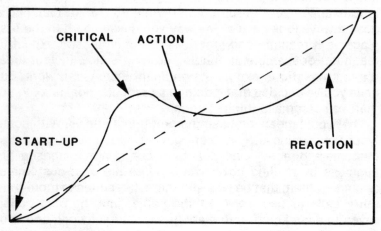

Figure 2-3

Critical point— There's a danger in charting. At some point, actual results will be far enough above your goal that you'll find yourself paying less attention to it from day to day. This is human nature. We tend to lose interest in a goal once it seems that we're going to succeed. At the critical point, there's enough of a lead so that you don't have to worry about going below that goal line.

Action point— Because you pay less attention when your actual line is far above the goal, you can expect to see the results of that neglect eventually. Your lack of attention will catch up with you. As the actual line levels out, it begins to approach the goal line. You realize what's happening and take action — by setting controls to decrease expenses or planning promotional efforts to increase income, for example — to correct the problem.

Reaction— Your actions don't have immediate results. There's a delay — a lag time — between taking the action and reaping the rewards. So you'll probably see the results line fall below the goal before it finally reacts by catching up.

Business owners who keep charts on a regular basis know that this sequence of events is unavoidable. Even when you're aware of the critical point/action/reaction sequence, you can't do much about it. If actual and goal relationships were predictable, the process of tracking would be pretty dull. And believe it or not, the actual tracking can become the most enjoyable part of business planning. It's exciting to try to anticipate that unknown and unseen factor that will come up next week.

During the time you're tracking a goal — updating your chart regularly and trying to stay above the line — you're getting into a good habit: planning. As you see a problem developing, you take action to correct it. If you don't take time for planning, you don't discover problems until they become critical. By then, it's often too late to avoid a loss.

There's nothing wrong with the actual results line falling below the goal line. It happens to everyone who keeps a progress chart sooner or later. And maybe it's just as well. That may be the only factor that will make you react. When you do finally decide it's time to take action, you'll often be at your most effective. Since the goal is important to you, your best personal talents come into play. And you discover that you can, in fact, control your financial destiny.

This tracking process applies to all types of goals, whether you're watching income, expenses, or the movement into new markets. Simply reduce the goal to a factor that can be tracked from one week to the next, plot your success, and decide how to act when the two lines on your chart get too close to one another.

DEADLINES AND YOUR PLAN

Time is a crucial part of your goals. It's one of the ways of measuring your success. Without it, you have no way to judge whether you're progressing. So put your project on a schedule.

But if it's a long, complicated project, don't try to tackle it all in one phase. Reduce it to a series of phases.

Let's say your goal is to reduce telephone expenses over the next six months. The cost of long distance calls has been excessive and you suspect some of your employees are using the company phone for personal calls. Here are a series of possible phases:

1) Research phone system alternatives for saving money and tracking calls by station. Decide on (a) an alternative system or (b) keeping the system now in place. *Deadline:* one month.

2) Design a telephone log to be used for all outgoing long distance calls. Write a procedure requiring that all employees log their phone calls, and delegate responsibility for enforcing it. *Deadline:* two months.

3) Write procedures for giving priority to incoming long distance calls, to reduce the need to return calls outside of the area. *Deadline:* two months.

4) Review average phone bills following the initiation of new procedures. Determine the effectiveness of the controls. Revise the current budget to continue expense reduction measures. *Deadline:* three months.

5) Delegate a procedure for a monthly analysis of the phone bill, including investigating all long distance calls not listed on the telephone log. You'll have to allow some time for employees to become accustomed to the new procedure. *Deadline:* four months.

6) Review the success of the procedure with new controls in place. Devise a new goal to continue or replace this one. *Deadline:* six months.

In this case, a progress chart could be prepared to show the monthly reduction. For example, if your monthly bill averages

$600, and you want to reduce it to $400 or less by the end of the year, your chart could look like this:

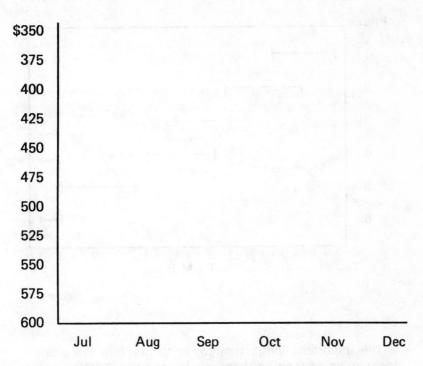

What happens to a goal like this if circumstances change? For example, what if you win a contract at a location that's a long distance call away from your office? Your phone bill will probably go up, not down. Your goal of reducing expenses is no longer valid, and it would be unreasonable to expect to reach it.

Flexibility is essential. The situation can change overnight, so no goal — even one planned for only a few months — will necessarily stay in effect for the entire time you've scheduled. You have to be ready to adjust to the circumstances as they change. That means each goal, your budgets and forecasts, and the business plan itself may be in a constant state of adjustment.

41

the deadline schedule

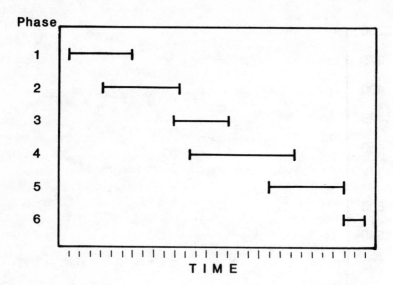

Figure 2-4

The important thing, though, is to practice the planning techniques as long as those goals are valid. That's what ensures profits in the long run.

The Deadline Schedule

A simple deadline scheduling chart is shown in Figure 2-4. You can use a chart like this to break down any goal you establish into phases. And the more complex a goal, the more important it is to break it down into manageable phases. Just as you read a book one chapter at a time, a goal can be reduced to a series of simple steps.

In the deadline schedule, the phases are identified down the left side, numbers 1 through 6. Let's see how it works using the the example of the telephone expense controls we've just discussed. You can now schedule and plan your time, breaking the problem into logical phases:

Phase 1: research
Phase 2: design log
Phase 3: procedure draft
Phase 4: review
Phase 5: analysis
Phase 6: final review

By the time you've completed all six phases, your goal will be realized. And rather than trying to tackle what could be an overwhelmingly complex problem all at once, the phasing technique allows you to manage it efficiently.

The chart is just a tool to help you manage the processes required to complete your task. The technique is similar to one you would use to control a complex construction project. When you complete one phase and begin the next at the right moment, the entire project is kept on schedule.

PITFALLS OF AN UNREALISTIC PLAN

There are limits on the goals you can set for yourself. If you don't keep your goals realistic, you could get rich on paper while your operation runs itself into the ground.

For example, one contractor who had just started his company decided to map out gross income for the coming year. He realized he couldn't start out with high volume. He had to build volume gradually. So he came up with the following breakdown:

January	$1,000	July	$25,000
February	2,000	August	30,000
March	4,000	September	35,000
April	8,000	October	40,000
May	16,000	November	45,000
June	20,000	December	50,000

43

This came out to $276,000 gross for the first full year in business. Now, it's not impossible for a novice business owner to reach this goal in one year — if the demand is there. But there were a number of flaws in this plan:

• The numbers double up for the first five months, then increase $5,000 through the end of the year. There's no allowance for seasonal changes, and no reasonable base of assumptions. The plan isn't based on work to be done for any identifiable customer groups or anything other than speculation. These are just numbers picked out of the air.

• There's no plan for the support services that would be needed to carry this volume of business. What about the office and warehouse, employees, transportation and storage facilities, not to mention capital to finance the growth?

• The plan isn't based on a market analysis. Until you've studied and understand the factors of competition, demand, and volume, you can't make a realistic plan.

Whenever your income increases, you must pay for that increase. More equipment, employees, promotion, internal controls — you have a whole range of matters to deal with. Volume doesn't grow by itself as if in a vacuum.

Inexperience and lack of understanding created the flaws in this plan. To plan effectively, whether for income, expenses, the number of jobs, or the rate of growth, you need to take an intelligent approach. That includes a consideration of these factors:

Cost of growth— How much do you need to invest in fixed assets, hiring of employees, or getting set up in an office?

Market conditions— What kind of demand is there for your services? How much competition is there? How wide a geographic influence do you want, and how will you manage it?

Personal risk— How much are you willing to go out on a limb to expand? Some people are simply more comfortable keeping their operation local, and staying in complete control. Unlimited growth is not always positive — and it's not always profitable. Only you can define your own comfort zone.

An assumption base— Every conclusion you reach and every goal you set must be based on an assumption you make about your market. Without that, you don't have a plan at all.

A tracking and evaluation system— By making charts, measuring results, and developing a way to respond to negative trends, you can design profits into your plan.

If you include all of these features in your plan, you won't fall into the trap of unrealistic goal setting. Remember, a plan is only as effective as it is realistic. It doesn't do any good to make a paper profit while you can't pay your employees.

THE ADVANTAGES OF PLANNING

To many business owners, the thought of making a plan and spending time tracking it might seem like too much administration. And I'll admit that the mechanical process of tracking won't create any profits. What it **will** do is provide you with *information* — and that's the stuff that profits are made of. It's the actions you take, based on the information you've gained, that justifies the time and effort spent on planning and tracking.

Planning puts you into a frame of mind for thinking about the future. When you actively plan and set goals for yourself, you've made it likely that you'll reach those goals. The passive business owner may or may not stay in business, but there's no way to measure his success. If goals aren't set, they can't be met.

You'll find that by thinking in terms of the plan and making decisions based on it, you'll increase your ability to identify and reach profit targets. The habit of thinking in terms of profit targets makes you a more capable manager of your business.

Having a series of successes also improves your confidence. That makes it easier to take the next step, earn a profit, save money on expenses, and expand. These individual successes add up, and contribute to the future.

Experienced planners know that through practice, the ability to "call the shots" correctly is sharpened. Why? Because you develop a sense of what will work, how long it will take, and exactly what needs to be done to get there from here.

There's really no secret to planning. It isn't a magic solution to every problem, and it isn't a way to get rich without working hard. But it is a sound technique for staying in control of your operation, for building the profits you want and deserve, and for making yourself think in terms of success.

_____CASE HISTORY: Working Without a Plan _____

Although Ted Bittner had a general contracting license, he ran a home inspection service. He didn't fix any of the problems he discovered for customers, he just issued inspection reports. His clients were homeowners, lenders, and real estate agents.

Business was good. There was a lot of demand for home inspection services, especially since some recent court decisions made real estate brokers liable for certain defects in a home. Ted was kept busy and was earning good money.

He'd been increasing his gross income each year, but finally reached a point where he just couldn't take on any more work. He started losing interest, since his ten-hour days weren't producing any growth. He charged about $250 for the average inspection. That was going rate among the competition. There was little flexibility in pricing.

Ted had done all right without a business plan up until now. He realized, however, that he had to do some planning if he wanted to keep his business growing. When he sat down to figure out what to do, he decided to take these steps:

1)   Apply for membership in the American Society of Home Inspectors (ASHI), the national organization that qualified professionals. A number of competitors had this license now. To continue competing effectively, he'd have to join also.

2)   Immediately hire one employee who was qualified to do inspections, and plan to hire a second within a year.

3)   Set inspection standards for employees, including the format of the inspection report.

4)   Get a word processing system. He'd been having his wife type up the reports. That took her five or six hours a day. Since they all followed the same format, using a word processor would be more efficient.

A year later, Ted's business was running smoothly. He had two employees. He devised a recording system in both company trucks so he and the other inspectors could dictate their inspection reports while going from one job to another. Most reports now took about fifteen minutes to type up, following a standard format. He was working from a complete business plan, with goals for number of jobs per week and total gross income. He had control systems for the highest general expenses. After one year of working from a plan, Ted's net profits grew 30 percent. Than was enough to make him a confirmed believer in business planning.

3 PREPARING YOUR PLAN

Your business plan shouldn't be complex — but it must be complete. It takes *planning* and *definition* to get the essential information you'll need to make your plan practical and comprehensive.

Start the planning process by defining ahead of time all of the elements that should go into your plan. List all the material you will need, and in what order you'll need it. Decide who will be delegated the responsibility for gathering facts for you. Finally, set a deadline for completing the plan. This chapter will help you identify what has to go into your plan.

PLANNING TO STAY IN CONTROL

A short but concise plan is best. And that's harder than it sounds. It takes a lot of effort to weed out unnecessary information. Remember that you'll be using your plan frequently throughout the year. It's easiest to use if it contains only what you need, arranged in a format that leads you to the information you want.

Writing your plan down on paper is best. That gives you a tangible outline for the future. It also makes your goals explicit so you can evaluate them realistically. Most of us start out with a pretty clear idea about where we want to be in the future. But the way to get there is a lot fuzzier. We don't know the first step to take, so we never get to the second step. That's why a written plan is necessary.

In too many businesses, however, a plan is done at the beginning of the year and then abandoned. It's foolish to spend time developing a workable plan that is put in a drawer and then forgotten for the next year. When that happens, the whole planning process was a waste of time — and a lost chance to increase future profits.

To avoid that waste, set up a tracking system for yourself. Assign deadlines for every goal and every step along the way. Build the tracking system into the plan itself, and record progress just as you carefully track progress on any job.

_____CASE HISTORY: Setting Deadlines _____

Harry Arnold wrote a business plan for the first time three years ago. He did some research on business planning, followed the steps carefully, and came up with a plan to increase profits.

The plan set goals and deadlines. It was well organized. And it included a tracking system. His plan was a good road map to success. But after the first couple of months, Harry let it go and forgot about the plan until it was time to look ahead to the next year. When he finally got around to his review, he discovered that he hadn't met any of his most important goals. He was close on a couple of them, but overall, the plan didn't come through.

That's when Harry realized the direct relationship between his profits and the plan. If he had followed the plan, he could have earned more profit during the year, probably without expending any more effort. One of his goals was to cut telephone expenses. He'd originally planned to put a phone log in the office, because he suspected that some employees were using the phone for personal calls. He never got around to doing that, of course. And phone bills for the year were higher than ever.

Harry realized that it was the same story for all of his goals. They were all reachable, but he hadn't enforced the steps and controls he had carefully developed in the plan.

The next year, Harry revised the plan and vowed to follow it faithfully throughout the year. He did — and he reached every one of his goals. They weren't that difficult. He cut expenses in some accounts (like telephone, office supplies, and transportation). He increased the volume in the most profitable line of business (residential maintenance and renovation work). And he eliminated a leftover inventory of material to free up storage space. Achieving those modest goals increased profits for the year by $15,000.

Harry's most ambitious goal was to emphasize the most profitable line of business. It kept his crews busy throughout the year because it was less affected by seasonal changes than the other types of work he did. And it had the highest percentage of profit showing at the bottom line. He also liked short-term work that was completed and paid for within sixty days in most cases. When Harry followed his plan, his profits improved and receivables came in sooner.

THE SECTIONS OF A PLAN

A complete plan includes nine sections. That may sound intimidating, but none of the sections needs to be very long. In fact, the entire plan could be as short as twenty pages or so. Since most of that is back-up information, the essence of the plan can be stated on even fewer pages and condensed into a one-page time-line schedule.

We'll look at the plan sections one at a time. Let's begin at the beginning — with the introduction.

Introduction

Assume the reader knows nothing about you, your business, or the origin of the operation. Even though you're doing the plan for yourself, put everything down on paper. Begin your plan with an introduction.

This section needs only a couple of paragraphs. It should tell who owns the company, your background, how long you've been in business, and the type of service you offer. Also name the primary customer, whether it's the homeowner, business owner, developer, or government.

Goals

Goals are the basic building blocks of the plan. They tell you what you hope to achieve during the year, and when. The goal statements must be specific, so you have a standard against which to measure results. Compare, for example, a weak goal stated in general terms to a specific one:

Weak goal: To increase sales during the year.
Strong goal: To increase sales by 5 percent per quarter.
Weak goal: To make more money after taxes.
Strong goal: To improve overall after-tax profits by 20 percent for the year.

The strong goal statement builds in a deadline, and helps you visualize the first step that needs to be taken. For example, you can improve overall profits right now by reducing general expenses. The first step might be to set up some policies designed to reduce waste and lost time. That leads to a lower level of expenses for the same level of gross sales. The result: more profits.

Assumptions

All goals are based on your assumptions. This section explains the assumption basis for your goals. You can't have one without the other. For example, let's assume you set a goal of increasing sales based on your assumption that there's a market for construction services that no contractor is now serving adequately. If your assumption is right, it's a matter of deciding how to reach the goal. And if your assumption is wrong, you should discover it during the preparation of this section.

You also assume it's possible to improve your after-tax profits. One way, of course, is to reduce expense levels. Another is to increase revenues without a corresponding increase in costs and expenses. Both of these ideas are based on the assumption that it's possible to hold expenses in check.

Marketing
This section explains what you plan to do during the year to maintain your existing level of business, or to expand, if that's part of your plan.

The marketing strategies you build into your plan make the entire job realistic. Many plans project much higher profits without stating the source or method. That's useless. You must be able to identify a market *and* the way you plan to reach it. Again, that calls for scheduling — breaking the goals down into workable units, assigning a deadline, and then following the plan to make it happen.

Graphics
Graphs and charts distill into a visual form your ideas about how to change the nature of your business. They don't need to be professional quality, unless you're trying to impress your banker or other outside expert. Even then, a carefully and neatly drawn chart is all you really need.

Here are some of the charts you can include:

• The mix of sales in your existing business, compared to the mix you expect to create in your plan.

• The level of general expenses in current problem accounts, and the estimated lower levels you hope to achieve in your plan.

- A summary of net profits for prior years with an estimate of profits at the end of the plan year.

Forecasts

This section predicts your gross revenues for the next year. A lot of forecasting is done arbitrarily, but try to be as specific as possible. List your current income by source, refer back to your assumptions about the market, and come up with a reasonable revenue forecast that can be plotted.

Most inexperienced planners use a forecasting technique that involves percentage increases over the past year. But that's too simple to be accurate. Break down your income by units you can identify and control. For example, if you work with residential customers, base your forecast on the number of jobs per year. Then estimate a reasonable increase, and base revenue forecasts on the average income per job. That way, if you fall short of your expectations, you'll be able to identify why, and take immediate action to correct the problem.

Allow for seasonal factors, competition, and other variables that could affect your income forecast. And be conservative. It's easy to be overly optimistic. For example, one plumbing contractor I know had a crew of three. When he started planning, he forecast a level of revenue growth that was impossible, because there simply wasn't enough time for three people to do that much work. There are only so many productive hours in a week. That limits how much work one plumber can handle. My friend's forecast for increased income wasn't practical because it wasn't based on a plan to hire any more employees. The plan was bound to fail.

Budgets

Map out budgets by the month. Be sure to base your estimates on realistic data. Don't simply carry over an average level. Base your budget estimate on realistic assumptions for each account. Be especially aware of the relationship between some expense accounts and your income.

Don't make the mistake my friend the plumbing contractor made. If you estimate a significant increase in gross income, also allow for higher payroll expenses. And if you plan to increase revenues in other ways, be sure to include an allowance for advertising or promotional expenses.

Projections

The most overlooked area in planning is control of cash flow. Yet, for many contractors, this is the most severe problem. That's especially true when the business is affected by seasonal highs and lows.

You need a monthly breakdown of cash flow projections, just like your monthly income forecast and expense budget. Plan for buying and selling of equipment, loan payments, new loans you expect to request during the year, increases in outstanding accounts receivable during expansion periods, and any other events that will affect your cash flow.

Financial

Your plan should include a set of financial statements: a balance sheet, income statement, and a statement of sources and applications of funds (your cash flow). It's best to prepare these in a comparative format, listing the latest year compared to the previous year, or even the previous two years, if the numbers are available.

Also include a summary of your plan in the form of a projected income statement. That's a forecast of the year's income, costs and expenses for the coming year. Compare this summary with actual income and profits for previous periods. This comparison can help you — and anyone else who reviews your plan — tell at a glance how realistic your entire plan really is.

If you want a complete, workable document, include each of these sections in your business plan. And don't forget to include a time line in the appropriate sections. Put yourself on a schedule for achieving your goals. That's how plans lead to higher profits.

the complete plan

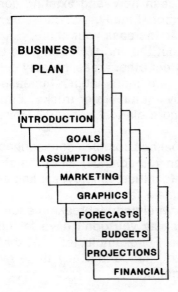

BUSINESS
PLAN

INTRODUCTION
GOALS
ASSUMPTIONS
MARKETING
GRAPHICS
FORECASTS
BUDGETS
PROJECTIONS
FINANCIAL

Figure 3-1

Figure 3-1 shows all the sections of a complete business plan.

DEFINING YOUR BUSINESS GOALS

Simplifying your major goal may be the hardest part of the entire planning process. You know in general terms what you want to achieve, but putting that down on paper requires organization and a carefully plotted summary.

Consider the simple goal statement, "To increase gross revenue 30 percent during the year."

What does that mean? First, you must be able to identify the source of that increase (the marketing section of the plan). You must establish that the demand is there, and that you can win your 30 percent away from the competition. Then you have to project when those increases will take place, considering seasonal factors, cash flow, and existing contracts that demand time and labor. Finally, you must decide how you'll reach that market to increase your share.

But even that's not the end. You still have to consider how your growth will affect other areas, notably general expenses. Will you need to hire more labor? Increase inventory and storage space? Buy equipment or trucks? Finance those new purchases? Hire more clerical support? Move to a larger office?

Even a simple goal has complex consequences. It can seem overwhelming when you consider all of the steps you have to take — financing, facilities, employees, and equipment lease or purchase, to name a few.

Avoid being overwhelmed by breaking each goal down into logical parts. That way you don't have to think about all of those steps at once. For example, let's say that as part of your goal, you'll have to finance and buy three more trucks. The stages for this might be:

1) Price trucks by March 1.
2) Arrange financing by March 15.
3) Take delivery by April 1.

You'll have to coordinate these stages, of course, with the date you need the equipment according to the plan. And it all depends on the assumption that you'll be able to obtain the financing you need.

Every goal is based on timing and assumptions. To manage progress toward a goal, break it down into steps and set a deadline for each step. Keep this schedule as realistic as possible, allowing plenty of time between steps so you can complete each before the next is due to start.

This is similar to controlling six or eight subs on a major building project. All the work has to be carefully scheduled and supervised to make sure the job is finished on schedule. One phase must be completed before another can begin. Any delay by one sub will affect subsequent work. Your schedule

```
┌─────────────────────────────────────────────────────┐
│              Business Goal Worksheet                  │
│                                                       │
│  Description _____ Date _____ │
│                                                       │
│  Steps                                      Deadline  │
│    1  _____  _____  │
│    2  _____  _____  │
│    3  _____  _____  │
│    4  _____  _____  │
│    5  _____  _____  │
│    6  _____  _____  │
│    7  _____  _____  │
│    8  _____  _____  │
│    9  _____  _____  │
│   10  _____  _____  │
│                                                       │
│  Time line                                            │
│                                                       │
│     STEP   ┬──┬──┬──┬──┬──┬──┬──┬──┬──┬──┬            │
│                                                       │
│     DATE   __ __ __ __ __ __ __ __ __ __              │
└─────────────────────────────────────────────────────┘
```

Figure 3-2

of deadlines works the same way.

To define and manage the stages, make up a business goals worksheet like the one shown in Figure 3-2. Start with a brief title or description of your goal. Then identify the logical steps necessary in reaching that goal. Assign deadlines to each. Then show all the steps toward that goal on a time line.

This helps you think through a goal and divide it into manageable phases. By approaching a major goal this way, you can keep yourself on schedule and are more likely to get where you want to go.

THE PRELIMINARY PLAN

Once you've broken your plan into phases or sections, start the process rolling by assigning each part to someone. This could mean delegating some parts to others, or giving yourself an assignment and — most importantly — a specific deadline.

It's always tempting to tell yourself that the whole plan can be done in a month. When you've finally made the commitment to planning, you want to see the results as soon as possible. That's only human. But don't do it! Instead, set a reasonable deadline, and assign procedures and phases on a one-by-one basis. That way, you will reach your final goal — even though it takes a little longer.

Approach this like the job of writing specs. Start with a listing of materials you'll need. This might include financial information from the past year, research on your market, a preliminary income forecast and expense budget, breakdowns of problem accounts, information about income (number of jobs, average size, the time it takes to collect money due), salary and wage information, estimates of future labor needs, equipment maintenance schedules, estimates of upcoming new purchases, and your need for outside financing.

Next, plan and delegate the work on each stage. Put down the name, a description of responsibilities, and a deadline. Typically, you might assign yourself the task of writing an introduction. At the same time, you give your accountant the job of putting together comparative financial statements. Your bookkeeper has the task of compiling a summary of jobs, average income, and the time required to collect.

Put the preliminary plan process on a schedule, broken down by the sections of the plan itself. Plan a start and end date for each section, and then track your progress. Don't let this fall behind schedule.

Use a worksheet like the one shown in Figure 3-3. Note the schedule in the last section. Here's where you can control the preparation stage most effectively. Each section's start and end date is broken down into "planned" and "actual." If the actual date isn't filled in by the planned deadline, someone is falling behind schedule. This section controls the writing of

Plan Work Schedule

Materials   ✓
_____   ___
_____   ___
_____   ___
_____   ___
_____   ___

Delegation:

Name	Responsibilities	Deadline
_____	_____	_____
_____	_____	_____
_____	_____	_____
_____	_____	_____
_____	_____	_____

Schedule

| | START DATE | | END DATE | |
Section	Planned	Actual	Planned	Actual

Figure 3-3

your preliminary plan, just as you'll have a control system to put the plan into effect once it's finished. This procedure will help you collect all the information needed by your target date.

Listing Your Assumptions

Before starting to draft your plan, list the assumptions you're making. These assumptions, which support the major goals, are the backbone of every plan.

If you discover that one of your assumptions is flawed, you'll have to go back, fix it, and then review the entire plan to that point. This happens. If you want your business plan to be realistic, be willing to review assumptions and make changes when needed.

The number of assumptions should match the number of major goals. Generally, you'll be able to support each goal with one assumption statement. For example:

Goal: To increase sales by 30 percent for the year.

Supporting assumption: There is a market demand for the type of service I provide. It's possible to grow by 30 percent, even with the current level of competition for the business.

Goal: To cut office expenses by 15 percent.

Supporting assumption: Supply expenses are too high, and I can institute controls to cut expense levels.

Goal: To eliminate one line of business.

Supporting assumption: Other, more profitable lines of business can be increased to maintain at least the current level of profits.

Goal: To get a loan for the purchase of new equipment worth $80,000.

Supporting assumption: A lender will be willing to loan me that much, based on my financial strength. I will have adequate cash flow and profits to repay the loan.

Just as assumptions back up the goal statements you include in your plan, your assumptions need supporting facts.

Include in your plan file the working papers supplied by your accountant or bookkeeper, your own notes, and other documents that are the support for your assumptions. These won't become part of the plan, but they will support the conclusions you draw and express through assumption statements.

While you're putting the plan together, you'll want to refer constantly to goal and assumption statements. So put your assumptions down on paper, using a worksheet like the one shown in Figure 3-4. This is nothing more than a concise list of your goals and assumptions.

For the coming year, you should have only three or four major goals. Beyond that, you may have additional, longer-term goals. Typically, these include a targeted retirement date or a plan to pay off a debt. If you have goals like these, include an additional section in your plan covering these longer-term goals. We'll cover this in more detail in later chapters.

For now, concentrate on the goals and assumptions with final deadlines within one year. Your business plan probably includes goals that extend five years or more into the future. But the greater emphasis should be put on what you have to do right now, what assumptions you're making, and how they affect your immediate plan.

Once you've gone through the preliminary draft, you'll know how valid your assumptions — and goals — are. Then go back and review what you started out with. If you need to change anything, you'll know more after going through the entire process of marketing, forecasts and budgets.

Testing Your Assumptions
After you've defined your goals and assumptions, go back through the preliminary plan. It's time to test what you've assumed. Why? There are four good reasons:

1)   An untested assumption might contain flaws that won't be discovered until it's too late, when your plan is not living up to expectations.

Assumptions

Goal _____

Assumption

_____

_____

_____

_____

Goal _____

Assumption

_____

_____

_____

_____

Goal _____

Assumption

_____

_____

_____

_____

Goal _____

Assumption

_____

_____

_____

_____

Figure 3-4

2) Once you're sure the assumptions are correct, you can proceed with confidence.

3) If unfavorable trends develop during the year, you will be certain that the fault is not with your assumptions.

4) It's easy to be overly optimistic in developing assumptions. But equally important, you could conclude you were too conservative. Finding and correcting that flaw early will help make the most of your plan.

For example, suppose you assume it will be possible to increase sales by 30 percent. But while working on your marketing strategy, you conclude that growth like that stretches your resources too thin. You'll need to modify the assumption. Or, you come to the conclusion that you won't be able to afford the expanded facilities, equipment, and labor force that your expansion plan will demand. Financial risks and cash flow limitations could force you to adopt a more gradual growth plan.

___CASE HISTORY: The Conservative Plan ___

David Williams runs a landscaping operation in a suburban area. Population in his city is 35,000 and the entire county (which he considers his territory) has about 80,000.

His business plan originally estimated annual sales growth at about 20 percent. After going all the way through his preliminary plan, he decided to increase that estimate. He found that he'd been holding back on the estimate of new jobs because he concentrated only on the immediate city. But he knew he could reach any part of the county within 30 minutes. During the marketing review section of the plan, David realized he'd underestimated the potential market.

There were twenty-eight landscape contractors listed in Dave's phone book with addresses in the county. Of this total, twenty-three were in his city, which was the major economic base of the entire area. But only about 44 percent of the population lived there. He figured that a little marketing effort in those other areas would probably increase revenues by 30 percent or more. So he came up with an idea for newspaper and radio advertising, an improved Yellow Pages ad, and distribution of flyers in outlying areas.

The plan had to be modified even more. David knew he'd have to plan for hiring more labor when his business started to grow, especially during the spring and summer season. He also would need to buy new trucks and tools.

The more optimistic plan succeeded, with most of the growth coming from areas outside of the city. And by following his plan, David was able to manage cash flow, anticipate future needs and cover them with bank financing. The result was higher profits.

____CASE HISTORY: The Unrealistic Plan ____

Pullman Construction had been in business eleven years when the owner, Mark Pullman, finally got around to doing a business plan. He decided he'd try to double profits in one year. This increase would come from several sources:

- An increase of 50 percent in gross sales
- Reduction of variable expenses
- Controls over some fixed expenses that seemed high
- Elimination of some expenses altogether

The plan looked good on paper. But going through it a second time, Mark realized it contained several flaws. The biggest mistake was the idea of reducing expenses while substantially increasing revenues. That just wasn't realistic.

He talked to his accountant, who explained that the purpose of planning growth was to retain a greater share of new profits. This, he said, could be done by stabilizing fixed overhead at one level while accepting higher variable expenses with higher sales.

The plan was revised accordingly. But there were more problems to face. The plan to increase revenues by 50 percent didn't consider market demand. There was plenty of competition in the area, making it unlikely that one small operation could grow that quickly. Also, Mark hadn't planned for any increase in direct labor, which made that section of the plan completely unrealistic.

There also was no plan for outside financing, although the level of growth would require a major increase in accounts receivable. If business increased 50 percent, it was reasonable to assume that the amount due Mark's company would increase by 50 percent. Unfortunately, cash wasn't available to finance that level of growth.

When Mark discovered these problems, he saw that his plan wasn't right. So he started over, building on the idea of gradual growth. He viewed expenses with an eye on the realities of the situation. And for the first time, he projected cash flow. This let him see where problems were likely to occur, even in a more conservative budget.

Over the next three years, Mark's operation grew slowly but steadily. His original goal, increasing business by 50 percent, finally was reached. It took thirty-six months instead of twelve. But he was still in business, and was earning a good profit. His cash flow was under control. And, best of all, he knew exactly where he was going. The assumptions were tested each year, proven and modified to be as realistic as possible. Mark ended up with a working plan, and used it to succeed.

THE PREPARATION SEQUENCE

There is a logical sequence in the preliminary phases of business planning. By using that sequence, you'll end up with a powerful tool for growth and profits. But without it, you'll spend a lot of time changing what was supposed to be your final plan, or proceeding with flawed assumptions.

There's another danger in a flawed plan, besides just wasting time. When you show it to a lender, your loan officer is probably going to spot the problems you overlooked. Your chances of getting a loan can drop to zero when that happens.

If a banker points out a flaw you hadn't considered, you lose credibility. And the entire plan is called into question.

Make sure your plan is valid *before* you show it to an outsider. Follow these seven steps:

Definition— Define everything before you begin. You must know what you want to do, what the deadlines will be, and what materials you need to get started on the preliminary plan.

Materials— Get all your information together before you start. You won't always need information in the order anticipated. So before beginning, make sure you have everything that's needed.

Deadlines— Build the idea of deadlines into every phase of your plan. Working from a target date will prompt you to action, give you danger signals ahead of time, and make it easy to measure progress.

Major goals— Base the entire plan on the major goals you build. Always keep these in mind. But be flexible. While putting together your preliminary plan, a new major goal may occur to you . . . or one goal you thought was important will drop in priority.

Assumptions— Back up your goals with assumption statements. These may only be one or two sentences long. But they must support the major goal. You'll use these throughout the plan-building process. In some cases, you'll want to modify a goal while you're examining the assumption.

Testing— Challenge yourself. Test the goals and assumptions before starting to draft the plan. Look for flaws, and if you find any, go back and modify the goals and assumptions.

The plan— Once your plan (and its preliminary elements) have been verified, tested, and modified, you're ready to start implementing it.

the preparation sequence

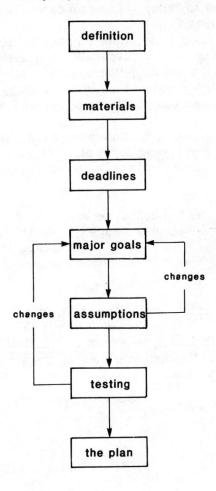

Figure 3-5

The preparation summary is shown in Figure 3-5. Note that changes can occur at two stages: when you're listing your assumptions, or when you're testing them. Keep an open mind during these parts of the preparation sequence. They might be the most important of all. When you find an error and correct it, you don't *lose* anything — you *gain* by validating your goals and assumptions.

How long should the entire preparation sequence take? That depends on how much validation and testing are needed. Remember that you'll be gathering basic information for nine segments of the plan, and then writing a rough draft for each segment. But also consider these points:

1) The sequence of gathering information, listing goals and assumptions, and testing, takes place only once. After that's completed, you'll be able to put together the plan sections fairly quickly.

2) The plan itself shouldn't be a lengthy document. Some sections will take up only a page or two. And the entire plan may be only twenty-five pages or so, several of which will be devoted to numbers. You won't have a great deal of narrative in the plan.

3) You may spend more time defining and checking the preliminaries than in actually doing the final plan itself. This initial phase is just as important as the final numbers you show. The more thorough you are here, the more realistic and useful your plan will be.

4

THE PRELIMINARY PLANNING

Before you begin putting your plan on paper, spend some time developing a few preliminary goals. Goals are the building blocks of a successful plan. The more time and effort you spend on this phase, the more useful your plan is likely to be. And there's another benefit of thorough preliminary planning: It makes actually writing the plan fast and easy.

Many experienced business planners will admit they spend much more time developing and modifying goals than writing the details of the plan itself. An engineer I know says the business planning process should be like putting up a building. On one of his recent projects, a high-rise was in the planning stages for over a year. Once construction started, structural work was finished in less than four months. The same is true in business planning. You can work out the sections of the plan in a day or two at the most, assuming you've spent several days thinking about where you want to go in the next year.

THE ELEMENTS OF GOALS

You might want to treat this preliminary stage as the actual start of the plan's first draft. A lot of it takes place in your head, but it's wise to keep notes and put your goals down on paper. There's a lot of work involved in the process, even though you end up with just a simple statement. Besides the brief goal statement, you must have a series of assumptions — worked out on paper, tested, and proven to your own satisfaction.

This process of developing your goals has three steps:

1) Developing a preliminary goal statement.

2) Building assumptions, testing them, and satisfying yourself that the goal is either as realistic as you thought it to be or it isn't at all. If it isn't, the next step is to modify the goal, either in scope or in the amount of time it will take.

3) Revision of the goal statement.

Now let's focus in on the second step, building assumptions to support your goals.

Developing Assumption Statements

Assumptions are the cornerstones that support the structure of the goal. While many planners think that the assumption base consists solely of financial information, there are a number of ways to build your assumptions. Financial data is an important part, of course. But your goal will be stronger and more likely to succeed if you consider other sources, also.

elements of goals

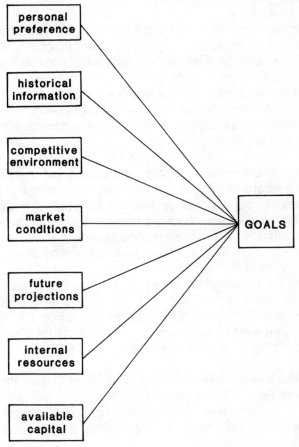

Figure 4-1

Figure 4-1 shows seven sources you can use in developing goals. Let's look at them one at a time.

Personal preference*—** Your goal should always be based on what ***you want. There's only one reason you're running your own operation, taking risks, and giving up the security of a regular paycheck signed by someone else. You made the decision to branch out on your own because you wanted more opportunity. Now make sure that the goals you set are meeting your expectations.

Think back to the time before you started your company. You wanted more personal freedom, better income and the increased self-esteem that comes from being your own boss. In some respects, the reality of being on your own might not meet your expectations. But you can change that. Keep in mind the personal satisfaction you were seeking when you started out — and structure the business plan around your original goals.

Historical information— A goal can be modified or expanded, based on what you have already learned. Your goal will be based largely on your experience: observations in the field and the office, analysis of your books and records, and knowledge of other profitable and not-so-profitable contractors. If you've made mistakes in the past, learn from them. And use your successes as the foundation for more success. Too many business owners start each year fresh, ignoring what happened in the recent past. Don't make that mistake. Keep good records, and base your future on what's taken place in the past. Recent events are often the best indicators of what you can expect in the near future.

Competitive environment— This is the best test of the goals you've set. For example, you plan to increase income substantially over the next year. But how much competition is there for the same business? Make your goals realistic by keeping an eye on the competition.

Stay in touch with other people in your field. Don't assume that you should never contact your own competition. Not only are they the best source of information you need, but you might both benefit by comparing notes.

Market conditions— You don't have a realistic goal if it's not based on actual conditions in your market. Is there a good demand for your service? If so, take a more aggressive approach in setting goals. But if that demand is low, your goal must be more modest. For example, few home builders can expect to build and sell more homes when demand for housing is weak. If there's a building moratorium in effect, a lot of existing homes for sale, and families and businesses moving away from the area, an optimistic growth goal isn't practical.

Successful planning requires a good forecast of market conditions. You can do this by being involved. You probably know a great deal more about trends and cycles than you give yourself credit for. For example, you deal with your market every day, talking with suppliers, subcontractors, and customers. You can see the trends developing if you're tuned in to the market. By comparing today's environment with six months ago, you can spot what's happening in your own organization. Now it's simply a matter of putting that information down on paper and seeing how it applies to your own goals.

Future projections— Good planning is *anticipating.* Forecasting and planning for the future puts you one step ahead of the competition. You're prepared for the next change in the economic cycle, and primed for success. You can judge the cycle by using historical perspectives, looking for shifts in supply and demand, and measuring the attitude and apprehension of your competitors.

Always keep the near future in mind. Many construction contractors get so preoccupied with putting out today's fires that they never have time to look ahead. Force yourself to think in terms of the future, planning for it, not merely taking it as it comes.

Internal resources— As part of the planning process, consider what needs to change in your business to reach the goals set. But don't forget that your internal resources are a support tool for your own growth. Your existing staff, facilities, equipment and procedures are the launching pad for reaching any goal. You may need to expand staff to meet future growth. But don't overlook the existing capacity to support the goals you set.

Some of your employees can probably offer good suggestions on the changes needed to reach new goals. Because your employees are closer to their jobs than anyone else, they're in the best position to advise you on ways to build assumptions. In most cases, you only have to ask for their participation. If your employees offer no new ideas, it's usually because they think you don't need or want their advice. If you invite suggestions, most employees will be happy to oblige.

Available capital— The best laid plans can't happen without money. This may be one of the hardest parts about planning for the future. Test your goals on the basis of time and cost. That should reveal whether or not you're being realistic. If the money is there, either from personal funds, income, or lenders, you'll be able to finance growth. If it isn't there, don't give up. Use the planning process to build up equity. Once your resources are in place, launch the more ambitious growth plan.

Don't let capital limitations discourage your most ambitious plans. There might be a way to arrange financing or investments to reach the goal you have in mind. But use capital limitations to keep your goals as realistic as possible. Trying to grow too rapidly has caused more than a little embarrassment for many construction companies. If your plan calls for rapid growth, you may be heading for trouble.

Testing Your Assumptions

In the last chapter, we talked about testing assumptions. Now let's look at how you actually test them, and why.

The method of testing is to work out the numbers, and make sure they fit into what you've learned from experience. You test to make sure your assumptions are realistic.

____CASE HISTORY: Faulty Assumptions ____

Joe Cambrini operated his landscaping business for three years before trying to put together his first business plan. He developed three goals for the coming year:

- To eliminate smaller residential jobs that were unprofitable.

- To win a larger market share and increase gross receipts by 20 percent.

- To reduce overhead by 10 percent for the year.

The first step Joe took was to project his goals in an estimated income statement for the year. He used a good technique. He started out with his actual income statement for the twelve months just ended. Then he subtracted the income from small residential jobs, increased his gross by 20 percent, and reduced overhead by 10 percent. This produced such a large projected profit that it made him wonder whether the goal was realistic.

He hadn't yet put down on paper the assumptions underlying his goals — so he tried to develop assumptions for his initial goal statements. Here's what he found out:

1) His smaller residential jobs weren't as unprofitable as he'd assumed. They filled in between larger jobs, keeping his regular crew of four men busy nearly all year. He liked being able to do that. And the income from those projects did help carry the overhead. If he turned down smaller jobs, most of his overhead would continue — with no cash coming in. So the effort spent on those jobs wasn't as pointless as he'd thought.

2) Increasing his market share by 20 percent in one year was too aggressive. Considering the large number of landscape contractors in the area (many of them more established, with larger crews, and more equipment and contracts), he decided that building a larger income base would take longer than one year.

3) Overhead could be reduced by at least 10 percent, and perhaps by more. There was a lot of fat in the budget, he suspected.

Based on the newly stated assumptions, he made some revisions to his plan. First, he decided to raise his rates slightly for residential jobs. He was charging less than most of his larger competitors. By increasing his income from the small jobs, he lost a few projects. But those he did handle were more profitable.

Second, Joe decided to go for a 5 percent growth in overall gross income. He wanted commercial work and recurring landscape jobs from the many condominium and apartment complexes in town, but he decided to retain a good mix of work, including some residential jobs.

Finally, he decided to place emphasis on controlling costs, hoping to increase profits by lowering the cost of doing business.

The Testing Process

Follow this process to develop realistic goals: First, define where you *think* you want to go. Then build your assumptions around the statements you develop. Test those assumptions with the information at hand, using the seven elements we've just discussed to validate or challenge what you've assumed. When that's completed, build a time line, breaking goals down into phases and giving yourself deadlines. Figure 4-2 shows these phases of goal development.

SETTING DEADLINES

When you've completed testing of your goals, you should have a definite, realistic set of goals for the coming year. Now the way is clear to build the best possible plan that will reach those goals.

But you're not likely to succeed in any plan without a schedule. And the best schedule is a series of little deadlines leading to final completion on schedule. Break your goal into distinct phases that you can track to make sure you're staying on schedule.

goal development

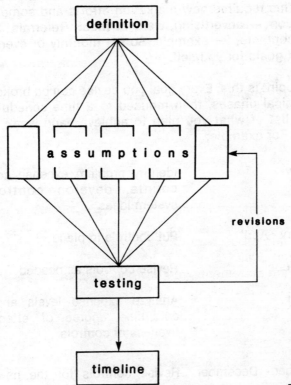

definition

assumptions

revisions

testing

timeline

Figure 4-2

1) A yearly income goal can be broken down into monthly goals. Be aware of seasonal variations. Few builders are equally busy every month of the year. If your goal is 20 percent more income, a good measure of your success would be comparing income this month with the same month last year. If the increase is 20 percent, you've met the monthly goal.

2) Phase in expense reductions in several logical steps. First, identify possible savings. Get ideas from your

77

employees, your accountant, and even from other contractors who have faced the same problems.

3) Building a new line of business has to be a gradual process. This requires new marketing efforts and some form of promotion — advertising, word of mouth referrals, and personal contacts, for example. So set monthly or even weekly contact goals for yourself.

The point is this: Every goal you devise can be broken down into logical phases, then reduced to a time schedule. Start with a list of what you plan to achieve each week or each month. For example:

January	Identify problem expense accounts, develop control system ideas
February - April	Put controls in place
May - June	Revise controls as needed
October	Analyze expense levels and determine degree of effectiveness of controls
November - December	Revise controls for the new year

Your schedule can be charted on a time line to make it easier to follow progress toward the goal. Figure 4-3 shows a typical time line. Follow these steps to use a time line:

1) Identify each phase by date and a brief description in the middle section.

2) Write in the deadline dates above the time line at the top, beginning with the start date, then the deadline date for the first phase, and so on.

the time line

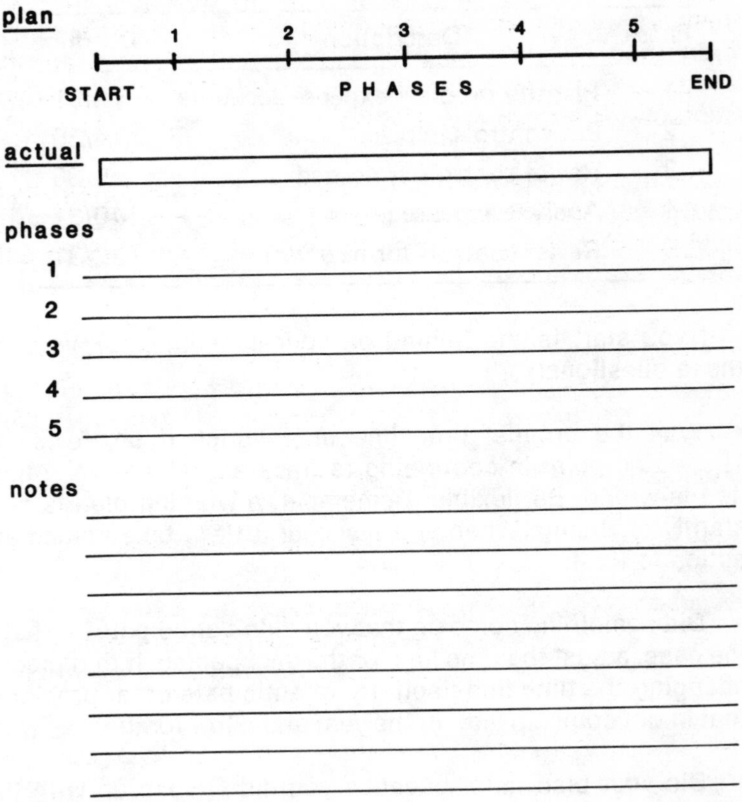
plan
1
2
3
4
5
START
P H A S E S
END
actual
phases
1
2
3
4
5
notes

Figure 4-3

3) As you progress toward your goal, darken in the block marked ***actual*** under the time line. You can tell at a glance if you're on schedule.

4) Keep notes in the bottom section, describing any unexpected problems and/or changes you've had to make along the way.

For example, the five-part goal described earlier would be listed on the time line like this:

Phase	Description	Deadline
1	Identify problem expense accounts	1/31
2	Put controls in place	4/30
3	Revise controls as needed	6/30
4	Analyze expense levels	10/31
5	Revise controls for new year	12/31

If you start falling behind on your schedule, ask yourself these questions:

• Was the original time line unrealistic? If so, revise it. There's no point in continuing to track a goal when the time line is wrong. Be flexible. Remember, a working plan is constantly changing. When you discover a flaw, take immediate action to fix it.

• Did something come up that you didn't anticipate? If that's the case, adjust the time line for the unexpected. If that means changing the time line itself, try to anticipate other problems that might come up later in the year and allow for them as well.

• Did your plan falter because you didn't keep up with the schedule? In this case, you need to catch up with the self-imposed deadline. A plan requires constant monitoring. It doesn't necessarily have to be a time-consuming process. But you do need to keep the plan in mind if you expect it to work.

Keep a running record of your progress throughout the year. This will be a valuable technique, both for managing your current goals and learning for the future. The successes and failures you have now in writing your plan will teach you how to be successful when you actually put the plan into effect.

```
+--------------------------------------------------------+
|                                                        |
|              goal management worksheet                 |
|                                                        |
|  goal _____ |
|                                                        |
|                                                        |
|  deadline   phase    date  comment                     |
|  _____   _____   ____  _____  |
|  _____   _____   ____  _____  |
|  _____   _____   ____  _____  |
|  _____   _____   ____  _____  |
|  _____   _____   ____  _____  |
|  _____   _____   ____  _____  |
|  _____   _____   ____  _____  |
|  _____   _____   ____  _____  |
|  _____   _____   ____  _____  |
|  _____   _____   ____  _____  |
|  _____   _____   ____  _____  |
|  _____   _____   ____  _____  |
|  _____   _____   ____  _____  |
|                                                        |
+--------------------------------------------------------+
```

Figure 4-4

Use a worksheet like the one shown in Figure 4-4 for this purpose.

List each deadline date and give each milestone a number on your time line. On a separate piece of paper, write down any problems you had meeting the goal at each intermediate point. Keep these worksheets in a loose-leaf binder. When you prepare to go through the planning process again next year, these notes will help you to develop the new plan.

REDUCING PAPERWORK

Does business planning require a lot of forms and charts? Will you be overwhelmed by paperwork, chained to your desk for hours at a time to keep on top of it?

The truth is, a good plan will *reduce* your paperwork. It will also save time and increase profits. You do need a few forms and charts to track your plan, of course — but you don't have to fill them out every day. Chances are, you'll only spend a few minutes each week reviewing your progress and updating the record.

If your plan is taking too much time, it isn't a good plan. A practical and efficient plan has these features:

1) It's easily managed. As the owner of a busy company, you can't afford to spend several hours each week stuck behind a desk, filling in forms and doing clerical work.

2) The forms and charts you use should show at a glance how the plan is proceeding. From this you should know what has to be done and when it has to be done to meet the plan goal.

3) It's coordinated. Your plan isn't something you do separately from day-to-day operations. It's an integrated system you practice as part of your management of the company. You don't just do a plan on paper. The paperwork is only a reminder and an aid in organizing your plan. You really carry your plan around with you, just as a carpenter hangs a hammer on his belt.

How do you turn the concepts in your plan into action? That requires keeping the plan in mind during your daily routine. Whenever a decision comes up, you ask yourself this important question: "How will this decision affect my business plan?"

A plan is only real when you act on what you discover. That means watching constantly. As the actual results begin to vary from the plan, you take actions to get back on track. If your goal is to reduce expenses and your overhead comes in higher than budget one month, *take action now.* Find out where the money was spent, why it happened, and what has to be done to prevent it from happening again.

Regular reviews of progress toward each plan goal will help you spot problems early, before they derail your progress completely. Taking action early puts you back on track before serious damage has been done. Your plan is a practical document, not just an intellectual exercise. The action you take after each plan review determines whether the plan fails or succeeds.

In the next chapter, we'll begin looking at the sections of the business plan one at a time, beginning with the introduction.

5 THE PLAN INTRODUCTION

Although the introduction to your plan should be short, it serves an important purpose. Here, in just one or two pages, you set the tone, present your major goals and arguments, and fill in a reader on what the plan is all about.

Business consultants don't all agree on when the introduction should be prepared. Some prefer to develop the goals and assumptions first, write a draft of each of the sections, and then finish up by writing the introduction. Others turn that process around. They write the introduction first (assuming goals have already been developed and tested), and use the introduction to set the theme for the entire plan.

Choose the method that works best for you. Some people don't like to write their plan until an introduction is behind them. Writing the introduction first may help establish the plan theme in your mind early in the process. This can be helpful in developing the other sections.

Other consultants prefer to write the introduction last, after the entire plan is finalized. You might be more comfortable writing this as a summary (even though it goes in the front of the plan). There's a chance you'll make changes to the plan as you draft the later stages.

As a compromise, you can draft your introduction first, proceed through the rest of the plan — and finally, go back and review the first section, making any changes you need at that point.

SET THE TONE

The tone you set in the introduction will affect a reader's impression of the entire plan. If it sounds confident and optimistic, that's how your entire plan will be viewed by the reader. And if it sounds unsure, or if you base the entire plan on poorly developed assumptions and goals, that will come through, too. And others will have less confidence in your plan. You'll probably have less confidence in it yourself!

Be careful in setting the tone. Assume that you will need to show your plan to others during the year. Even though you think you're going through this just for your own use, you may decide later that you need a bank loan, for example. You should have a valid, working plan ready to show a loan officer when that time comes.

Few things impress a lending officer more than seeing a business owner with a complete, practical, working business plan. Most people don't plan ahead. Walking in with a well-thought-out plan is a good start to getting that loan.

The banker's primary concern is whether or not you'll be able to repay the loan. It's a matter of risk. Are you solvent enough to afford loan payments with your cash flow? Are you profitable? What's the competition, the demand in the market, and the likelihood that you'll be able to survive in business? Those are the subjects every business plan should cover.

Your plan will help prove you're a good risk. It shows that you're a progressive professional, with goals set and a plan to reach those goals. Just having a plan places you above the average applicant for a loan. You reduce your chance of failure by planning for the future.

If you don't expect to need a bank loan, you still have a considerable advantage with a plan. It's that element of anticipation — trying to figure out what will happen during the next twelve months — that gives you an edge over your competition. A plan shows that you understand trends in the market, are planning cash flow for the inevitable slow periods, and have anticipated the need for more labor and new equipment. You're no longer just a contractor following the competition. You're anticipating the future and planning to take advantage of it.

Even if you don't share your plan with someone else, the tone you set in your introduction should put you in a productive frame of mind. If the introduction shows doubt and indecision, it will probably affect your ability to reach the goals set. If you're worried about being able to write a strong, positive introduction, read on. When you focus on the key areas worth highlighting, the job won't be difficult.

INTRODUCE THE KEY AREAS OF THE PLAN

The introduction is a narrative section. It brings the reader into the plan, points out the highlights, and identifies three key areas of your plan:

1) *Major goals:* You may have only one goal, or a series of targets for the year. Regardless of the number or their complexity, you must base all of your planning activities around these major points.

Your goal doesn't have to be for expansion. Some contractors have realized that too much growth, or growing too quickly, can be more hazardous than not growing at all. So your goal might be to increase profitability without taking on any new lines of work.

Your major goals don't even have to be financial. You might want to build a specific level of quality, for example. That's a good goal but doesn't involve higher income, higher profits, or cash flow.

2) *Assumptions:* It's not enough to simply state a goal and expect to reach it. Your goals must be supported by assumptions. For example, when you set the goal of increasing income, you make a series of assumptions: that there's a demand; that you can win more work than your competition; that you have or can accumulate the money, tradesmen, subcontractors and equipment needed to handle that growth; and that you can keep costs and expenses under control.

Think of assumptions as the proof of your goals. As long as you make a convincing case, through historical and current information, your projection of the future will be valid.

Developing assumptions also makes you think about what could go wrong. With some goals, you'll discover flaws just by going through the process of building an assumption base. That forces a change, and strengthens your plan.

3) *Actions:* You'll identify what actions are needed for the plan to succeed. That's where your time line comes in. Include a precise statement of the actions you'll take.

Many plans go almost far enough and then stop. They identify goals and assumptions that are strong and realistic . . . then they fail to come up with an action plan. As a result, nothing really happens. The entire planning process is a waste of time and effort if you don't identify the steps that are required — and then take those steps.

Coming up with the right actions is the hard part of planning. Many concepts look good on paper. To turn them into reality, you have to decide what has to be done and when it's going to be done.

WHAT TO INCLUDE

Your introduction can say a great deal in only one or two pages. Concentrate on these five major areas: the plan overview, company history, resources, current status, and the future. Let's look at them one at a time.

The Plan Overview

Start out by telling the reader what the plan is, what it includes, and what you hope to achieve with it.

Give the reader your purpose. Why are you doing the plan? Your purpose could be to map out a way to expand your markets, reduce expenses, or finance the purchase of new equipment.

Also specify the scope of your plan. If you include budgets and forecasts, or a marketing plan, say so.

Finally, include any special notes on the methods you've used in your plan. Keep this section brief, while giving the reader enough knowledge to understand exactly how you developed your details.

Company History

Assume the reader knows nothing about your company. Describe what form of organization you use (corporation, partnership or sole proprietorship), the year founded, and the name of all owners if you have partners. Explain briefly the type of work you do, and how you developed your markets to this point.

Resources

Explain what you have to work with. This section should include a discussion of four points:

Personnel— How many people work for you, and in what capacity?

Systems— Are you automated? Do you have an unusual telephone system or method for communicating with remote crews? How do your systems help you on jobs?

Experience— Briefly explain your own background and qualifications.

Capital— Every builder needs working capital. You have money invested in equipment, receivables, work in progress, and cash on hand. How much do you have invested in each of these and in other assets?

Status

Describe operations today. What type of work do you perform, who are your customers, and what's the competition? What has your growth rate been during the time you've been in business? This establishes a foundation to support a reasonable and realistic projection of the future.

The Future

How do you predict your operation will change? Will you be doing a different kind of work? Will you see a shift in customers, or an increase or decrease in competition? Tie your discussion down in terms of specific goals, assumptions, and an active plan.

The five major areas of the introduction are illustrated in Figure 5-1.

CHOOSE THE PRESENTATION

The introduction leads the reader into the plan. The last section, the future, is especially related to the goals, assumptions and actions you'll lay out in subsequent sections.

There are several ways you can present the essential elements of your plan. Consider each of them. Then pick the method that seems right for you. You can emphasize your *goals,* your *assumptions,* or the *action* and time schedule you've built into the plan — or a combination of all three. The method you choose depends on how complex your plan is.

For example, one builder's plan was quite simple. The only goal was to reduce expenses for the year. He worked out a forecast and budget so that his profits would increase by 11

introduction topics

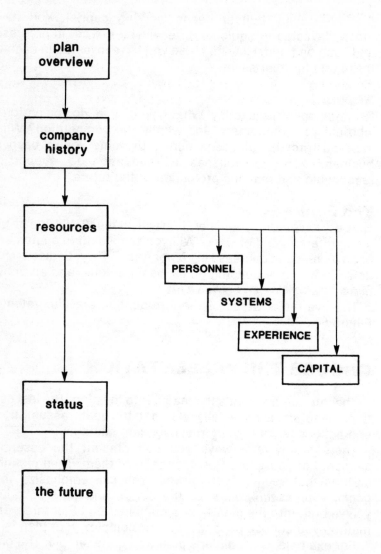

Figure 5-1

percent — just from expense controls. He used the direct approach, discussing this goal in the introduction, his assumptions, and the action plan.

In another case, a builder planned a major expansion for the year. It would involve forecasting significant growth in income, increases in variable expenses, new controls over fixed expense areas, investment in new equipment, hiring more employees, and automating a good part of the administrative chores. This complex plan was introduced with a discussion of the major goals. Major assumptions were mentioned in support of the goals. An action plan was laid out very briefly. (Remember, the introduction should be relatively short, with the details included in each of the other sections.)

Regardless of the approach you use, you'll need to cover the five major areas we listed earlier. The approach just changes the emphasis you put on each area. First we'll look at the integrated approach.

The Integrated Approach

This involves discussing your goals, assumptions and action plan as a collective unit. The advantage here is that the three parts — goals, assumptions and actions — are tied together and made inseparable. This adds continuity to your plan and stresses the relationship between those three points. For example, a statement of the future might read:

"During the coming year, we will earn the same amount of gross revenues **Goal** as during the past year. However, we will increase profits by reducing the **Assumption** level of overhead expenses. Control systems will be put into place during **Action** the first quarter."

The integrated approach is shown in Figure 5-2.

91

the integrated approach

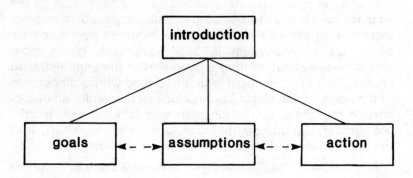

Figure 5-2

The Goals Approach

With this method, the goal itself is the primary subject covered. Assumptions and actions are included, but only in the context of the goal itself. This points out the importance of goals as the guiding principles of your entire plan. Everything hinges on goals, without exception. Using the same example, let's see how it might read if you use the goals approach:

"During the coming year, we will
achieve the same level of gross   **Goal**
revenues as during the past year.
Our purpose is to control growth   **Assumption**
but increase profits by careful and
direct control of overhead ex-   **Action**
penses."

The goals approach is illustrated in Figure 5-3.

the goals approach

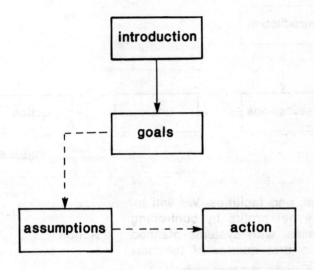

Figure 5-3

The Assumption Approach

Here, the approach is much different. The assumptions of your plan are emphasized, with goals and actions secondary. When discussing the future, speaking in terms of assumptions demonstrates that you have a realistic point of view. You're not simply making up goals out of thin air. For example:

"We believe our level of overhead expenses during past years was too high, and that profits can be increased with the use of internal controls. We also believe that our current level of income is an acceptable level, given our staff,

Assumption

Goal

93

the assumption approach

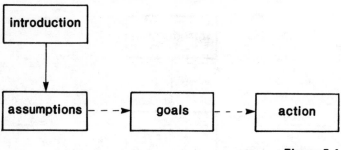

Figure 5-4

capital, and facilities. We will increase net profits by controlling
expenses, with systems planned   **Action**
for the first quarter of the new
year."

Figure 5-4 depicts the assumption approach.

The Action Approach
The final approach to the introduction is placing your emphasis on actions. With this approach, you emphasize what's
going to be done. This focuses the reader's mind on what will
happen. It adds a touch of reality to the difficult task of projec-
ting the future. For example:

"We have developed overhead control systems, and will install them
during the first quarter of   **Action**
the new year. These internal con-
trols will increase net profits for
the year without the need for   **Goal**
a corresponding growth in gross

94

the action approach

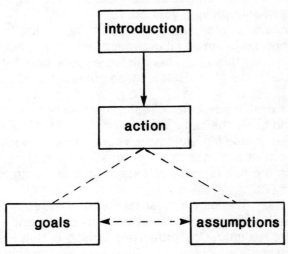

Figure 5-5

income. We believe a significant improvement in net profits is possible under present circumstances, and that attempting to expand revenues would be a mistake in today's market.

Assumption

The action approach is illustrated in Figure 5-5.

THE IMPORTANCE OF THE INTRODUCTION

The way you write your introduction and the points you make will set the tone for your plan. Emphasize the positive.

Write as though you're completely confident your goals will be reached. But make only your major points. This is just the introduction. The details come later.

It's enough to mention major goals, assumptions and actions within the context of the introduction. Later you'll be concerned with proving your point.

Assume your plan will go to a lending institution for the most important loan you'll ever need, even if you don't plan to borrow money this year. This will force you to fight for your major points in the plan. Follow these guidelines:

• **Be a devil's advocate.**   Test and challenge your assumptions and goals the same way a lender would. Show your plan to someone else (an employee, your spouse, or your accountant, for example). Ask them for ideas and criticism. Then improve on the points that don't stand up under criticism.

• **Revise.**   Change your plan as much as necessary to make it valid. Be sure your assumptions are strong and that your goals are realistic. One pitfall of planning is that it's hard to maintain your own objectivity. Only by reviewing your assumptions and your goals can you end up with a solid, absolute plan that you're sure will work.

• **Look for negatives.**   There's always something that can go wrong. What will happen to your plan if part of it doesn't work out? Going through this phase brings out any weaknesses. It forces you to justify and prove the major points you make in the plan.

• **Organize and then reorganize.**   Once you have laid out your plan, does it make sense? Look for ways to make important points first and leave details until later. You'll know you're on the right track when your introduction says a great deal in a very small amount of space, and all the details and projections are in other parts of the plan.

• **Simplify.**   Your plan should be so easy to follow that anyone will be able to see at a glance exactly who you are, where you're going, and what you will achieve in the coming year. If anyone has questions after reviewing your plan, you haven't gone far enough. Even after you think you've done everything you can to make the plan simple, look at it one last time and try to cut the length wherever possible.

FOLLOW THESE STEPS IN WRITING YOUR PLAN

The introduction needs to be just long enough to cover the major points and introduce a reader to you, your operation, and the resources you have available.

What's the best way to express these ideas? You don't have to be a polished technical writer to put together a good introduction. You just need to write what you know, then edit it. I'll break the process down into six steps, beginning with organization.

Organize the Material

What are you going to say? Make a list of what you want to cover in your introduction. Then put it in the most logical order.

The more organized you are before you begin to write, the better your first draft will be. You'll save time because you won't need to do so much editing later. And organization will make it easier to write and to focus on a specific topic.

Figure 5-6 is a listing of the points one contractor wanted to cover in his introduction. Notice that the list is organized by the five major topics we discussed earlier.

Write Your First Draft

Simply write your introduction, in the order you've organized it. Keep to one subject at a time, following your outline carefully.

Don't be too concerned at this point with a polished, final version. Just get down on paper all of the important points you need to make. If you're not sure about statements, phrasing, or the best way to communicate an idea, underline that section and come back to it later.

the introduction list

Plan overview:

      purpose - map out ideas for higher profits
               - cutting overhead expenses
               - shifting business to residential

      marketing plan - ideas for reaching customers

      budget and forecast - method

Company history:

      form - sole proprietorship, then corporation
      year founded - 1986, incorporated 1988
      owner - Karl Sterling

Resources:

      personnel - crews, office staff, estimator
      systems - computer for job cost, scheduling
      experience - construction background
      capital - line of credit, expected new loans
            - investment in equipment

Current status:

      work - type of work done
          - profitability
      customers - residential
              - commercial
      growth rate - summary of volume and profits

The future:

      changes in operations - shift to residential
                         - reduce commercial jobs
                         - reduce overhead
                         - same volume, higher profits

      kinds of work - profitable and unprofitable
      customers - rates of profit
            - market demand

Figure 5-6

Figure 5-7 shows the first draft the contractor wrote, following his outline in Figure 5-6. At this point, he wasn't concerned with style or organization — he just wanted to get all of his ideas down on paper.

Smooth It Out

Go back over what you've written and read it back to yourself, aloud if that helps. Look for awkward phrases or words that don't sound right to you. Think of a better way to say what you want. Make the changes that seem necessary.

Once you have something down on paper, editing yourself isn't too difficult. Most people struggle with a first draft. But going back over something and improving it is much easier than getting it down on paper in the first place.

Make Easy Transitions

Look at the end of each section and the beginning of the next one. As you change subjects, be aware that the reader needs to be led from one point to another. The purpose of adding transitions is to make the introduction easy to read. Without proper transitions, it will seem choppy and disorganized, even if you've put a lot of work into it. Writing transitions is a fairly simple technique, but it will improve the quality of your writing substantially.

Let's look at a couple of examples. Here's how one first draft read:

"...field crew consists of 23 men organized in three primary crews. In addition, an estimator and office manager are on staff.

"Job cost records are kept on an automated system that the owner designed with the help of outside consultants. This system . . . ."

Notice how the discussion suddenly shifts from one topic to another. The reader is concentrating on staff and then sudden-

the first draft

The company hopes to change this year, by cutting out commercial accounts, that are not as profitable as the residential accounts the company also serves. We could do this by cutting the overhead expenses, which seem to grow at a faster pace than volume of sales each year. We will also try to keep overall volume at about the same level as last year, but hopefully with a higher profit.

We will reach customers by using our present customers for referrals, and by advertising. We also plan to make contact with other sources, including real estate brokers, developers, and homeowner lending institutions in the area.

Included in this plan is the company's budget and forecast for the new year. It was developed by the company using tested assumptions, and we hope it will prove to be accurate.

The company was formed as a sole proprietorship in 1986 and incorporated in 1988. Karl Sterling is the owner and sole stockholder.

Resources include 25 fulltime field workers and three foremen. The company also has two office workers, and one estimator.

Job cost records and scheduling are on the computer, which means the company can save a lot of time in recording information and getting reports, even if the volume of business increases. The company will not have to hire new office employees just to keep records.

The owner has many years of experience in the construction field. Before starting this company, he was a foreman with Crowell Construction, a job he had for more than 10 years.

The company has a $35,000 line of credit with its bank, enough to take care of temporary cash flow problems during the year, and to buy needed new equipment. The company will try to get a new loan for the one major equipment purchase it wants to make this year. The investment in equipment is now $285,000, and the company expects to buy about $20,000 in new equipment this year.

We now do about 40% commercial and 60% residential work. The demand for residential is increasing, and the margin of profit is better than commercial jobs. The business plan includes a summary of last year's volume and profits in each group.

Figure 5-7

first draft (page 2)

On average, commercial work yields a 5% profit and residential work ends up at about 10%. If we are right about the market, we should be able to replace the level of commercial work over the next 12 to 24 months, and have strictly residential contracts. The volume of new home construction and renovation among existing home-owners is high, and demand for residential work is growing.

In the near future, the company would like to shift away from commercial contract work. At the same time, they should be able to reduce overhead, since the expense mix seems to be heavier on the commercial side. This could be achieved with good internal controls and by following the budget closely. As a result, the company hopes to achieve higher profits with approximately the same level of gross volume.

One goal is for the company to emphasize volume that is more profitable. The company does not want to expand its operations just to become larger, but wants to be a more profitable company.

The combination of the rate of profit and the demand on the residential side leads the company to set its goal for the new year. They should be able to do this by going through a gradual transition. It will take time to build up the volume of residential work, and a schedule is included in the marketing plan. By the end of the year, we hope to improve profits by 2%. And by the end of two years, the company estimates it will improve profits by 4% above last year's level.

Figure 5-7 (continued)

ly is facing a discussion of job cost records. Here's how to rewrite it with a transition:

". . . field crew consists of 23 men organized in three primary crews. In addition, an estimator and office manager are on staff.

"Having multiple crews enables the company to work on several jobs at the same time, which requires efficient support systems. With that in mind, the owner developed an automated job cost system with the help of outside consultants."

Here's another example:

". . . with seven years as foreman for a major contractor, and another five years operating his own company.

"During the coming year, the operation will expand considerably. That will require a considerable investment in equipment . . ."

In this case, the discussion goes from a summary of the owner's background, into expansion and investment needs. That's a drastic change that needs a transition to help the reader:

". . . with seven years as a foreman for a major contractor, and another five years operating his own company.

"The owner has learned throughout this period that growth is not possible without investment of capital. During the coming year, the operation will expand considerable, requiring. . ."

Put It in the Active Voice
Try to use the active rather than passive voice. Add action to your explanations.

It's easy to fall into the trap of believing we have to qualify everything we say. Rather than making a definite statement ("we will"), there's a tendency to leave room for error ("we would like"). But that weakens the style of writing. Make definite, positive statements that add strength and power to your introduction. Some examples:

Passive statement	Active statement
The firm hopes to grow by about 10%	We will grow by no less than 10%

If the company does make this goal . . .	When we make this goal . . .
It is hoped that we will reduce expenses.	We will reduce expenses.
The company will attempt to increase its revenues . . .	We will increase revenues . . .
The company would like to grow by . . .	We will grow by . . .

Also make your introduction friendly and personal by using the first person (words like "we" and "our") and avoiding the third person ("the company").

Do Your Final Edit

A day or two after you've completed the introduction, read it again. Look for words, phrases or paragraphs that can be deleted. If possible, cut its length in half. I'm not kidding. You'll find that it's possible in most cases to cut out half the words you use without reducing the value of what you've written. This may help make the introduction an efficient, clear expression that sets a tone for your entire plan.

Nearly all writing can be improved by eliminating unnecessary words. Most people tend to write too much and include too little meaning in what they've written. That's what editing is for. Write as much as you like. Then go back to cut out the excess. You should end up with a concise, clear explanation of the major points you're trying to make.

Perhaps the hardest part of self-editing is being objective about your work. It helps to put some time between each of the steps. When you pick up the pages a day or two later, you're looking at the words with fresh eyes more likely to find weaknesses.

the edited first draft

passive voice

The company hopes to change this year, by cutting out commercial accounts, that are not as profitable as the residential accounts the company also serves. We could do this by cutting the overhead expenses, which seem to grow at a faster pace than volume of sales each year. We will also try to keep overall volume at about the same level as last year, but hopefully with a higher profit.

will — *WEAK BEGINNING*

should be stated more strongly

We will reach customers by using our present customers for referrals, and by advertising. We also plan to make contact with other sources, including real estate brokers, developers, and homeowner lending institutions in the area.

← repeats
will

Included in this plan is the company's budget and forecast for the new year. It was developed by the company using tested assumptions, and we hope it will prove to be accurate.

passive
NEEDS A transition

The company was formed as a sole proprietorship in 1986 and incorporated in 1988. Karl Sterling is the owner and sole stockholder.

SAY this differently

Resources include 25 fulltime field workers and three foremen. The company also has two office workers, and one estimator.

combine

strengthen

Job cost records and scheduling are on the computer, which means the company can save a lot of time in recording information and getting reports, even if the volume of business increases. The company will not have to hire new office employees just to keep records.

The owner has many years of experience in the construction field. Before starting this company, he was a foreman with Crowell Construction, a job he had for more than 10 years.

PASSIVE

The company has a $35,000 line of credit with its bank, enough to take care of temporary cash flow problems during the year, and to buy needed new equipment. The company will try to get a new loan for the one major equipment purchase it wants to make this year. The investment in equipment is now $285,000, and the company expects to buy about $20,000 in new equipment this year.

SAY in some other way

repeats

We now do about 40% commercial and 60% residential work. The demand for residential is increasing, and the margin of profit is better than commercial jobs. The business plan includes a summary of last year's volume and profits in each group.

how can we prove this? statistics, etc.

Figure 5-8

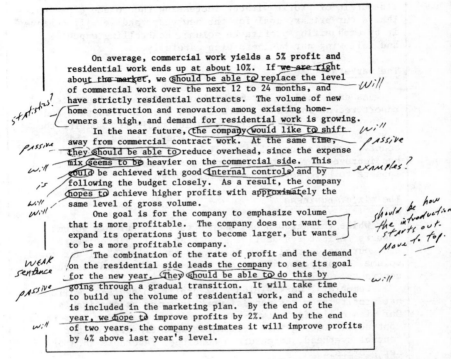

edited first draft (page 2)

On average, commercial work yields a 5% profit and residential work ends up at about 10%. If ~~we are right~~ about ~~the market~~, we ~~should be able to~~ replace the level of commercial work over the next 12 to 24 months, and have strictly residential contracts. The volume of new home construction and renovation among existing homeowners is high, and demand for residential work is growing.

statistics? *Will*

In the near future, ~~the company~~ ~~would like to~~ shift away from commercial contract work. At the same time, ~~they~~ ~~should be able to~~ reduce overhead, since the expense mix ~~seems to be~~ heavier on the commercial side. This ~~could~~ be achieved with good ~~internal controls~~ and by following the budget closely. As a result, the company ~~hopes to~~ achieve higher profits with ~~approximately~~ the same level of gross volume.

passive *will* *passive* *will* *examples?* *is* *will* *will*

One goal is for the company to emphasize volume that is more profitable. The company does not want to expand its operations just to become larger, but wants to be a more profitable company.

should be how the introduction starts out. Move to top.

The combination of the rate of profit and the demand on the residential side leads the company to set its goal for the new year. ~~They~~ ~~should be able to~~ do this by going through a gradual transition. It will take time to build up the volume of residential work, and a schedule is included in the marketing plan. By the end of the year, we ~~hope to~~ improve profits by 2%. And by the end of two years, the company estimates it will improve profits by 4% above last year's level.

WEAK sentence *passive* *will* *will*

Figure 5-8 (continued)

In Figure 5-8, you can follow the editing our contractor did to his first draft. He moved things around to emphasize the important points, changed some passive language to active, and generally made it a stronger section.

As part of the final edit, prepare the introduction for typing in an attractive format. Break it down into appropriate sections, with headings for each subject. Underline the headings or leave space around them to make it easy for the reader to follow the organization. Make it as visually inviting as possible, even when it's only a couple of pages long.

the final version

This will be the year that Sterling Construction improves its margin of profit without increasing the volume of sales. That's our primary goal for the new year, and we will achieve it by emphasizing profitable volume, controlling expenses, and following our business plan carefully.

The markets

As explained in our marketing section, local studies report recent increases, both in new home construction and in the volume of homeowner renovation projects. During the last two years, 25 new companies opened offices in this county, creating over 500 new jobs. The employment rate has improved during the same two years, and the growth trend appears to have several more years to go.

The mix of business

While this growth has been occurring, our own volume results reflect residential growth as well. Three years ago, our residential work accounted for only 15% of our total volume. Last year, 60% of all revenues came from residential contracts.

Commercial work yields a 5% profit on average, while our net profit from residential work is twice as profitable. Our plan calls for a two-year transition away from commercial contracts. During this period, we will closely monitor and control overhead, to ensure a continued favorable rate of net profits.

Controlling volume and expenses

This business plan emphasizes the importance of controlled expenses during the period of changing income. We will achieve this through installation of expense controls, tracking the budget, and following our own schedule for contacting and attracting new residential accounts. We will utilize our existing customer base for referrals, as well as approaching the market through other means (see the marketing plan).

Resources

The success of this plan depends on the right mixture of experience, professional employees, equipment and capital. Sterling Construction originally formed as a partnership in

Figure 5-9

1986, was incorporated in 1988. Karl Sterling, president and sole stockholder, began this firm with more than 10 years of construction experience. His background, plus the experience of the estimator, office staff of two, and three 8-man crews, places the company in an excellent position to address the needs of its customers.

Growth in the number of accounts will not pose a problem or an added expense for the company. We have automated our accounting, job cost and scheduling records, enabling us to quickly determine the status and profitability of any on-going project.

Our expansion into the residential field will, however, require investment of $20,000 in capital assets this year. We will finance this by seeking a new loan to add to our present investment level of $285,000 in equipment and machinery.

We are protected against slower cash flow periods, and against the contingency that we will not obtain an equipment loan, by our existing $35,000 line of credit. Our plan will succeed without additional debt capital.

Summary

Sterling Construction has identified a market opportunity. The growth in demand for residential construction in our area will help make this plan a successful and profitable one. We already know that residential work is more profitable than commercial, and that we have the experience and resources to provide quality services to our customers.

We will grow in profits, without expanding our volume or fixed overhead. The key to this success is outlined in the following plan, including a schedule and time line for each of the action steps we will follow during the year.

Figure 5-9 (continued)

Set up pages with ample margins on the left and right as well as top and bottom. Use the same margins for the rest of the plan. To help the reader find what he wants, number each page and include a brief table of contents.

Follow these basic techniques and your introduction will be a convincing, direct, clear explanation of your plan and your operation — like the final version shown in Figure 5-9.

In the next chapter, we'll look at the second section of the business plan, the statement of your major goals.

MAJOR GOALS

Although you can choose when to write the introduction, there's no choice about putting the goals down on paper. They **must** be developed before you can outline the plan of action.

Setting goals is like putting up a building. You have to know where it's going, who will pay for it, what materials and labor will cost, how long it's going to take, and what the building should look like. That's a form of goal setting. You do the same thing in your plan, working with ideas and experience instead of materials and labor.

COMPONENTS OF GOALS

I suggest that you define your goals completely before putting them down on paper. There are three parts to defining any goal:

1) *The problem:* What do you want to improve or solve? You might be unhappy with your level of net profits, or need outside financing for the purchase of equipment. Maybe you want to start up a new service.

2) *The solution:* Once you understand what the problem is, you can devise the ideal solution. Of course, that means identifying resources, defining exactly what you want, and mapping out the process for getting there.

3) *The deadline:* You need to set a reasonable time for reaching the goal. When thinking about problems and solutions, time is always an important consideration. Don't expect your business to change overnight. You make it change gradually, with control and coordination, while keeping an eye on other responsibilities, the limits of your capital and manpower, and the customers you serve.

These three elements — problem, solution and deadline — are linked together. You can't separate them. Without goals and a specific plan, what happens? Most business owners say to themselves at some point, "I'd like to earn more money." Then what? All too often, that's about as far as it goes. Thinking about a problem isn't enough.

Here's a series of observations and opinions that could lead to a goal. But by themselves, they're of little value. **There's a lot of competition out there . . . But I don't have the money to grow any bigger . . . It takes too much time to manage bigger jobs and labor forces . . . I'll get there some day . . . I'm too busy to think about it right now.**

So what happens? Nothing! The goals aren't worked out. Solutions are never developed. The business owner might think the problem has been analyzed. But all that's been developed is an excuse for not solving the problem.

Most of the contractors I know don't intentionally avoid the process of setting and reaching goals. They just don't understand the procedure for doing it. But most of those same contractors who have used business planning to grow and prosper would describe the process as defining the future, mapping out a way to get there, and then taking action.

PUTTING IT ON PAPER

To develop your major goals, start out by putting all your thoughts on paper. You want to create a picture of the future. Writing everything down helps you build that picture. As long as the goal is no more than a vague notion, you won't start tackling the problem and solving it. Writing everything down lets you:

- Firm up the idea, making it concrete.

- Identify unrealistic ideas and correct them before you proceed.

- Break a big goal down into logical steps.

- See how you can actually get from here to there, through a controlled, methodical process.

Begin to Define the Goal

Let's take a typical idea and see how it can be developed into a goal. You start out with the thought, "I'd like to earn more money next year." Well, who wouldn't? We all have that goal. But how many of us set down and **plan how we're going to make it happen**? Your first step is defining your goal. Begin your first draft by writing down the subject and date:

Net profits   Today's date

Now describe the current status. Write down the problem as you understand it. For example:

"Net profit last year was about the same as the year before. But sales were higher. With increasing personal expenses, my real earning power is lower."

This simple statement says a lot. You've identified the problem. As you study the statement, you might realize that part of the problem is rising expenses. You solve a large part of the

110

problem by identifying expenses that can be controlled better. And to increase income, you'll have to study your markets and see where opportunities for more work can be found.

Describe the Ideal

Now you've defined the problem. Next, write down what you would consider your ideal position at the end of the plan. For example:

"Fixed overhead should be highly predictable, with sales rising slightly each year. Net income should also rise to the point where there's never a severe cash flow problem. I'd also like to put away some money for retirement, and have some cash in reserve for emergencies and slow months."

That might seem like a big order. And, in fact, you've expanded the scope of the issue. Your goal, as defined so far, has several parts:

1) Revenues should increase each year.
2) Fixed overhead should be controlled.
3) Cash flow should be predictable.
4) A cash reserve should be set up.
5) Money should be put away for retirement.

You can consider these five points as components of a single goal. Or, you can break them out into separate goals, and come up with a plan for each. There's more on this choice later in this chapter. For now, you have fully defined the scope of your challenge. You've told yourself where you are, and where you'd like to be. You've fine-tuned your goal, which sets up the next phase in developing a complete, workable plan.

Develop the Steps to Take

Write down the steps you need to take. Don't be concerned now with the order. You can rearrange your steps later when you develop a time line. Your steps might include:

- Identify ways to increase revenues.
- Set up a schedule for revenue growth.
- Study overhead accounts to identify problems.
- Put controls in place to reduce expense levels.
- Develop a cash flow projection for the year.
- Budget for deposits to a cash reserve fund.
- Start a retirement plan and fund it.

Details for these steps are developed in other parts of your plan. For now, you've identified the process for getting from the problem to the solution. You're ready to write your statement. It could read:

> Within the coming twelve months, I will increase revenues by no less than 10 percent over last year, and net profits by no less than 5 percent. Through control of cash flow, I will set up a cash reserve, and start my retirement plan.

If this seems like a simplified version of your goal, that's exactly what it is. A goal statement should be very simple and straightforward, including no details or specifics. Those come later. It should just state as clearly as possible what you're going to achieve in the next twelve months.

Use a worksheet like Figure 6-1 to define your own goals.

THE GOAL TIME LINE

After fully defining your preliminary goals, the next step is to place them on a schedule. Whether you have one primary goal or a number of related goals, this is a crucial step in getting from here to there.

You can start by simply listing what you know has to be done. Then rearrange your list so that the order is logical. Break goals down into a series of simple phases, making them manageable and respecting the limits of your time and abilities.

goal development worksheet

Subject _____ Date _____

Current status

_____

_____

_____

Ideal status

_____

_____

_____

Steps

1 _____

2 _____

3 _____

4 _____

5 _____

6 _____

Goal statement

_____

_____

_____

_____

Figure 6-1

For example, the goal may be reducing fixed overhead expenses. You have specific ideas for control systems, but you'll have to define and install them, train your staff, and monitor progress. Eventually, a part of the control process can be delegated to others. This all takes time. Although you can't make changes overnight, you can develop a reasonable schedule.

Maybe you'll want to tackle the biggest problems — the most wasteful part of the problem — first. Then take on the next problem, and so forth. Schedule it. Break down a big process into manageable phases.

Write up a time schedule as shown in Figure 6-2. Start by listing your goal in column 1. Assign a reference to the first phase, beginning with *A.* Describe the step. Reserve the last column for the date you expect to have finished that phase. For example, you might have three major goals: to reduce fixed overhead expenses, set up a retirement account, and increase revenues.

Look at Figure 6-3. It shows the time line schedule filled in with the steps you'll take to achieve those three goals.

These steps may look simplistic — and they are, to a degree. Just as a goal statement itself is a pared-down expression of where you're going, these summarized steps don't tell the whole story. They're one more step in the structure of a complete, working goal. In the initial stages, keep each phase clear and simple. The details come later.

For example, in the third goal, the **marketing plan** is a big job. You'll have to find a way of promoting your services to potential customers. The details on this may fill an entire section in your plan. For now, you only need to know that you have to schedule that phase. It may take several months to accomplish. And you might have to modify your initial time schedule once you get into the details. At this point, the important thing is to get through the time line itself.

Once you've developed a time line for each step of each goal, put the entire process on a single chart. See Figure 6-4.

Now, no matter how many goals you have, you'll be able to see your plan at a glance. Just enter the goal name on the ap-

time line schedule

Goal	Ref	Description	Actual (✓)

Figure 6-2

time line schedule

Goal	Ref	Description	Actual (✓)
REDUCE	A	WRITE UP CONTROLS	
EXPENSES	B	INSTALL CONTROLS	
	C	TRAIN EMPLOYEES	
	D	DEVELOP MONITORING SYSTEM	
	E	DELEGATE RESPONSIBILITY	
	F	EVALUATE SUCCESS	
	G	MODIFY PROCEDURE	
RETIREMENT	A	DISCUSS WITH EXPERTS	
FUND	B	SELECT FUND	
	C	BUDGET CONTRIBUTIONS	
	D	ADJUST BUDGETS	
INCREASE	A	IDENTIFY MARKETS	
SALES	B	DEVELOP FORECAST	
	C	MARKETING PLAN	
	D	MONITOR GROWTH	
	E	EVALUATE & REVISE	

Figure 6-3

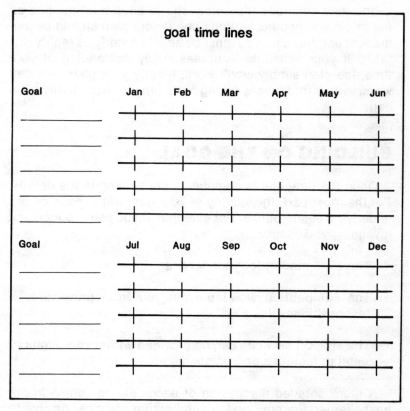

Figure 6-4

propriate line and place your reference step (A, B, or C) in the month you plan to complete it. By looking at this time line summary, you'll get a good sense of how realistic your initial plan is.

For example, you might have three or four goals for the year, with several steps planned for June and July. But you also know these are your busiest months. You'll be spending most of your time at job sites or estimating on a short deadline. In that case, is it realistic to schedule a lot of administrative and planning time in the office?

You may conclude it's unrealistic to keep the time line on the original schedule. Nothing about your plan should be permanent or inflexible. You must be able to modify as reality dictates. If your schedule is unreasonably demanding of your time, the plan simply won't work. Modify your plan so it can work, even if that means taking more time than originally planned.

BUILDING ON THE GOAL

Once the time line is completed, start filling in the details. For the most part, the validity of your goal will depend on the underlying assumptions. For example, if you want to increase revenues, you assume:

- There's a market for your services

- The competition won't prevent you from growing to a reasonable level

- The support services can be provided within your limits of capital, facilities and personnel

A more detailed discussion of assumptions comes in the next chapter. For now, just remember that you must be able to validate your goals in several ways before going on to the detailed assumptions.

After developing your goals statement and time line, check them against these factors:

1) *Financial resources:* Have you considered the demands your goal will make on available cash? Do you have the capital available to reach the goal as you've defined it? Will you need a loan or a line of credit?

2) *Personnel:* What labor or office resources do you have now? Will you need to increase the size of the staff to reach the goal?

```
+------------------------------------------+
|                                          |
|   goal checklist                         |
|                                          |
|     _____   statement                    |
|     _____   time line                    |
|     _____   financial resources:         |
|                                          |
|             _____   cash flow            |
|             _____   capital              |
|             _____   loan                 |
|             _____   line of credit       |
|                                          |
|     _____   personnel                    |
|     _____   facilities                   |
|     _____   forecasts and budgets        |
|                                          |
+------------------------------------------+
```

Figure 6-5

3) **Facilities:** Are your present office and storage space adequate for the operation as laid out in your plan? Remember that growth and expansion usually require a proportional expansion of facilities — desk space, filing space, storage space, work space, etc.

4) **Forecasts and budgets:** If you're working from a budget today, how will your plan change it? If your goal is increasing revenues, several expense categories will be affected as sales grow.

Use the goal checklist in Figure 6-5 to make sure you've considered all the important points in developing your goals and time line.

Is Your Goal Achievable?

Consider all of these related issues — financial, personnel, facilities, and budgets — when you start breaking your goal into manageable parts. If you keep them in mind, you'll be able to develop realistic and reachable goals for the year, and stay in control of the process.

For example, a drywall contractor who wanted to increase sales decided to bid on some insulation jobs. He did a fairly complete marketing plan and made some income projections. It was a good plan, as far as it went. But he didn't foresee some expensive changes:

1)   The new business required investment in trucks and specialized equipment. He didn't have the money on hand and was forced to ask for a bank loan. Because he hadn't planned this as part of his cash flow for the year, he had to change his plan.

2)   The growth meant a greater volume of phone calls, job cost records, and other administrative duties. He had to hire an additional employee. That wasn't part of the plan.

3)   He had to keep inventory for the first time and was forced to rent storage space. Because he hadn't planned that far ahead, the only storage available at short notice was inconvenient, located several blocks away from his office.

4)   The budget was invalid because the plan didn't look ahead far enough to see the extra rent, salary, interest, and other expenses related to growth.

Some goals might require investing money for several months — even for more than a full year. You could actually have negative cash flow and a drain on profits while building volume in a new specialty, for example. You can only know this by following your goal all the way through to its realistic conclusion. You might discover that you simply can't afford to increase or expand right now, or that the way you planned to expand isn't going to produce higher profits during the first year or two.

No plan will work if you don't understand precisely the consequences of each change you make. You can certainly see how increasing income will produce higher profits — assuming you don't have to increase overhead to support a higher volume. But if you do need more space, more employees, a loan, and other expenses, you might not be able to justify growth at the level you first estimated.

Avoid these problems by gathering the facts before you begin. There are always alternatives if you discover problems while still in the planning stage. Either change the strategy or give yourself more time to meet the goal.

PLANNING FORMATS

There are three ways to approach the plan once you have specific goals: in a single goal format, a segmented format, or a tied-in format. We'll look at all three.

The Single Goal Format

The single goal format is illustrated in Figure 6-6. This is the most appropriate format when your entire plan is based on one primary goal. All other goals are considered secondary. The assumptions you make are all tied to that one, primary goal.

When you use this format, base the entire plan on the single goal. For example, your primary goal might be to increase revenues and net profits. Secondary goals could be the reduction of fixed overhead, setting up a retirement fund, and establishing a cash emergency reserve. All of your assumptions — like the secondary goals — are tied directly to the primary goal. The entire plan is based on the idea of that one, specific purpose.

The advantages of the single goal format are:

• It gives the reader (and you) a focus that is carried throughout the plan.

single goal format

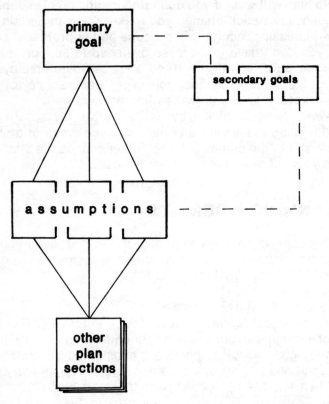

Figure 6-6

- It ties all secondary goals into the master plan, making them part of a target.

- It reduces distraction and conflict between unlike goals.

  The main disadvantage of this format is inflexibility. It excludes any goals that aren't related to the primary goal.

segmented format

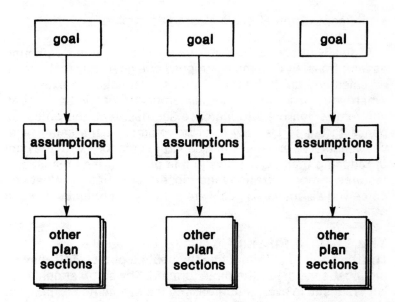

Figure 6-7

The Segmented Format

When goals are not related directly to one another, divide them into segments. This second format is shown in Figure 6-7.

This is most appropriate when your goals are totally unrelated and there's no reason to tie them together. This would extend to every part of your plan. Essentially, you would need to develop a partial plan for each of the unrelated goals. When two or more goals are not directly tied together, simplify your plan by treating each separately.

The advantages of this format are:

- It's easier to grasp unrelated matters if they're covered separately in the same plan.

123

• You can develop, prove and plan separately and then bring all your goals together in the form of forecasts and budgets.

• It keeps different goals clear in your mind.

A disadvantage is that you might end up with conflicting assumptions. For example, suppose one goal calls for increased sales and another for a 10 percent reduction in expenses. When you carry through the assumptions of the sales goal, you realize you need to increase salaries, rent and office expense to support a new level of volume. At the same time, you've isolated expenses in a separate category, with the goal of reducing them. Collectively, this plan just isn't realistic. It requires a reorganization, and closer coordination. What you perceived as unrelated goals are actually in conflict with each other.

The Tied-in Format

The third and final format ties the goals together. This may be the most sensible of the three formats. The singular goal idea isn't realistic in every situation, and the segmented format can lead to conflicts. But with a tied-in format, you can incorporate the best of both ideas. See Figure 6-8.

Here, separate goals — whether related to each other or not — are tied in to one another. This gives you the chance to examine any conflicts and resolve them. Collectively, you develop a broad base of assumptions and then develop a truly coordinated plan.

Advantages include:

• Every goal is developed, analyzed and revised in harmony with limitations set by other goals in the same plan.

• You can coordinate your assumptions to make all of the goal fit within the plan.

• Priorities can be set in your time line, not only within each goal, but for all goals as a part of the same coordinated plan and schedule.

tied-in format

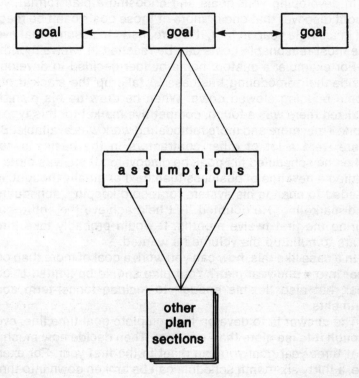

Figure 6-8

A disadvantage of this format is the danger that the plan will lack a central focus. A reader might not get as strong a sense of direction as you'd like. For example, there should be a strong, focused idea or theme to your business plan. What is the major goal, the primary objective, for the coming year?

You can overcome this possible disadvantage by stating your primary goal strongly, both in the introduction and goal sections. Be sure that all assumptions are based on the major goal, and that your marketing plan refers back to the central theme.

LONG-TERM GOALS

In developing your goals and choosing a plan format, you might discover that one or more of those goals can't be reached in a single year. In fact, it's unrealistic to assume that even the most reasonable goals can be reached in twelve months.

For example, a custom home builder decided to develop a residential remodeling business to take up the slack if new home building slowed down. When he drew up his plan, he realized there was a tough, competitive market for this type of work. True, more and more remodeling work was available. But there were a lot of other contractors in the business, too. When he scheduled his goal, he discovered there was more to adding a new line of business than he'd originally thought. He needed to change his system for record keeping, scheduling, and marketing. He doubted that he'd achieve the entire goal during the first twelve months. It would probably take three years to build up the volume he wanted.

In a case like this, how can you work a goal of more than one year into a one-year plan? Your plan should be limited to one year, but also flexible enough to include longer-term commitments.

The answer is to develop the complete goal time line, even though it takes more than one year. Then decide how much of that three-year goal you can meet in the first year. For example, a thirty-six-month schedule can be broken down into three segments.

For the first year, plan to proceed through the schedule as you would for any goal, trying to complete each step on time. At the end of the year, modify your long-term goal, if necessary, to conform with your actual progress to date and any problems you've discovered. Then lay out the progress expected in the next twelve months.

Let's look again at the custom builder getting into the remodeling business: He could break his goal down into three segments, and carry out his plan through the first year. At the end of that year, he might discover that he's progressing faster than he'd planned — requiring a modification of the original time line. Or he might find that the market is even tougher than he thought. Now, he has to either extend the deadline further into the future or come up with a more aggressive plan. He might increase his marketing effort, identify new ways to approach the market, and make other mid-course corrections.

A long-term goal can be covered in a series of one-year plans. It's probably a mistake to expand the scope of any single plan beyond twelve months. The longer a period you try to project, the less accurate it becomes. It's difficult enough to see twelve months ahead. By limiting the scope of your plan to the immediate future, you stay in touch with your goals, and stress — for your own benefit — the importance of staying on schedule.

Two- or three-year plans invite delay and excuses for failure. If you fall behind one month, you have another thirty-five to make it up. Right? That's just human nature. You may not feel there's any immediate need to get back on track. And before you know it, your plan has fallen so far behind that it's no longer a workable document.

The goals you develop at the beginning of your plan define, limit and expand everything else you do. The purpose of starting with goals is to provide the actual framework from which you develop and fill in the rest of that plan. A strong beginning makes reaching the end on schedule more likely. And any weaknesses that go unfixed will threaten the strength and structure of the entire plan.

For your plan to succeed, you have to keep one eye on the future. You have to lay out logical steps and follow them in sequence. Without monthly milestones and regular reminders of where you're going, a goal is nothing more than an idea. But with the steps defined and scheduled, your goal is a reality waiting for you to put it into action.

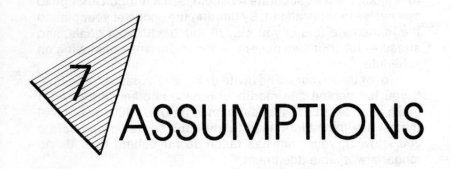

7

ASSUMPTIONS

Now our goals are defined and down on paper. The next section of your business plan gives the details that support the goals. The assumptions are named, tested, and refined. In their final form, they serve as the action points for the remainder of the plan.

Every time you set a goal — whether it's in your business or in your personal life — you base that goal on a series of underlying beliefs. I'll call them **assumptions**. When you decided to take a chance and start your own business, what were some of your goals and their related assumptions?

Goal	Assumption
Independence	You will have more independence in your own business.
Financial gain	You can make more money on your own than working for someone else.
Early retirement	You can save enough money to retire early.

EXPECT YOUR ASSUMPTIONS TO CHANGE

To show how your assumptions change over time, let's look at each of these reasons for going into business in the first place:

Original assumption: You will have more independence in your own business.

Changes: You discover that there's actually a greater commitment than there was as an employee. You work longer hours and have more responsibilities than you did working for someone else. But they're *your* hours. Even though you can't take off and go fishing whenever you want, you still have a form of independence you can accept.

Original assumption: You can make more money on your own than working for someone else.

Changes: During the early years in a new business, most builders earn less money, not more. But you believe that by staying with it, you will eventually be better off. This idea might take longer than you thought, but it's still valid.

Original assumption: You can save enough money to retire early.

Changes: This idea might prove true, but your goal could change. Many people who own their own business find out they don't want to retire at all, much less retire early. So while you can save enough to be able to retire when you choose, you may be motivated to keep working instead.

Assumptions you make about the coming year will probably change, just as your long-term assumptions do. At the time an assumption is developed, it's based on a goal as you understand or believe it at that time. As time passes, your perceptions change. So do the realities. Things happen in ways you can't possibly anticipate. This doesn't mean that your entire plan will necessarily be obsolete. It might just need fine-tuning in the face of changing assumptions.

_____CASE HISTORY: Minor Changes _____

Steve Reeder developed a plan for his plumbing service based on his primary goal: To increase the volume of residential plumbing work handled each month. He had bought the business from his father and uncle the year before. They had allowed the volume of business to settle at a comfortable level, and did all the work themselves. Steve's plans were based on three assumptions:

1) He would need to hire two new employees, one about three months into the year and another by summer.

2) He would need to buy an additional truck for each employee.

3) He would have to promote his service to find new customers.

As it turned out, a little extra promotion brought in more work than he had expected. Steve had to hire his second employee within weeks after the first one was put on the payroll. And before summer, he needed two more.

The plan had to be changed. First, Steve needed to buy extra trucks for the new employees. This required bank loans for two more trucks than were in the plan.

Second, he had to turn down some business to avoid spreading his resources too thin. He was tempted to buy five new trucks and hire five new plumbers. If business didn't slow down, he could have kept all five busy every day. But he decided to wait a while before adding too much capacity. As it turned out, that was a good decision. The level of business stabilized — but at a very profitable point.

The extra office work made it necessary to hire a full-time office manager. In the past, a bookkeeper came in at the end of each month to do the billings. But now, the volume of business was so high that something other than the company's telephone answering machine was needed. And the monthly billing procedure had to be revised.

These changes were minor, from Steve's point of view. His primary goal was to expand. He didn't plan for as much growth as he experienced, but he was happy to have the additional profits. He realized, however, that running too many jobs at once would make it hard to maintain the quality he expected and was known for.

CASE HISTORY: Invalid Assumptions

Bill Matthews had been in business for more than fifteen years before he did his first formal business plan. He saw at once the benefits of mapping out the year ahead.

His business started the same year he got his contractor's license. That first year, he'd bought an old house, fixed it up and sold it at a considerable profit. Now, many years later, he was still in the same business, but in a bigger way. He had a staff of seven, including a plumber and an electrician.

During the previous year, Bill noticed that his houses weren't selling as quickly as they had in the past. Usually he had the house sold well before work was completed. But he went ahead with his plan on the assumption that the house being renovated would sell within two months. That allowed one month to complete the work and another to close the sale.

About four months into the year, Bill realized his assumption had been wrong. Home sales were slow all over the state. He went to the loan officer he'd been working with for years and explained the problem. The loan officer kept statistics that showed declining demand for homes like Bill was trying to sell. And there were more homes for sale, meaning it was a buyer's market. Prices weren't rising as they had done in the past, either. And the average swing between the asking price and the sales price was increasing. While it used to be under 5 percent, it was closer to 10 percent now.

All of these statistics told Bill that the market wasn't right for buying and reselling homes, at least not at the volume Bill had planned. Market conditions made his assumptions wrong. He revised the plan, deciding to test a new line of business. The plan included offering home improvement services, which, Bill found, was a market with a lot of demand. If people couldn't afford to move up to a larger home, many would add on to or improve the home they had.

CASE HISTORY: A New Goal

Larry Hobbs owned the largest heating and sheet metal operation in the county. When he did his plan for the year, his most important goal was to increase revenue. As a subcontractor, most work was done for a core group of fifteen to twenty general contractors in the area.

Major projects in the area included three new shopping centers, an industrial park, and two buildings at the local college. It looked like a good year. But as summer began, the housing market started picking up, bringing opportunities in smaller but more profitable residential jobs.

Larry believed that he could turn a greater net profit in a shorter period of time if he took more of this residential work. With the labor force and equipment at his disposal, he could certainly finance the work. He decided to change his plan. Instead of bidding on the commercial jobs alone, he had to choose between taking both types of work or specializing in residential jobs. He decided to bid both types of work for a number of reasons. First, the housing market was volatile, rising and falling with changes in employment at the three major manufacturing plants in the region. Larry was concerned that a competitor would steal all the commercial work if he abandoned that field completely. He might not be able to get it back later. But doing both types of work also meant investing in more equipment, hiring more people, and renting some additional office space.

All of this meant changing the plan drastically. This was the expansion opportunity he'd been waiting for. He could divide his time and efforts between two different markets, increase profits, and do a lot of growing in the coming two years — if it was planned and capitalized properly.

Larry concluded that his plan was inadequate. He started from scratch and revised it entirely. He now had a new goal. The old plan simply didn't apply.

METHODS OF CHANGING ASSUMPTIONS

Your assumptions can change as months pass. It's even possible that the assumption you make today will be obsolete before you finish writing your plan. When assumptions change, go back and change your original goals.

For example, let's say your goal is to increase revenues by 30 percent in the coming year. This will require a group of assumptions, such as:

- There's a market for your service.
- The competition won't keep you from reaching this goal.

- You can afford to invest money needed for this much growth.
- You have the equipment to handle the increase.
- The personnel you need are either on hand or can be hired.
- You can survive any cash flow problems caused by growth.

These initial assumptions are indicators. Once you think through all of the beliefs underlying your goal, you can research and test them.

Research means studying the market, your own facilities and resources. Can you support growth of 30 percent in one year? Is demand for your work growing? If you do a lot of residential work, are more homes being built or improved this year than last? What are the construction trends in your area? Is the local economy improving, staying the same, or on the decline? Are there a high number of commercial vacancies? Or is there a shortage of good commercial space?

Testing is matching reality against the statements you've put down on paper. Do you have the cash, equipment and personnel needed to do 30 percent more business? You may discover that you can't afford as much growth as you want. You'll have to take it slower.

If testing of the assumptions shows that a goal is unrealistic, modify or change that goal. For example, you might conclude that there isn't enough business available to grow 30 percent this year. Maybe you don't have enough cash available to expand that fast. So you modify your assumptions and extend your goal over a two-year period. Maybe growth of 15 percent is enough this year.

I prefer to start with optimistic goals and then scale them down as necessary. Begin by setting high standards. Then test each assumption required to meet that goal. Hold these assumptions up to the harsh light of reality. Be brutally frank

changing your assumption

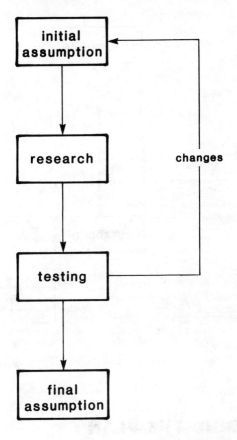

Figure 7-1

with yourself. Examine everything that's likely to affect your assumptions. As you discover flaws in assumptions, make your changes. The end product will be realistic assumptions that can be used to set reasonable goals for the coming year. This process is summarized in Figure 7-1.

effects on the plan

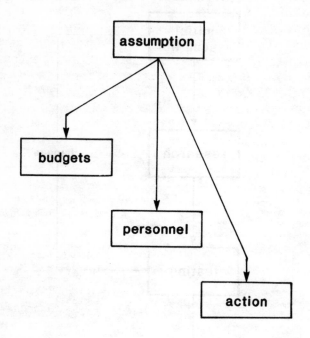

Figure 7-2

CHANGING THE PLAN

If you discover it's necessary to change an assumption after you've developed your full plan, you'll also have to change the marketing, forecasting, budgeting, and time line sections of your plan.

The areas that will be most affected by changes in assumptions are shown in Figure 7-2. These are budgets, personnel, and action.

Budgets

Your expense budgets for the year are based on the timing of your goals and assumptions. As changes occur in them, your budgets will have to change as well. Some parts of the budgets will be based on fixed overhead at levels you have already identified (such as office salaries, rent, and telephone). Others, however, are variable (like travel and direct labor), and will change as you change your plan.

Budgets require assumptions, just like the plan itself. Each expense budget should be based on an assumption. For office supplies, for example, it's safe to assume that you'll have to spend at least 30 percent more if volume increases 30 percent in a year. The same is true for salaries of office employees. Your telephone budget depends on expected cost increases, controls you plan to put into effect, and maybe expansion into areas that require more toll calls.

Personnel

Many assumptions will be based on the size of your labor force. For example, increasing revenue will require increases in payroll. If your plans call for cutting back on unprofitable work, a major reduction in the labor force might be possible. In any case, you must be prepared to revise your plan as assumptions change.

It's probably a mistake to plan for growth without also allowing for labor cost increases. There's a limit to how much work anyone can do — even if that person is the boss.

Action

Even the best assumption may contain a key flaw: timing. You might need fifteen, eighteen or twenty-four months to reach a goal you originally thought would take only one year. So be sure to change your action plan and time line whenever you modify an assumption.

Be willing to modify your action plan to keep it on a realistic footing. A plan that won't work demands change. The action plan is a dated checklist of things you need to do, clarifying the actions needed and setting deadlines for completion. But it only works if it's based on realistic performance standards. Don't overlook the need to continue with existing work, in addition to developing your new plans.

Make Changes Whenever They're Needed

No plan is permanent and final. Even with a well-prepared plan for the coming year, you'll discover flaws and will want to make at least slight changes. A plan should be an active, working guide to running your operation. Just as the goals you develop are the guidelines of the entire plan, the assumptions are the connection between those goals and the steps you must take to achieve them.

That's the disadvantage with going outside of your operation to have a plan prepared. You can hire a planning consultant and pay several thousand dollars to have a full plan developed. Then, in theory, you have twelve months' worth of planning. In fact, though, that entire plan could be obsolete in one month. As changes occur — either in your thinking or in the timing of the plan — the basic assumptions become outdated.

A plan prepared by a consultant can be set up so that modification is easier. But it's still better to do your own plan. Only you can understand the details of your operation well enough to keep the plan realistic and flexible. That means understanding the assumptions you need to develop, and knowing when and how to make the changes needed.

You can't do a plan today and leave it alone for the entire year. Before you're through, it will look very different from the original version. Consider, for example, how even a single change can affect the entire plan: You set the goal of increasing revenue by 30 percent, based on the belief that a lot of homebuilding activity will take place in the coming year. You write out a series of assumptions, develop a marketing plan, forecasts and budgets, and a time line. Then, in the first month of the year, your county slaps a moratorium on building. Now you need to shift emphasis to some other line of work.

When that occurs, how realistic is your goal? With virtually all of your assumptions now changed, you'll have to rethink the entire plan. An unforeseen event has changed the market, forcing a revision of your goal, your assumptions, and every other aspect of your plan.

BUILDING WORKING ASSUMPTIONS

The uncertainties of the coming year — or even of next month — present a problem. You can't come up with a plan today that will always work in the future. But is that a reason to avoid doing any planning at all? Not really. A plan is the best tool available for adapting to the future. True, it has to be based on what you know today. But failing to plan is nearly as bad as planning to fail.

A valid assumption based on today's market and operating environment will work only as long as that environment doesn't change. As changes do occur, the plan has to be modified. Most assumptions in a plan can be modified without invalidating the entire idea. Your primary goals can continue to be valid. Even with the uncertainties we must live with, the planning process is essential to stay in control of your operation.

Assumptions, to work, have to have these attributes:

- They must be tied to goals.

- They must be flexible. As goals change, so must your assumptions.

- They must be useful as action points, leading you into the steps you can take to put the plan into action.

Use a worksheet like Figure 7-3 to develop your working assumptions. Show the date on which your assumptions were developed. That may be important information if revisions are needed later. Then write a brief statement that describes the assumption itself. Be sure to include notes on budgets or forecasts that will be affected by your assumption. For example, increases in income will usually come only after payroll and other expenses have increased.

The last step will be to write out the action plan, including dates and the work that will be required.

Here are some examples of assumption statements used in business plans:

Sales can be increased by at least 10 percent over the coming year, without needing larger facilities, more employees, or new equipment.

A new line of work will require investment in two trucks and other heavy equipment, inventory and a 15 percent increase in direct labor.

Cash flow will be adequate to fund planned growth, except during the months of November through January. Short-term borrowing will be necessary for this period.

There is a growing demand for residential contract work, and a declining demand for commercial contracts.

Planned expansion will require the addition of a full-time estimator and one more clerical employee.

Assumptions, like goals, should be simple statements that are supported by the background, research and market factors you've studied. Once they're stated, they're incorporated into the details of the plan, including the forecasts, budgets, and the marketing expansion section.

assumption worksheet

date _____

assumption statement

_____
_____
_____
_____
_____

budget notes

_____
_____
_____
_____
_____
_____
_____
_____

action

DATE	EXPLANATION
_____	_____
_____	_____
_____	_____
_____	_____
_____	_____

Figure 7-3

DEALING WITH MIDYEAR REVISIONS

Once you've finished drafting, testing and revising assumptions, it's time to begin the next section of your plan. The marketing expansion section of your detailed plan will include a description of the actions you'll take and when you'll take them. But any marketing strategy will require changes as you determine what works and what doesn't. Several times during the year you'll probably have to revise your marketing assumptions. That means the rest of your plan will have to be modified as well.

This revising marketing assumptions doesn't mean that the entire detailed marketing expansion plan has to be redone in its entirety. It's more likely that some parts of the plan will be modified. Perhaps you'll have to:

• Increase the time required to make the expansion plan happen.

• Abandon one aspect of the plan and replace it with another.

• Recognize and incorporate new ideas into the plan. (For example, you might find a new marketing opportunity and discover it belongs in your plan.)

• Change the budget for expansion.

• Borrow money, when you'd originally thought you could afford expansion without going into debt.

• Shift emphasis from one line of service to another.

midyear revisions

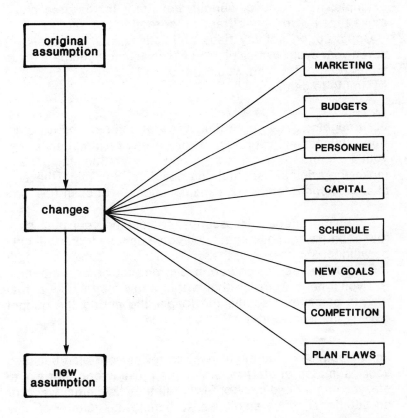

Figure 7-4

Expect to make midyear revisions. The original assumptions will have to change because the way your company operates has changed. Figure 7-4 summarizes the factors that can make revisions necessary. Let's look at them one at a time, beginning with market conditions.

1) **Markets:** The markets available today might change during the year. With a plan, you'll be able to anticipate these changes and react to them before your competition can. For example, a tornado or serious hailstorm in the area could make repair work very attractive for roofing contractors.

Construction activity rises and falls, usually in a six- or seven-year cycle. With a plan, you'll be able to anticipate these shifts. Without a plan, you'll be taken by surprise, forced to scramble to catch up.

2) **Budgets:** You might discover that some of the assumptions you made in your budget will have to be modified. Either your assumptions prove to be wrong, or something happens to make the original assumptions obsolete. You might have to change income forecasts, expense budgets, or cash flow projections.

Modifying budgets is essential to keeping your plan on a realistic footing. The budget you come up with today will only be valid for about six months, at the most. You can do a budget for an entire year, of course, based on today's assumptions. But you'll need to revise that within a few months, as actual results come in. Usually, the longer the period the budget covers, the less valid it will prove to be.

3) **Personnel:** You might need to revise your plan because your estimates of staff requirements prove wrong. For example, you might need more or fewer full-time field employees, or an additional office employee, to handle the volume of new business you create as part of your plan.

Develop a rough idea of the relationship between manhours and revenue. You probably have a fairly good idea now of the number of people you need to generate a specific level of income. For example, many builders need about one full-time employee for each $70,000 to $100,000 of gross income. Office staff requirements change with volume, too. Be sure to consider the need for support staff if you plan major changes in income.

4) **Capital:** Your original assumption might have overlooked cash shortages. You'll have to revise the plan, extending deadlines or perhaps looking for a loan. Capital limitations should be part of every business plan. In fact, every assumption should be based on a clear idea of what capital is available or will be needed during the year. Don't forget seasonal factors, also. Cash availability isn't a constant. It changes with the time of year.

5) **Schedule:** For a number of reasons, you might not be able to stay on your original schedule. Either other obligations take time away from the development of your plan, or the plan schedule is simply too ambitious. You might find that as you begin meeting the goals in your plan, little time is left to manage the plan itself. The success of the plan can actually delay progress.

Think of your time line as the most flexible part of your plan. It can be expanded or constricted as your schedule, progress, and outside influences dictate. Don't try to live with an inflexible schedule for your plan. Just as you allow some room for delays in a job schedule, build a comfortable margin for error into the time line for the business plan.

6) **New goals:** Plans can change because your goals change. For example, you might review your primary goals six months into the year and realize they're wrong. They were right for you at the time they were developed, but you now have a different perspective. That means changing your assumptions and each part of the plan, to the extent that new goals demand.

Outside influences — like a changing market, competition, or opportunities for new work — can affect your goals. But you'll change, too. Your perspective will change during the year, maybe making your original goal seem too ambitious. Maybe your priorities have changed, making some goals irrelevant.

7) **Competition:** It's hard to predict what the competition will do. You can't possibly know today what the competition

will be doing tomorrow. Of course, you can estimate and base your assumptions on those estimates. You might discover during the year that the competition is, in fact, much different than you thought.

How does competition affect your plan? If too many similar contractors are chasing the same, limited market, there will invariably be too little work for some. This probably sets limits on your growth. You might estimate too much or too little potential growth based on your understanding of competitive factors.

8) *Plan flaws:* You will find flaws in your plan, demanding changes in basic assumptions. For example, suppose you assume that income will increase every month. But as the new year begins, you realize you didn't allow for seasonal variations. Bad weather makes the first two or three months of the year slow for most construction contractors. You need to adjust the time line for reaching your goal.

A flaw doesn't mean a plan was done badly, only that something was overlooked. It could also be that a valid plan develops flaws as conditions change. For example, the assumption you make today about the market demand for your services might be perfect. But six months later they could be unrealistic.

You can't be expected to see the future perfectly. If you could, there would be no need for planning at all. The plan's purpose is not to remove uncertainty from your operation, but to better prepare for it. Assumptions help you anticipate problems before they occur. By working from a base of well-considered assumptions, you'll be better able to stay a step ahead of your competitors. That's going to help build profits and increase your sense of accomplishment and personal satisfaction.

THE MARKET EXPANSION PLAN

If the goal of a business plan is growth, a part of that plan should include an explanation of where the growth will come from. This is usually called a *market expansion plan*. Your plan has to identify the potential for growth while still being realistic about the limitations you face. I'll go into detail about this later in the chapter.

Don't repeat the mistake many business owners have made. It's easy to concentrate on only part of the growth issue. For example, anyone can forecast good growth prospects for a particular area over the next few years. But that's just part of the picture. Will larger competitors move into the area? Do you have the cash available to take advantage of the opportunities? How many days a week and hours a day are you willing to work? Can you attract and train capable, reliable tradesmen and skilled supervisors? These are important parts of your market expansion planning.

But don't be too conservative. Don't focus exclusively on the limitations. Begin by assuming that you can afford to expand. Set a realistic goal and then evaluate the market thoroughly to see how your goal can be reached.

I call this process "market expansion planning." But maybe market *improvement* planning is a better term. Your plan doesn't have to assume higher income. The goal could be a higher percentage of profit on the same income. Either way, you need good planning and research to make it happen.

EXPLORING THE LIMITATIONS

There are limits to how much any company can grow in one year. To plan and control any form of expansion, you have to understand these limits:

Competition— Unless you have the only shop in town, you must be aware of your competitors. They, like you, own a share of the market. And even if you offer a unique service, the more success you have, the more likely it is that others will move in to compete with you.

Chances are, however, there's plenty of competition from contractors working in your area, chasing the same customers. Each contractor is limited by this competition. Each one will capture only a portion of the available jobs in any one year.

The best way to track your competition is to stay in touch with them. Join your local building associations and societies — every organization geared to contractors you think of as competition. Visit with competitors. Talk to them. Not only will you get a feel for how they're doing, but it could also lead to joint venturing or sub work in the future. And subscribe to regional construction magazines.

What do you look for when you're checking out the competition? Here are signs that they're doing well:

1) They hire many tradesmen in a short period of time.

2) They're so busy that they refer smaller jobs to you, or to other contractors.

3) They expand into larger quarters or warehouse space.

The signs of success are easy to spot. It's human nature to want to announce healthy growth. If competitors get quiet, that could be a sign that they're not doing as well as they were.

Demand— Few construction contractors double in volume from one year to the next. You can only expect to expand so much in one year. There are practical limits to how much you can (or even want to) grow in any year. These limits are reflected in a realistic growth plan.

A home builder I know had enough money and could get enough tradesmen to triple his gross volume one year — so he made a plan forecasting that expansion. But the demand for housing in his area weakened as the year began. With too many homes on the market, some employers laying off staff, and pressure on prices from a large developer who was having financial troubles, it wasn't realistic to expect a huge increase in volume. He didn't reach his goal, even with the money and tradesmen needed to grow quickly.

Make sure your plan is based on research and an understanding of changes in the market. If you expect a weak housing market, you can beat the competition by offering a different service. For example, it's possible to expand by changing your emphasis to another line of work that's more in demand.

Demand can work the other way, too. For example, when a sudden demand for new construction hits, you must be ready to meet it if you want to maximize your growth. That means having capital in reserve to purchase materials, hire new workers and supervisors, and support the sudden growth in volume with clerical staff. If you haven't planned and saved during the lean times, you can't capitalize on the good times.

Check building trends by talking to bankers and real estate brokers. They're in the best position to know what's going on. Bankers review loan applications and must stay on top of a developing — or declining — market for homes and commercial construction. Real estate brokers also watch trends closely.

If a friendly real estate broker lets you know that there's a housing glut, it may be time to shift to another emphasis. Perhaps renovation or commercial work is on the increase. When commercial development is growing because new businesses are moving into the area, you can expect housing demand to follow. New businesses attract employees who need housing.

Also keep an eye on the direction of your local economy. Bankers follow these trends, including population, employment levels, traffic, and other indicators.

Capital— Growth costs money. You need it to make your plan a reality — and you need it in predictable amounts. Part of the process of making your plan succeed is managing cash flow.

It's common to have cash problems during a period of expansion. For example, I know of a heating and sheet metal contractor who prepared a business plan aimed at increasing his market share. That meant buying new trucks, investing in inventory, and hiring new crews. The work was there, but receivables increased even faster than the volume of work. He was forced to settle for a more modest level of growth because of his limited capital.

The lack of capital can ruin even the best of plans. Don't ignore the problems that come with higher volume. It's easy to get so busy trying to keep your new jobs on schedule that you don't take the time to manage your cash flow.

Manpower— You must coordinate growth with available manpower. That doesn't just mean hiring people to fill out crews. It also means having the cash to pay them on time, providing the equipment they need, and controlling their schedules.

One landscaper ran into problems when he doubled up his crews one year. He simply didn't have the trucks to get crews, equipment and inventory to the job sites. That meant delays and excessive idle time. The result was losses that he didn't expect. Even though the market was there, profits fell.

Growth must be controlled and planned. Hiring more people will usually create as many problems as it solves for the first few days or weeks. Don't expect that new staff to be as productive as existing staff — at least not until they've been trained and integrated into your team.

Time — It's easy to forget how important supervision can be on a construction site. But someone has to keep the work on schedule and be sure the tools, materials and tradesmen are available. A responsible foreman or supervisor will be able to reduce your supervision burden. But you still need to spend some time on each job. Doubling volume will usually more than double the supervision required.

A successful general contractor in my community found himself with more jobs than he'd expected. Against my advice, he continued to take on everything that came his way. What he didn't understand was that much of his success was built on his own ability as a supervisor. When he ran into problems on a key job, he had to spend several days working out of trouble. That left him with less time available for other work. The result was predictable. Unfortunately, the loss wasn't just financial. His reputation in the community took more of a beating than his bank account.

Understand your limits. Be sure your limits are part of the plan. Your business will grow only if you can find or develop experienced field supervisors, establish good reporting systems, and schedule your jobs effectively. Begin with the people needed to handle growth, not the growth itself.

Quality — Growth for its own sake can be as destructive as a deterioration in profits. Every growth plan needs to address the issue of maintaining standards of quality. An architect friend of mine accepted more work than he could handle. He had always prided himself on the personalized care and creative attention he gave to every job. But as work in his shop grew, he gave more responsibility to designers who weren't used to working with owners and contractors. He found later that some customers had been offended by working with less experienced designers and draftsmen. The lesson was obvious: Growth that erodes quality usually means loss of future business. There's no point in simply increasing volume if that

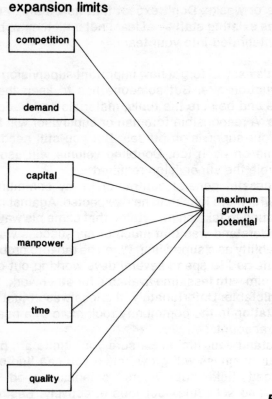

Figure 8-1

means loss of future business and a decline in your reputation.

The six major limits to expansion are summarized in Figure 8-1.

BUILDING YOUR EXPANSION PLAN

Start your expansion plan by estimating the number of new contracts you can expect during the coming year. Estimate what that expansion will produce in extra income. Keep these points in mind:

1)   Immediate growth might mean deferred profits. Be sure you can afford to carry new business long enough for future profits to come in.

2)   Certain types of business might be less profitable than others. Be sure you're concentrating on *profitable* growth.

3)   Your first plan might not be the best alternative available. On paper, try several different levels of growth for the coming year.

One contractor came up with a comfortable estimate of growth in two different types of business. He broke these lines into broad categories of commercial and residential work. The reason: Commercial work was more profitable in the long run, but there were fewer jobs available and the competition was more intense. It was also more difficult to forecast income for commercial work. Any estimate of sales growth had to be conservative.

He didn't have too much trouble estimating the possible gross income. But he failed to realize that gross profits would probably be lower as volume increased. He didn't anticipate higher shrinkage in inventory, the depreciation of new equipment, or higher labor costs with increasing idle time.

In other words, the cost of doing business is higher when volume expands. The contractor learned this lesson: He couldn't expect the same level of gross profit after expansion as he had with a smaller, more directly controllable operation.

When he realized that, he had to decide what level of volume would justify the probability of higher costs. He couldn't know the exact escalation of costs in advance, so — like all business ventures — there was a degree of risk involved.

That's the problem with market expansion. In most cases, you haven't been in this territory before, so you're likely to make a few mistakes. The purpose of planning for expansion is to identify problem areas, and then to keep an eye on them. Reduce future losses by finding a logical and comfortable balance between the risks of growth and careful control over financial commitment. Hiring new people, buying capital

```
┌─────────────────────────────────────────────────────────────┐
│                                                             │
│                    market estimates                         │
│                                                             │
│                                                             │
│   source of income _____ │
│                                                             │
│                                                             │
│                        PLAN 1      PLAN 2      PLAN 3        │
│                                                             │
│        number of contracts  _____   _____   _____     │
│        average income    $_____  $_____  $_____     │
│        gross income      $_____  $_____  $_____     │
│        costs             _____   _____   _____      │
│        gross profit      $_____  $_____  $_____     │
│                                                             │
└─────────────────────────────────────────────────────────────┘
```

Figure 8-2

assets, and going into debt might all be necessary in order to expand. You can control the rate of growth, and face only risks that you anticipated. Or you can jump in with both feet before you know how deep the pond is.

To help him make this decision, the contractor used a worksheet (Figure 8-2) to break down his estimates into three possible levels. The first was for very little growth, the second was moderate, and the third was for the highest volume.

His three-part growth plan is shown in Figure 8-3. It included the number of contracts, average income per contract, estimated gross income, costs, and gross profit. That's as far as the estimate went. Actual budgets for fixed and variable expenses would come later, when the forecast and budget were finalized. At this point, the purpose was strictly a comparison of options. That's best done by comparing gross profits. Considering all the factors (the need for investment in inventory and new equipment, and hiring new employees), the most aggressive plan wasn't the most attractive. He decided to take the middle path, setting his sights on moderate growth. The first plan would bring in a higher percentage of net profits, because costs would probably come in at about the level he

market estimates

source of income __RESIDENTIAL__

	PLAN 1	PLAN 2	PLAN 3
number of contracts	10	15	25
average income	$14,100	$14,100	$14,100
gross income	$141,100	$211,500	$352,500
costs	84,600	126,900	211,500
gross profit	$ 56,400	$ 84,600	$ 141,000

Figure 8-3

assumed. But the amount of that profit would be much smaller than either of the other two alternatives. And the third plan would *probably* end up the most profitable of all. But there were too many unknowns, including the need to make some very heavy capital commitments. The chance of complete failure just wasn't worth the risk.

A three-part estimate like this can help you decide on the best level of growth, based on the degree of risk involved. When you expand, you take risks in several forms. Of course, there's the chance the growth won't be there, even after you invest a lot of money in new equipment, inventory and work crews. You also risk loss of quality, expose yourself to more risk at a higher volume level, and take the chance that a cash crisis could bring operations to a halt.

When an expansion plan means investing in a larger operation, you have to consider:

• How much time will be required to recapture your investment? For example, if you have to buy three new trucks for growth during the next year, will you be able to justify that investment over the next three, five or ten years? If income is for

155

the short term, that investment might not pay off.

• Will growth mean larger facilities? If a new line of business will require a higher level of clerical support, a storage area or workshop, will you need to lease a larger space? And will the higher level of work be permanent enough to justify the added overhead?

• Is bigger always better? If it's possible to make a good living with a moderate growth plan, why take the additional risk?

USING YOUR FINANCIAL RECORDS

Your company's financial records will help reveal how reasonable the plan seems. Compare gross income for the last two years to the plan you develop for the coming year. Consider the quality of growth and the accuracy of your plan by comparing net profits over time. If you're controlling overhead and keeping costs at reasonable levels, both the dollar amount and the percentage of net profits should show an improvement from one year to the next.

But don't set goals that are too conservative. There's no advantage in setting a goal that will produce lower profits for the coming year. The whole point of most growth plans is to produce more capital for the business — and put more money in your pocket. Plan to maintain at least your current level of profitability, even if you don't plan to grow.

The comparison is an easy one if you have only one line of business. But if you have two or more specialties, it gets more complicated. Recall the general contractor I mentioned earlier in this chapter who planned to take on both more residential *and* more commercial work. How could he judge growth? Commercial work in this case yielded a higher percentage of net profit, but residential income came in more quickly and was necessary to keep the operation afloat. Most of his growth was in residential work. But the profit margin was lower than on commercial jobs. This isn't necessarily bad, as long as total earnings are increasing.

When you do two different types of work, costs will probably be different for each type. That makes your analysis a little more difficult. How do you distribute expenses between the two markets? For example, where do you assign your telephone, clerical salaries, and rent? Any division you make of fixed overhead expenses must be arbitrary, because there is no relationship between a particular line of business and your expense commitments. For example, you pay a fixed amount of rent every month. As long as that lease is in effect, you can't logically commit a portion of that expense to any one line of business.

The solution is to perform any analysis strictly on the basis of gross profit — sales minus directly assigned costs. On this level, you can accurately judge performance and profits by line of business. So keep records of all expenses, but do the comparisons only on gross profit. For example:

	Year 1	Year 2	Year 3
Commercial Work			
gross income	$116,800	$194,500	$248,600
costs	67,900	115,100	141,700
gross profit	$48,900	$79,400	$106,900
margin	42%	41%	43%
Residential Work			
gross income	$188,200	$357,400	$434,900
costs	146,700	257,600	291,400
gross profit	$41,500	$99,800	$143,500
margin	22%	28%	33%

In this case, the margin for commercial work remains around 42 percent, while residential work is much lower. But over time, the volume of residential income has grown substantially. This line of business obviously carries a greater portion of the fixed overhead. But again, this can be a misleading statistic.

Your overhead must be paid every month, regardless of the

volume of income. If a line of business is carrying some of the overhead, it may be to your advantage to continue that business, even if the gross margin is smaller.

Don't decide to expand or to abandon a line of business strictly on the basis of dollar volume. For example, what if volume is increasing but gross margin is falling? That means that the cost of doing business is rising. But fewer dollars are available to pay overhead. If you're spending more time on that business and taking more risks, further expansion may be foolish. Growth may be at the expense of other, more profitable work.

If you're doing more than one line of business, compare income and costs to find the gross margin for each line. If you're not keeping your books this way, using a simple job cost system would help. The only way to accurately track gross income by lines of work is by keeping accurate job cost records. These records **must** indicate where your direct costs are assigned. What you learn may speak volumes about the true profitability and volume trends of each line of work.

If you offer only one primary service, the job is much easier. Compare annual results for at least the last two years to your forecast for the coming year. Use a worksheet like the one shown in Figure 8-4. It's similar to the worksheet in Figure 8-2. But in that section you were comparing three levels of possible future growth. On this worksheet, you're comparing two years of actual income and costs to next year's estimated income and costs, as forecast by your plan.

In this case, costs, variable expenses and net profits are all summarized in both dollar amount and percentage of sales. This helps you to spot trends when you're comparing actual results for two previous years to the estimate you've prepared for next year. Are you forecasting an improvement or a decline in gross income and net profit?

If there is a deterioration in the percentage of net profit, decide whether or not the decrease is acceptable. You might be willing to accept a lower margin or net profit because volume and the dollar amount of profits are higher. But if both the percentage and the amount decline, you need to take action. That could mean changing the plan to:

income plan

	YEAR	YEAR	PLAN
gross income	$ _____	$ _____	$ _____
costs	_____	_____	_____
% costs	_____ %	_____ %	_____ %
variable expenses	_____	_____	_____
% variables	_____ %	_____ %	_____ %
fixed expenses	_____	_____	_____
total expenses	$ _____	$ _____	$ _____
net profit	$ _____	$ _____	$ _____
% net	_____ %	_____ %	_____ %

Figure 8-4

1) Control the level of overhead, so that profits can increase with volume.

2) Take another look at growth, and decide what level will produce the best results for you.

3) Select a manageable level of volume and then control it to produce maximum profits.

4) Abandon the idea of growth if it simply isn't profitable enough to justify the risks.

THE TIME FACTOR

The market expansion plan must be based on an understanding of your own financial records and your forecast of future trends. Once you're satisfied that the volume you're planning for will bring in an acceptable gross margin and net profit, the next step is to put your plan onto a schedule.

Scheduling is an important part of your market expansion plan. Knowing what you expect to do is only the first step in the process. The second step is to impose a deadline on yourself. If you're not used to planning and carrying through, that deadline might seem overwhelming at first. After all, you've set a goal for yourself that, by today's standards, is both ambitious and aggressive. Now, you have to decide how to get there.

You've heard this before in this book, but it bears repeating. Whenever you're facing a large, complex task, break it down into smaller, more manageable steps. Once you have the steps, you can assign a reasonable deadline to each one. Then the larger goal won't seem as distant — or as intimidating.

When you have your final market expansion plan, prepare a time line that shows each of the intermediate goals. See Figure 8-5. These worksheets help you control the entire planning process. They're the working documents in the business plan. Don't treat the plan as if it's written in stone. You should work on it every month, updating your time lines and taking actions to make sure you reach your goals.

Most plans have several components, so you might need to divide your time line into different sections. For example, an expansion plan might include promotion (direct mail and newspaper advertising), investment (in equipment, facilities and inventory); and control (your direct involvement, building systems to track income and manage costs, for example).

Using the worksheet in Figure 8-5, you might break those three parts out into steps like these:

Promotion

1) January: write newspaper ad and direct mail copy; place ads in paper

2) February: begin direct mail campaign; a selective mailing

3) March: judge the results of the mail campaign; modify the ad

4) July: review first six months; decide on subsequent approach

detailed time line

market _____

description	JAN	FEB	MAR	APR	MAY	JUN
_____						
_____						
_____						

	JUL	AUG	SEP	OCT	NOV	DEC
_____						
_____						
_____						

notes

_____

_____

_____

_____

_____

_____

_____

Figure 8-5

Investment

1) February: purchase two trucks

2) March: hire additional crew

3) May: order inventory for expected summer volume

4) August: current lease expires; move to larger facilities

Control

1) January: design income tracking system

2) February: begin new job cost system

3) March: quarterly income review

4) June: review six month expense control system; modify as
needed

Enter each of these phases on the schedule and explain
them in brief notes in the bottom section of the form. Now you
can tell at a glance what has to be accomplished each month
in order to achieve the goal by the end of the year. Figure 8-6
shows these steps entered on the time line.

Monitor your success throughout the year by following the
planned time schedule, and comparing actual results. If you've
broken the expansion program down into specific steps,
checking progress against the schedule will be easy.

Figure 8-7 shows how even a multi-part expansion plan can
be summarized at a glance. Using the time line we just
described, you would enter each step in the appropriate section, on the *estimated* line. Then, as each month ends, enter
the corresponding number on the *actual* line. If you fall behind
schedule, concentrate on catching up or you won't reach your
goal for the year.

detailed time line

market **RESIDENTIAL**

description	JAN	FEB	MAR	APR	MAY	JUN
PROMOTION	1	2	3			
INVESTMENT		1	2		3	
CONTROL	1	2	3			4

	JUL	AUG	SEP	OCT	NOV	DEC
PROMOTION	4					
INVESTMENT		4				
CONTROL						

notes

PROMOTION — 1. WRITE NEWSPAPER AD
2. BEGIN DIRECT MAIL
3. JUDGE THE RESULTS
4. REVIEW FIRST SIX MONTHS

INVESTMENT — 1. PURCHASE TWO TRUCKS
2. HIRE ADDITIONAL CREW
3. ORDER INVENTORY
4. MOVE TO LARGER FACILITY

CONTROL — 1. DESIGN SYSTEM   3. REVIEW INCOME
2. START JOB COST SYSTEM   4. REVIEW 6 MONTHS

Figure 8-6

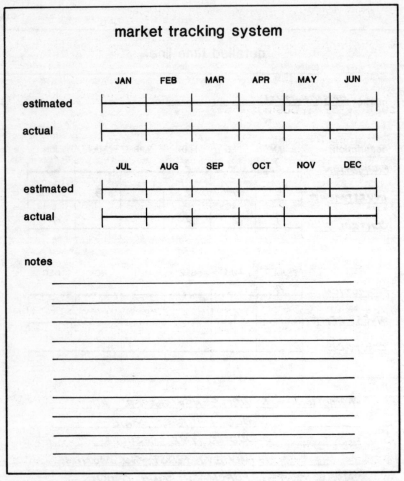

Figure 8-7

PLANNING FOR NO GROWTH

We tend to assume that a plan must include more income than in the previous year. But is that always best? You might study the financial records for your last three years, and discover that:

- Your gross volume has grown each year.

- Profits have stayed about the same or have even declined.

- You're spending more time than ever just managing jobs, handling administrative chores, and scraping together enough cash to stay in business.

- You have more at risk now than ever before.

In situations where rapid growth occurs over a three- to five-year period, it isn't uncommon for these problems to develop. You might realize you were happier and more in control several years ago. And you may even have made more money when your gross volume was lower.

Your marketing expansion plan doesn't have to mean higher volume. You might decide, instead, to expand profits while stabilizing gross income. In this case, the emphasis is placed on controlling costs and expenses rather than revenues. The result will be higher margins and more real profit, with these advantages:

1) Stable or lowered volume means you can control your own time better.

2) Your emphasis shifts from volume to quality. That means a more solid customer base, a better reputation, and better overall management of the operation.

3) You will identify a core of work that is best suited to your operation. Any additional customers will serve as replacements, rather than additional work.

4) The pressure is off of you. There's no longer that basic but often flawed assumption that there *must* be growth in volume, or you're failing. Emphasis will be on profits rather than mere growth.

But how can you reconcile the idea of no growth in volume with the inevitable increase in the cost of doing business? Rents go up, salaries and wages have to be increased, and material costs rise. All of that cuts into your margin of profit. Don't you need higher volume in order to keep your profit level the same?

In some cases, you don't. With more control over your time, you can hold down fixed overhead levels and offset increased prices with better controls, resulting in savings.

In time, you will have to increase volume to maintain an acceptable level of profits, or to create real and permanent growth. But when that growth is gradual and controlled, you'll still be in control. By taking a balanced approach, planning both your overhead and the volume of business, you'll be able to preserve the quality of work you produce, gradually increase your volume *and* your profits, and still have a sense of personal control over your operation.

That's an ideal expansion plan — one that keeps you in control, lets you decide on future volume and profits, and ensures that you're satisfied and happy with the mix of business that comes your way. Market expansion doesn't mean growth for its own sake. It's a process of control and planning that looks ahead to both the immediate future, and to the long-term growth of operations. I strongly recommend that you review the market expansion plan at the end of this book to see how these principles should be applied.

PLAN
GRAPHICS

*E*very business plan has a goal. Reaching any ambitious goal requires motivation and hard work. Making the sacrifices required will be easier if you can see progress toward the goal — day by day and step by step. The best way to make progress obvious is to put it in graphic form, either as a chart or graph.

Many of the goals in a business plan can be illustrated with charts and graphs. Progress toward your goal shouldn't require reading a complex report. Make it easy to grasp all the essential information at a glance. A graph can show many of the key elements in your plan. That will help you and everyone on your payroll focus on the most important parts of your plan for the future.

WHY USE GRAPHICS?

There are several advantages to using graphics in your business plan. First, a plan that includes graphics is more likely to be read. An attractive plan broken up by charts and graphs is a lot more inviting than visually boring pages of text. So if you're preparing your plan to give to a loan officer, for example, having visual aids will improve the chances that he or she will read the entire report.

Here's the second reason for using graphics: It's widely accepted that people retain information better when it's presented in a visual form. And to communicate the complexities of a business plan, graphics also help you in other ways.

1) *They convey what you want to emphasize.* Graphs should carry the reader from one main point to another and keep the focus on the issue you consider most important.

For example, you believe it's realistic to forecast a 30 percent increase in gross revenue, while your overhead grows by only 10 percent. That's a very promising claim, and difficult to explain in purely narrative form. But graphs can show quickly what you expect to do in the coming year.

2) *They make the text more understandable.* When you read a document filled with a lot of numbers, it may be difficult to understand exactly what's being said. Simple graphs and charts present the important data, and then the text explains the details.

Let's say you're making a case for a 30 percent increase in gross revenue. You start by showing on a graph both the revenues for last year and what you expect in the coming twelve months. That might seem too optimistic to the reader at first glance. But in the text, you explain your reasoning, listing the market conditions, competitive situation, and other realities that have led you to your conclusion.

3) *They make your plan more readable.* Your plan is basically a financial document, by its nature involving a lot of numbers.

To make it truly readable, you need to separate the discussion from the numbers.

Many plan writers try to do that by dividing the plan into two parts: text and statements. All of the financial projections, budgets, and other purely numerical information go together at the back of the report. The first part of the plan contains only narrative. The reader has to plod through pages of unbroken text, occasionally referring to a table in the back to help decipher a difficult section of the report. Most readers won't remember much of what's in those pages. Including graphics in the body of the report makes it more interesting and easier to read.

4) *Putting life into the numbers.* Pictures can say something much more vividly than words. And in a business plan, charts and graphs are your pictures. Imagine trying to describe a construction project without a blueprint. You would expect your crews to draw the wrong conclusions, to make mistakes, and generally to have a long and difficult job. The drawing has a specific purpose and use in a construction project. The same is true in a business plan.

The ideas you want to convey in the plan have to be made clear, or they'll be misunderstood. People simply won't take the effort to interpret what you're *trying* to say. You have to not only tell them, but show them as well.

WHAT GRAPHICS CAN DO FOR YOU

Consider graphics essential if your plan will go to any outsider, like a loan officer or potential partner. You want as much clarity as possible in your plan, and graphs will help you achieve it.

When your plan includes visual aids, it stands out from the pack. Most contractors believe they don't have the resources to produce professional quality business charts and graphs, so they shy away from using them. But you can do simple charts, even if it means simply drawing lines around a summary of financial information and putting a title on it. Anything that breaks up a long series of paragraphs is an advantage.

The Supplies You Need

You can add a professional touch to hand-drawn graphics in your business plan, even with very little experience. And it doesn't cost much. The basic supplies you need to create simple but high-quality charts and graphs include:

	Approximate cost
2 rapidograph pens	$20.00
press-on letters sheet	10.00
graph paper	3.00
total	$33.00

Rapidograph pens come in a range of different line widths. With two pens (I recommend the 0.50 and 0.25 sizes), you can draw thick and thin lines to add variety in your graphics. Most of the graphs in this book were prepared using Rotring brand rapidograph pens.

For even less money, you can use line tape for graphics. A roll of black tape, which costs only a few dollars, gives you a consistently straight line. The disadvantage is that you can't make curved lines with tape, so you have less flexibility in your design.

Figure 9-1 shows the different quality of lines using a variety of different pens and tape.

You can prepare the titles and words or numbers in graphs on a good quality typewriter. Make sure you have a new black ribbon. Or you can use press-on letters, which come in sheets that cost about $10.00 each. It takes some practice to achieve consistency and quality with press-on letters, so it takes more time to prepare graphs if you use them. If you need to prepare

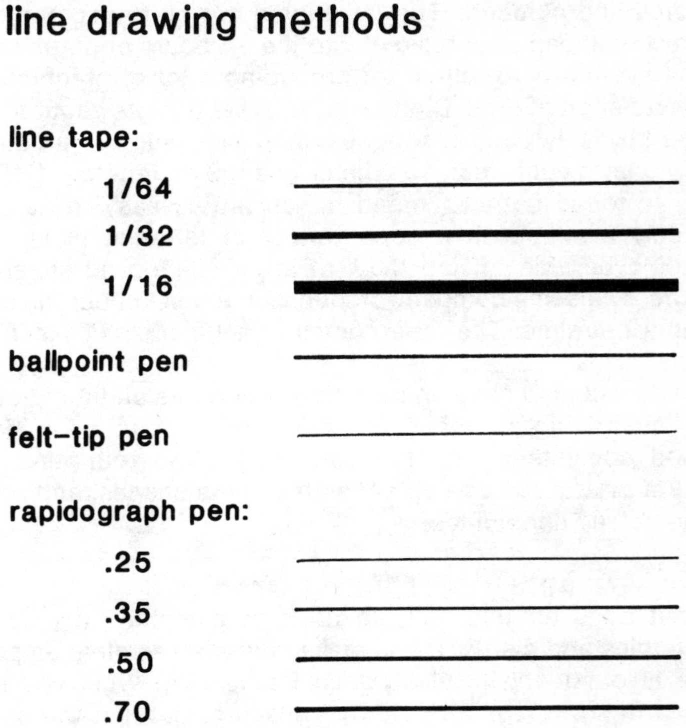

line drawing methods

line tape:

1/64	————————————
1/32	————————————
1/16	━━━━━━━━━━━━

ballpoint pen ————————————

felt–tip pen ————————————

rapidograph pen:

.25	————————————
.35	————————————
.50	————————————
.70	————————————

Figure 9-1

a large number of charts and graphs, typing the words and figures is a better alternative.

The graphics in this book were prepared using rapidograph pens and a number of other graphics tools. I have art board printed to my specifications rather than using thinner graphic paper. Art board is expensive to buy — about thirty cents each. I can print a large number for one-third that cost. Of course, I also prepare an average of fifty charts and graphs every month, so the expense is justified. If you're just doing a few charts, you can use standard graph paper.

For the lettering, I use a Kroy brand lettering system. This is a fast and high-quality method for producing the graph's words and numbers. They're printed out on transparent tape which you can attach directly to the art board or graph paper. The system is excellent for producing a lot of graphics in a short period of time. But the entire system costs about $1,200. You probably can't justify spending that much to produce a few charts each year, so type or use rub-on letters.

I've found Letraset brand rub-on letters easy to use, and widely available in a good variety of lettering styles. You should be able to find them at any well-stocked art supply store. The same company produces line tape, under the brand name Letraline. The tape comes in 1/16, 1/32, 1/64-inch and other sizes.

You will also need an assortment of rulers and templates. I suggest using a metal-edged ruler with a cork underside for good, consistent lines that won't wear down your pens. Also buy a protractor, a template with various shapes, and one or two curved-line guides.

The Advantages of Using Graphics

What does all this have to do with planning? It's simple. Graphics add clarity. If you make your plan as clear as possible, an outsider will quickly grasp its meaning. When you apply for a line of credit, you're more likely to get it if the banker doesn't have to ask you to explain what the plan is trying to say. And if you're trying to raise capital by bringing in a partner, the plan will tell the whole story clearly.

What if your plan is just for your own use? You'll find it easier to use throughout the year if you take the time to summarize important points with charts and graphs. This gives you a means of comparison, quick review, and easy reference.

For example, one builder broke out his income forecast with a simple line graph. He put down the estimate for each month on a graph, using a solid black line. Then, as each month's actual results came in, he tracked it with a red line. From this comparison, he could tell at a glance:

- Exactly how close the actual income was to the forecast.

- When it was above or below forecast.

172

- How the whole year was shaping up.

- How accurately he'd forecast income for the year (helping him achieve even greater accuracy the next year).

When the builder saw that actual income was slipping below forecast, he went back to the budget and looked at the original assumptions. He found the problem: Residential work wasn't coming in at the expected pace. He put some additional emphasis on marketing residential work, sending letters to previous customers. He reminded them that he was available for renovation and maintenance work. The direct mail campaign brought in enough new work to boost income to the forecast level for the rest of the year.

Graphing sales helped the builder stay on target toward the goal he'd set for the year. In this case, a graph in the business plan helped spot a trend before it got out of hand.

Don't think that graphs and charts are in your plan only to impress a loan officer. They also help you follow the plan, to modify it when needed, and to spot problems early, when there's still time to make corrections.

WHICH GRAPHICS SHOULD YOU USE?

The easiest visual aid is the chart. This is nothing more than a listing of information, complete with a title and descriptions. And it will probably be the most common form of graphic you'll use in your business plan.

In one business plan, the contractor wanted to describe how the forecast would exceed the previous year's budget. In the market expansion plan section, he wrote this paragraph:

> Revenues for the last year were $1,541,800. The forecast for the coming year is $1,890,000. This includes estimates for increases in all four quarters, with the biggest increase in the summer months (third quarter). A summary of the forecast is included in the last section of this plan.

That simple paragraph contains all the pertinent information. But it's not necessarily complete, easy to understand or to remember. I would prefer to supplement that narrative with a chart and put that chart right below your explanation.

For example, I would rewrite the paragraph to be a valuable lead-in to the information in the chart. There's no need to tell the reader what's in the chart — that's redundant. Instead, use the narrative to make observations and point out the importance of data in the chart. Here's how I'd write it:

> The forecast for next year estimates a 22.6 percent increase in revenues over last year. We expect significant increases in every quarter, as summarized below.

Forecast of Revenues		
Quarter	Last Year	Forecast
1	$ 218,400	$ 325,000
2	312,100	355,000
3	627,100	750,000
4	384,200	460,000
Total	$1,541,800	$1,890,000

The lead-in is much shorter and points out the dramatic level of growth being projected. This is **highlighting.** It's much more convincing than burying the reader in pages of narrative.

A table like this is an easy format to work with. It's usually just a list of numbers and labels. But once you draw a square around it, this financial forecast becomes a chart. This type of information is included in many business plans. But too often it's buried among several other statements in the back section. Put it in the relevant section, where the reader can't miss it. Make your point in a way that helps the reader notice and remember what's been said.

You can use smaller forms of charts to highlight facts, making your plan interesting and attractive at the same time. You can use a chart like the one just shown to break up the text, but you can also work text around a smaller chart, perhaps one that has only one or two bits of information.

For example, you're going through your assumptions that support the idea of a 22.6 percent increase in revenues for the coming year. In that section of your plan, it's important to summarize the financial result of this projection. But at the same time, you don't want to get too far off the subject. You'll be giving full details in the market expansion plan, so there's no need to get into the specific numbers. But you want the reader to know what your assumptions mean. So you might make a small chart like this:

```
Forecast    $1,890,000
Increase     22.6%
```

You can include a chart like this right in the text, either centering it or setting it off to one side. You can wrap the text around a small chart, as shown in Figure 9-2. This format produces an informative report. It also:

- Makes your report interesting for the reader

- Varies the narrative to heighten interest

- Conveys important conclusions

- Directs the reader's attention

- Shows the results of assumptions

THE LINE GRAPH

To show changes in financial information, the line graph is the best format. This consists of a square or rectangle, with a title or caption that describes it. The left side is usually marked off to denote value, such as dollars of sales or numbers of contracts. The bottom line generally shows time (years, quarters or months). You could set up a line graph another

175

charts in text

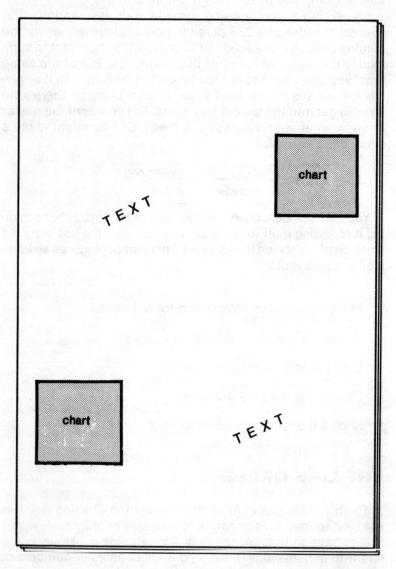

Figure 9-2

line graph

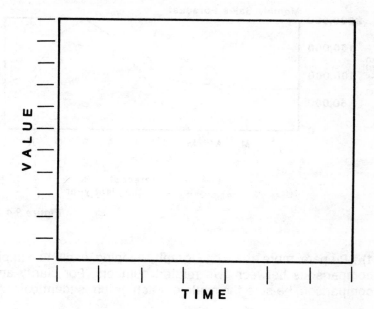

Figure 9-3

way, but this format is what most people are used to seeing. It's probably best to stick to it, to avoid confusion. The setup for a typical line graph is shown in Figure 9-3.

You can use a solid line, dotted line, dots, or dashes to show value. If you're reporting more than one type of information on a graph, you can combine these choices. For example, you could use a solid line to show your revenue forecast and a dotted line to indicate the estimated cost of sales.

Don't try to put too much on a line graph, as it will only confuse the reader. All graphs should be as simple as possible. When you do need to report on more than one bit of information, consider these choices:

rectangular line graph

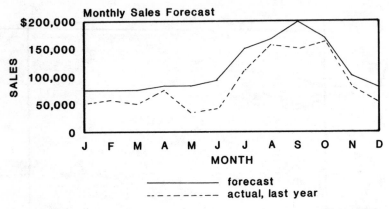

Figure 9-4

1) Prepare more than one graph, keeping each to simple comparisons between two related numbers. For clarity and comparison, be sure the scale of each graph is identical.

2) Use a different form than the line graph. (See the next section on bar graphs.)

3) Combine information into a single figure (income from different sources combined into one revenue total, for example) to simplify and clarify your graph.

Keep your line graph to a reasonable scale. You want a graph that's small enough to fit onto one page, but large enough so that the reader can easily comprehend it.

In selecting the increments you report, try to make your line graph as square as possible. For example, one contractor broke down a forecast by month, making a total of twelve time elements along the bottom of the graph. He needed to show sales up to a maximum of $200,000, so he indicated five divisions along the left edge, using an increment of $50,000. Figure 9-4 shows his chart.

squared line graph

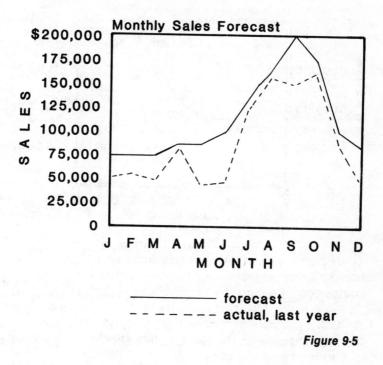

forecast
actual, last year

Figure 9-5

In this graph, the field is too narrow to make a good representation. It would be much better to make the graph more square by using an increment of $25,000, creating nine divisions along the sales line. Look at Figure 9-5.

There are two advantages to the second format: it creates a bigger field for reporting the financial results, and it allows a much more accurate representation. You want your graph to be as accurate as possible, *not* misleading. This requires keeping the scale of the graph consistent. For example, one contractor wanted to compare revenues to costs. She set up the graph with two scales: the left side represented income

two-scale line graph

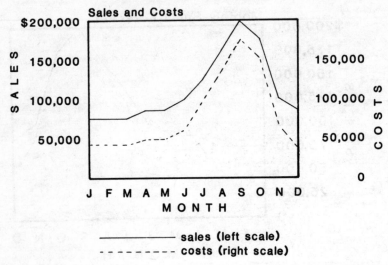

Figure 9-6

and the right side, costs. Her graph is shown in Figure 9-6. It's easy to read and accurate.

If you use a two-scale line graph, both scales must be the same. If one division indicates $50,000 in one scale, it must also represent $50,000 in the other scale. If they're not the same, the relationship between the two scales (income and costs, in this case) will be distorted. For example, if the two sides of Figure 9-6 were set up with different scales — say $50,000 increments for sales and $25,000 increments for costs — it wouldn't show the relationship accurately.

THE BAR GRAPH

Another form of graph that works well in business plans is the bar graph. This form gives you more flexibility than the line

horizontal bar graph

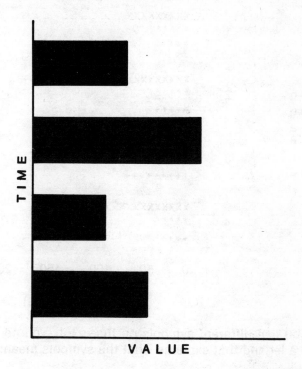

Figure 9-7

graph because it can handle several pieces of information.

There are two types of bar graph: horizontal and vertical. You can use either one, depending on your personal preference and the nature of the information you're reporting. Choose whichever form shows the results accurately and in a way that's easier to understand.

The format for a simple horizontal bar graph is shown in Figure 9-7. But you can use more than one type of bar to represent different data. For example, one builder with three sources of income used a horizontal bar graph to compare quarterly income for one year:

```
                     XXXXXXXXX
                1    * * * * * *

                     + + + +


                     XXXXXXXXXXX
   q            2    * * * * * * *
   u
   a                 + + + + +
   r
   t                 XXXXXXXXXXXXXXXXXXX
   e            3    * * * * * * * * * *
   r
                     + + + + + + + + +


                     XXXXXXXXXXXX
                4    * * * *

                     + + + + + +


                0    50    100    150    200

                     Income (thousands)
```

If you use different symbols on the graph, you need to include a legend that explains what the symbols mean:

```
        XXXXX    residential
        *****    commercial
        +++++    subcontracting
```

The vertical bar graph is more similar to the line graph, expressing time on the horizontal line and value on the vertical line. Many people prefer it for this reason. Figure 9-8 shows a sample vertical bar graph.

THE PIE CHART

There's one final graphic you can consider including in your business plan: the pie chart, also known as the circle graph.

vertical bar graph

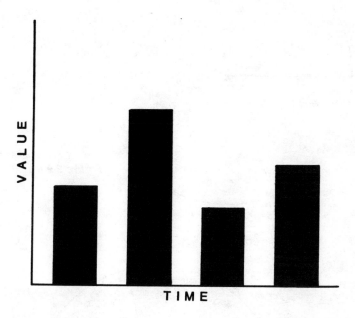

Figure 9-8

Figure 9-9 shows a sample.

With this type of graph, you can represent the elements that make up a financial total. You can divide sales by source, for example, or break down each dollar of income into costs, expenses, taxes and profits.

In addition to showing a full circle, you can emphasize one segment by separating it from the rest. For example, to show the portion of total income that's left for profits, the profit "slice" of the pie can be drawn away from the remainder of the circle. Figure 9-10 shows an example.

pie chart

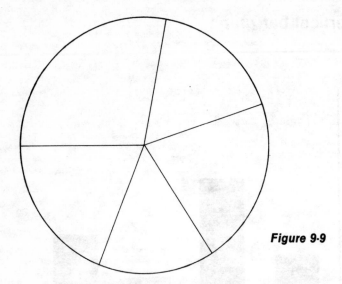

Figure 9-9

sliced pie chart

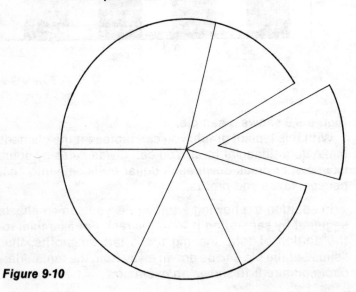

Figure 9-10

To develop an accurate pie chart, convert percentages to degrees of the circle. For example, let's make a pie chart of the following expenses:

Salaries and wages	28%
Rent	17%
Maintenance	21%
Taxes and licenses	15%
Other expenses	19%
Total	100%

To show this information on a pie chart, convert the percentages to the appropriate number of degrees. Since a circle has 360 degrees, multiply 360 by the percentage:

28% x 360 =	101 degrees
17% x 360 =	61 degrees
21% x 360 =	76 degrees
15% x 360 =	54 degrees
19% x 360 =	68 degrees
Total	360 degrees

To make a simple pie chart, you'll need a compass and a protractor. Use the compass to draw a circle that will fit on a page of your plan. Then draw a base line from the center of the circle to the edge. This base line represents zero degrees. Place the protractor on your base line, and locate the point for 101 degrees. Draw a line from the center of the circle to that point.

degrees of the circle

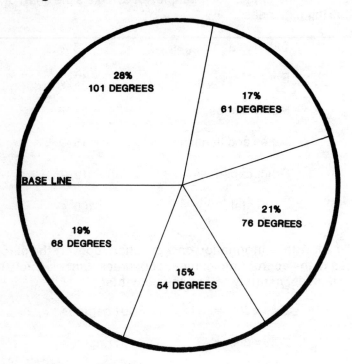

Figure 9-11

Use your second line as the new base line, and line up your protractor. Locate 61 degrees and draw a third line, from the center of the circle to that point. Proceed around the circle until all segments have been divided. Then label each one by name and percentage. Figure 9-11 shows the circle divided into degrees by the percentages given above.

Be sure the information you're conveying is appropriate for the pie chart format. This is a specialized graph that won't work for everything you have to report. And don't overuse any one type of graph in your plan. Even attractive graphics will lose the reader's attention if they're used too often.

CHOOSING YOUR FORMAT

Which kind of graph you'll choose depends on the nature of the information you're reporting. The purpose of graphics in your plan is to simplify and summarize. Choose the form that achieves that in the best possible way.

Here are some guidelines to help you make the choice:

Charts— Use charts to convey summarized financial information that clarifies or adds to the narrative of the plan. You can include comparisons, but for the most dramatic trends or estimates of the future, consider a graph. Reserve the use of charts primarily for information that doesn't work in purely narrative form, but isn't dramatic enough to make a good graph.

Line graphs— These are most effective for showing trends. Use a line graph to show historical information for a single item (like sales), or projections. Avoid complicating the graph by including too much. You can include two related numbers (like last year's sales and an estimate of the coming year), but don't go beyond two factors on the line graph.

Bar graphs— This form of graph is most appropriate when you need to compare several different financial facts. For example, you might use a bar graph to show income from three or more sources, or several types of expenses compared to the budget. You can show the information in either horizontal or vertical form. Use vertical graphs for the simpler material, and reserve horizontal reporting for the more complex.

Pie charts— They're more accurately called circle graphs. You'll probably use pie charts less frequently than the other graphs. A pie chart is appropriate for showing parts of a whole (such as income by source, the breakdown of each dollar in income, or a division of major expenses). Include pie charts in your business report only when they're the best way to communicate a particular type of information.

KEEPING IT VALID

Don't include charts and graphs just to make your plan look impressive. Don't let them complicate your plan. Graphics should simplify your business plan and make it easier to read and understand. Rather than placing a series of financial reports together at the end of the report, incorporate graphics into the body of the plan. That makes it easier for the reviewer (or you) to grasp the information and get the most from what's revealed.

There's a simple rule for deciding where and when to put information into visual terms. Whenever your discussion starts to talk about numbers, and the point you're trying to make becomes complex, there's probably a graph that can do the job. Don't look for opportunities in the plan to make a graph. Rather, let the nature of the discussion dictate where it's appropriate.

You won't be able to reduce every point to a visual aid — and you wouldn't want to even if you could. It's just as bad to clutter your report with too many graphics as to have none at all. Your business plan should be balanced, using graphs and charts where they do the job.

Your graphics don't have to be perfect. They only need to convey information effectively. You can do your own visual aids without hiring a professional. Simply drawing a square around a chart and placing it in the plan itself is one easy method. And the time required to put together a good line or bar graph is well worth the effort.

You can produce graphics on a variety of specialized computer programs. But be aware that the process isn't as easy as it sounds in the sales literature. You must be willing to invest the time required to master the program before you'll be able to quickly produce high-quality graphics. In addition, you'll need to invest several thousand dollars in hardware, including a plotter to draw the graphs. For the limited number of visual aids you probably produce in one year, it's unlikely you'll be able to justify such a large investment of time and money.

A small effort to improve the ideas and information conveyed in your plan can make a large difference. The banker you deal with probably isn't expecting a thorough and well-thought-out document. He's more often given nothing at all. Too many people want to borrow money without even knowing exactly what they need it for. When you enter that bank with a complete plan — one that also includes relevant charts and graphs — you are the exception to the rule. And even more important, it means you'll be able to better track and compare your plan to actual results. That boosts your chances of reaching your financial and personal goals.

SUMMARIZED INCOME FORECASTS

The plan sections we've covered so far describe how you intend to create company growth, and control that growth when it occurs. Of course, any growth will have an effect on your income and expenses. That's why a section of your plan must anticipate changes in income and suggest how those changes will be handled.

Of course you'll prepare a detailed budget that includes estimates of income, expenses and cash flow. But this isn't part of the business plan — it's one of your basic business tools, whether you do any planning or not. We'll cover the detailed budget in a later chapter. For the plan itself, however, you need only a summary of the highlights.

The income forecast supports your marketing expansion plan. It's an outline of your basic assumptions for the entire plan. It also becomes a schedule that you can use to measure progress toward the final goal.

WHAT TO INCLUDE

In this chapter (and the next two), I'll show you how to include budget information in your plan. These budget sections should be concise but packed with information. That requires a brief but complete listing of assumptions, sources of growth, and the effects of all the changes on your costs, expenses and cash flow.

Keep It Short

Remember, these are summary sections. Don't include every detail of your forecast in the plan. If you make it too long, a reader is more likely to skip over it. If someone who's reviewing your plan does want more information, you can show more data on the detailed worksheets. But for most people, the summarized version will be enough.

Example: A contractor started out his income section with a one-page chart. Each line represented one month. Each column showed the estimated receipts from each source for that month. On the next page, he explained the basic assumptions that went into the forecast. The entire explanation took two pages.

Back Up Your Estimate

Yes, keep it short — but not *too* short. Too little detail will hurt your plan. You want to convey not only the numbers, but the basis for their development as well. You'll probably need about half a page to explain the assumptions that went into your income forecast.

For example, here's an income forecast you might find in a typical business plan:

Income Forecasts

	Residential	Commercial	Total
January	$ 14,000	$ 10,000	$ 24,000
February	14,000	—	14,000
March	12,500	—	12,500
April	15,000	15,000	30,000
May	14,500	22,000	36,500
June	16,000	37,000	53,000
July	17,000	42,000	59,000
August	16,500	31,000	47,500
September	16,500	19,000	35,500
October	14,000	17,000	31,000
November	14,000	13,000	27,000
December	14,000	—	14,000
TOTAL	**$178,000**	**$206,000**	**$384,000**

Forecast Explanation:

Estimated gross receipts for the year total $384,000. Residential work accounts for 46%, while 54% comes from commercial contracts.

Residential: The six months between October and March are a slow but stable season for residential work. Most of the income from this source comes from the renovation in owner-occupied homes, an activity that always builds in volume during the warmer months.

In the past three years, our volume and seasonal levels have been predictable. This forecast is a conservative estimate of growth that follows the trend established in the past.

Commercial: Estimates through August exceed the previous year. They are based on existing contracts and our schedule of completion on three jobs.

We estimate two additional projects in the summer season, based on historical patterns and averages. The total forecast exceeds last year by 15%, based solely on work already under contract.

You'll understand the importance of including supporting detail when you submit your plan with a loan application. The loan officer will probably turn down the request if the income forecast is unreasonably high. But a forecast based on a detailed and realistic budget should help get loan approval without delay.

Connect Income and Assumptions

Anyone reviewing your plan is going to be at least a little skeptical. When you forecast the future, you tend to make the most favorable assumptions. But you should be as accurate as possible, showing income that's neither too high nor too low. Prove your point by showing the components of your estimated income, supported by sound assumptions.

Example: One contractor came up with an easy solution. He reported income forecasts in two ways. First, he prepared a typical monthly summary. Second, he showed how the forecast was developed, to validate its accuracy. He included a worksheet breaking out each month. The first line showed income for the previous year. Each line below that was an adjustment of one type or another: increases for new sources of income, decreases for one-time contracts, and changes due to the discovery of new opportunities. He supported each line with an explanation of the assumptions on which the figures were based. Here's what it looked like:

Income Forecasts

	Current Year	Adjustments		Forecast
January	$ 26,800	$ (2,800)	(1)	$ 24,000
February	21,400	(7,400)	(1)	14,000
March	19,000	(6,500)	(1)	12,500
April	22,300	7,700		30,000
May	21,900	14,600	(2)	36,500
June	32,000	21,000	(2)	53,000
July	41,600	17,400	(2)	59,000
August	39,500	8,000	(3)	47,5000

193

Income Forecasts (continued)

	Current Year	Adjustments		Forecast
September	34,000	1,500		35,500
October	23,800	7,200	(3)	31,000
November	21,400	5,600		27,000
December	19,600	(5,600)	(1)	14,000
Total	$323,300	$60,700		$384,000

(1)   Slow-season month estimates are conservatively lower than the previous year, assuming residential work will not be as high in the future.

(2)   Increases are due to income that will be earned on commercial jobs already under contract.

(3)   Commercial work is expected during the summer in addition to contracts already in progress.

Relate Income to Expenses and Cash Flow

Your forecast of income will affect other sections of the budget. Costs will vary with income. If you estimate a large volume of growth for the year, even your fixed expenses may increase. Cash flow will also be affected. Remember that your accounts receivable will grow as sales increase. Will you need to borrow money to put your plan into effect?

Example: The president of a construction firm planned a direct mail campaign to boost sales. This would make the advertising budget higher than the year before. To explain this change, he included a cross-reference in the plan. More promotion would mean higher cash receipts. But these would be partially offset by increases in accounts receivable. And finally, the increase in income required a loan. That meant repayments (affecting cash flow) and interest expenses. All of these factors were cross-referenced in the summarized income report.

HOW TO PRESENT YOUR FORECAST

You can probably show a summary income forecast on two pages or less. That's all you need in the plan. Remember that details belong somewhere else. Anyone reviewing your plan wants to see everything at a glance. Even for your own use, details can get in the way.

Show Income by Source

Even in a very brief income section, show the monthly breakdown for income by source. Use a worksheet like Figure 10-1 to show up to four sources of income. Include a one or two sentence summary for each assumption at the bottom of the page.

This worksheet can be simplified even more if you have only one or two sources of income. By source of income, I mean a particular market you serve or type of work you do. For example, you might do both commercial and residential projects, some home maintenance and repair work, or renovate and improve homes. The more sources you have, the more important it is to itemize income by source. Don't make the mistake of reporting too little, even if you've worked out the details and have an airtight forecast.

Remember that someone on the outside doesn't know your market as well as you do. It's your job to educate and convince others who'll be reading your plan.

A typical worksheet might look like this:

Month	1	2	3	4	Total
Jan	$3,200	$1,400	$5,600	$8,000	$18,200
Feb	3,200	1,600	6,000	0	10,800
Mar	3,200	1,600	5,600	0	10,400
Apr	3,200	2,000	5,600	7,000	17,800
May	3,200	2,400	3,500	0	9,100
Jun	3,200	3,800	3,500	0	10,500
Jul	3,900	3,900	3,500	0	11,300
Aug	3,900	4,200	3,500	9,000	20,600
Sep	3,900	4,200	2,500	0	10,600
Oct	3,900	2,800	2,500	8,000	17,200
Nov	3,900	2,200	2,500	0	8,600
Dec	3,900	1,400	2,500	8,000	15,800
Total	$42,600	$31,500	$46,800	$40,000	$160,900

income assumptions

month	1	2	3	4	total
Jan					
Feb					
Mar					
Apr					
May					
Jun					
Jul					
Aug					
Sep					
Oct					
Nov					
Dec					
total					

explanation

1 _____

_____

2 _____

_____

3 _____

_____

4 _____

_____

Figure 10-1

Explain Your Figures

Below the income breakdown, include a short explanation section to support the figures. Keep your explanations short, but make sure all the important elements are represented:

- A description of exactly what type of income is included in the column.

- The basis for the forecast (historical records, market factors, increases over the last year, other sources).

- Variations during the year (for seasonal factors, increases in volume, and so forth).

- A mention of the effect on expenses and cash flow, especially if that effect will be a large one.

The entire explanation can include all of these elements in only two or three sentences. For example, here's the explanation section written by a contractor who had four sources of income: residential maintenance, home improvement, subcontracting, and commercial contracts:

Residential maintenance will continue for the first six months at about the same level as last year. Income will increase starting in July. Most of this income is paid in cash.

Home improvement contracts have been made throughout the year in the past. This year, we will reduce that line of income. Payments generally occur at the time of completion.

The firm serves as subcontractor on a regular basis for another builder. Income from this varies due to seasonal activity, and is paid on average within the month following completion.

Ongoing commercial contracts and an estimate of new jobs will account for about $40,000 in revenues, assuming two contracts in addition to work in process. Income is booked as earned, and usually paid within 30 days.

coordinating the forecast

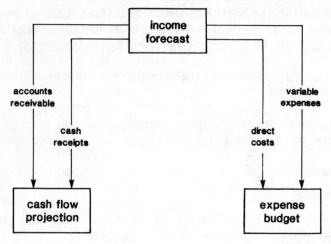

Figure 10-2

Of course, the complete income forecast includes much more detail than this. The purpose of this income summary is just to highlight the results. But all of the supporting detail must be included in other sections of the plan. Your brief mention of assumptions will be fully explained in the assumption section, the forecast will be in line with your market expansion plan, and the expense and cash flow sections will be cross-referenced to your income summary. Let's look at how to do that cross-referencing.

THE CROSS-REFERENCING SYSTEM

Cross-reference your income forecast — even a very brief one — to other sections of the plan and to basic assumptions. Point out the relationships between income and other budget and cash flow estimates. Cash flow will be affected by the amount and timing of cash receipts, as well as by changes in levels of accounts receivable. Your expense budget will change with changes in direct costs and variable expenses. Figure 10-2 shows a diagram of these relationships.

Although this income forecast is just a brief summary, you still have to support it with clear assumptions. Now I don't mean that you have to prove your forecast at this point. A plan can't verify every figure you project: It only presents a course of action you intend to follow. If a bank officer wants verification, he'll ask for it. In writing your business plan, concentrate on laying out a realistic and reasonable case. Although it will only be one or two pages long, the income forecast section must include these three divisions:

1) **The forecast:** This contains only the numbers, broken out by the month. A quarterly or annual income forecast isn't specific enough. There are too many variables, including the seasonal factor that affects most businesses. You might anticipate a gradual increase or decrease in one particular source of income. And income from some sources won't be received every month.

2) **Components:** Your forecast is more convincing when it's broken down by components (the sources of revenue). Break out and describe each source of income for each month.

3) **Assumptions:** Because each component is different, you need to mention the assumptions that go into the forecast. In our example, residential maintenance includes fairly level receipts, with a gradual increase during the year. Subcontracting varies by season. The builder in the example plans to reduce home improvement work. Note that income from commercial contracts comes in lump sums throughout the year.

Build your income forecast section with these three categories in mind. Figure 10-3 shows the elements you use in building an income forecast.

MAKING THE FORECAST REALISTIC

Remember that anyone reviewing your plan will always be looking for flaws. That's because most business plans are too optimistic. But you're the expert on your industry and, more specifically, on your business. You're in the best position to

elements of the forecast

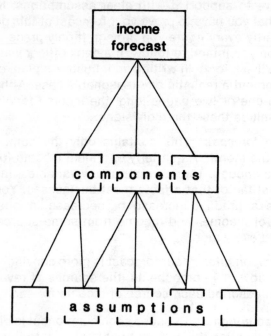

Figure 10-3

prepare an accurate forecast. If you base it on sound information and logical assumptions, your reader will have little to complain about.

Although estimating the future is difficult, you're also an expert at that. You estimate the costs of future jobs every day — and if you're still in business, you must be doing something right.

When you prepare an estimate for a customer, you begin by gathering all the facts: labor, material and equipment costs, how long the work will take, and what percentage to add for profit. The same is true when you're preparing an income forecast. In fact, it's exactly the same process.

When preparing an estimate, you're concerned with labor and material costs. Your income forecast is based on:

Market conditions— You understand what's going on in your own region. You know what types of work are available, the demand for your services, and the competitors who'll be trying to get their slice of the same pie.

Resources— You also know what you can handle. You have a certain amount of capital, equipment and manpower available. You can expand beyond those limits only if you can find more capital, equipment and manpower. That limits how fast you can grow in a year.

Time— If you're handling thirty major contracts this year, you probably aren't prepared to take on a hundred next year. That just wouldn't be realistic. Even if you could raise the money and hire the crews, you have a limited amount of time to devote to your jobs. And you know that your direct involvement is essential to maintaining quality.

You want your forecast to be reasonable. No one would believe an overly optimistic forecast, and *you* can't use wishful thinking as a guide to growth. To reach your goals, you need a realistic road map to success.

SEASONAL CHANGES

If you're like most builders, summer is your busy season and winter is slower. Your forecast should consider changes from season to season. That's not always easy. The best source of information is your record of work done for the last two or three years. Use as much historical data as possible to make your forecast realistic. Your own experience with seasonal changes in the past is the best guide for anticipating seasonal changes in the future.

The forecast is your best guess, nothing more. Base your plan on what's reasonable, the income each job is likely to bring in, and how much time is involved. Then map out your increases over the year.

For example, a landscaper currently has eighteen jobs underway. He completed 124 jobs last year, including a wide range of residential and commercial work. This year, he's estimating that he'll do about 156 jobs. He could have set up his income forecast by assuming he'd finish thirteen jobs each month, then multiplying that number by last year's average price per job. But he knew (as you do) that this would be misleading. His work varies by the season.

Instead of assuming a steady volume all year long, he could predict a gradual increase through the year. The schedule might look like this:

Month	Jobs	Month	Jobs	Month	Jobs
Jan	10	May	12	Sep	15
Feb	10	Jun	12	Oct	16
Mar	11	Jul	13	Nov	16
Apr	11	Aug	14	Dec	16

There's a problem with this method, too. No landscape contractor should expect a steady increase in business. It's unrealistic to expect ten new jobs in January. Of course, that's the monthly average based on all the work done last year — including the summer months. The example shows the landscape contractor ending the year with the highest monthly volume, sixteen contracts. January and December are slow months for most landscape contractors in most of the U.S.

An estimate of 156 new jobs for the year may be pretty close to the mark. It's based on past growth trends, an understanding of market demand, competition, and ideas about promoting services and getting more customers. A plan that well considered shouldn't overlook seasonal changes. The plan should anticipate the busy summer season, timing promotions to coincide with natural business peaks.

Even if you're not a landscaper, consider the seasonal volume changes in your income forecast. Here's how:

1) Summarize total income and the number of jobs during the last three years. Break out the totals by month. If you're estimating income on an as-earned basis, be sure to use accrual records. And if you're doing your forecast on a cash basis, use records of cash receipts. Keep in mind that an exceptionally harsh or mild winter will affect the results. But you're looking for averages, and using three years (or more) will make your best guess more accurate.

2) Decide whether to base your average on actual dollars earned or on the number of jobs. You might have to modify averages, especially if you've changed the mix of business during the three-year period, if the hourly or job charges have risen, or if one of the years in your average isn't typical, causing the resulting numbers to be distorted.

3) Plot your modified average on a graph. You'll need to track the average dollars or jobs, whichever one you decide to use. But the important goal here is to develop a predictable average *curve* that's affected by the seasons. The past numbers aren't as important at this stage as spotting the trends.

4) Base your current forecast on the seasonal curve you develop.

Using this method made the landscape contractor's forecast much more realistic. First, he analyzed his jobs for the past three years to compute monthly totals. Since he recorded sales as soon as the work was billed out, he based estimates on his sales journal for each month. He calculated total income and the number of jobs for each month. If he reported on the cash basis, recording income only when it was actually received, he would have based the forecast on his cash receipts journal.

Because he'd raised his rates twice during the three years, he decided to use the number of jobs as a basis for his seasonal calculations. He figured the average number of jobs each month over the three years. He put the totals on a graph, plotting a "typical" year.

seasonal tracking

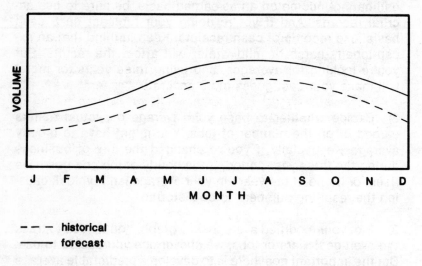

Figure 10-4

Finally, he forecast his current year's income based on the curve, estimating a higher volume of work for the summer months, and a lower average for the winter. This seasonal graph is shown in Figure 10-4.

USING A TIME LINE

Your business plan should be a practical working document, not just an estimate of the future. What features can you build into the plan to make it more of a practical working document?

With a time line, you can track your income through the year and compare actual results to your forecast. Remember, every goal can be broken down into simple steps. If you do this with your forecast, you'll be able to measure and control results.

For example, suppose you forecast an increase in income, based on a direct mail campaign to homeowners in your city. You identify four steps in this process:

1) Design and print two letters, one each for initial contact and follow-up.

2) Develop a system for telephone response and follow-up calling to prospective new customers.

3) Mail out a test batch.

4) Evaluate results.

Plan the timing of this four-part project with seasonal demand factors in mind. For example, you serve a residential market and people start thinking about hiring a contractor during the summer. You decide the best time to mail letters is during the months of May and June. You forecast income on the same schedule.

Divide your time line into *forecast* and *actual* lines. Put each phase of your plan on the forecast line, and track it as you actually complete the work. In the example above, you might decide to design your letters in March, to develop follow-up systems in April, to mail out a test batch in May, and to evaluate results in the first part of June.

This direct mail idea might be only one of three ideas for controlling income during the year. Besides the direct mail campaign, let's say you plan a series of newspaper ads and a program of personal contacts. In this case, you'll need three separate time lines. You could develop an income forecast time line like the one in Figure 10-5, incorporating your three promotional ideas.

Let's take a look at how this three-part promotional forecast might work out throughout the year.

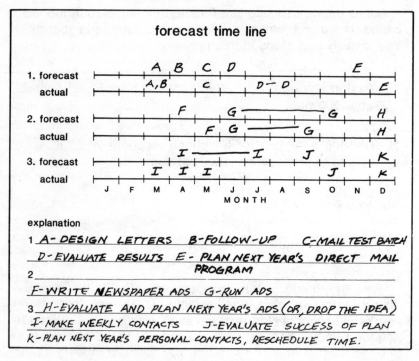

forecast time line

1. forecast / actual
2. forecast / actual
3. forecast / actual

explanation

1 A- DESIGN LETTERS   B-FOLLOW-UP   C-MAIL TEST BATCH
  D- EVALUATE RESULTS   E- PLAN NEXT YEAR'S   DIRECT MAIL
2   PROGRAM

F- WRITE NEWSPAPER ADS   G- RUN ADS

3 H- EVALUATE AND PLAN NEXT YEAR'S ADS (OR, DROP THE IDEA)
I- MAKE WEEKLY CONTACTS   J- EVALUATE SUCCESS OF PLAN
K- PLAN NEXT YEAR'S PERSONAL CONTACTS, RESCHEDULE TIME.

Figure 10-5

Direct mail— You may discover that the design (A) and follow-up (B) can be done together in a single month. That puts you ahead of schedule. Then you send out the mailing on schedule, in May. But you can't start evaluating the results in June because you don't have enough responses yet. You delay the evaluation until July and August. And you slip a little on the plan for next year's campaign, completing it in December instead of November. What's important is that you got it done before the end of the year.

Newspaper ads— You planned to write your ads (F) in April, but didn't get it done until May. The ads were placed in June (G) to run every week. But the forecast originally called for keeping ads in the paper through October, and you pulled them a month early. As it turned out, business started dropping off and you felt that they were no longer paying off. In December, you evaluated the ads along with the direct mail campaign.

Personal contact— This program was the most difficult of the three to evaluate. You started making contact (I) earlier than planned, and stopped in May. Once the busy season started, you just didn't have time to keep it up.

Evaluate Your Time Line

When you begin to do your time line, look at it and *think about it.* See if you can spot any trouble before you finalize your plan. Spread the work out so you have time to complete each step. Will you be busy with other projects in months when you've scheduled several steps?

For example, one contractor realized that his four-part time line required a heavy amount of administrative work during June and July. This was when his busy season started. He rearranged the forecast so that a lot of the preliminary work could be done in early spring. That freed up his time for other work during the summer. During the year, he tracked each of his four goals and made sure he stayed on target.

You'll probably have to make some modifications during the year. Make your income forecast as realistic as possible — but be flexible enough to change your plan as you discover flaws.

To succeed as a business planner, you need simple but usable systems for tracking. If you can track progress and make adjustments as needed, you'll be able to both predict and control future income. And that practically guarantees success.

11 SUMMARIZED EXPENSE BUDGETS

*I*n this section of your business plan, you summarize projected costs and expenses. Later in the plan you'll provide details on each cost item. This section should also include enough supporting information so your reader can see that the estimates are reasonable.

EXPENSES AND YOUR PLAN

This section includes a forecast of costs and expenses, demonstrates that your estimates are realistic, describes measures that will be used to control costs, and suggests how expenses will be matched against cash flow. Let's look at each of these areas.

Forecasting Costs and Expenses

There's no need to include all of the details you used in developing your complete budget. In this section, you only need to show the totals and explain significant changes.

For example, a contractor forecasts a major change in both income and the emphasis of his operation. Part of the plan calls for an expansion of markets, which will require a larger field and office staff. That means higher labor costs. It also means a higher budget for rent, as he'll have to move to a larger office. The expense summary section of his plan explains these changes, and summarizes other costs and expenses.

Show That Your Estimates Are Realistic

Of course you want your plan to be as realistic as possible, both for your own purposes and to convince any outside reviewer. The process of preparing the plan forces you to test your assumptions and prove that your estimates are reasonable.

For example, one builder had estimated a large increase in net profit due to expanding volume in the coming year. But when he got into the expense budgets, he realized that he'd have to spend much more than he'd planned to support the increased volume of business, reducing the anticipated net profit. Going through the planning process helped him see the flaws in his idea.

Develop Control Measures

Explain how you intend to control your costs and expenses, to make sure they stay within your estimate. In other words, take command of your future. Use your plan to develop controls and to put them into effect.

One contractor had chronic problems with printing and telephone expenses. These expenses had always run over budget in the past. When the owner prepared his plan for the new year, he estimated a moderate growth in volume. He also decided to try and keep these expenses in line. In the summarized expense section, he described controls he planned to put into effect at the start of the new year. The budget was put together with those controls in mind. He used the plan to develop ideas for cutting expenses.

A realistic plan is the key to profits. It's the stress test of your business plan. If you put up a house without enough support, it won't stand on its own. You'll have to strengthen it. A business plan works the same way. Your costs and expenses are the structural components of your operation. They must be strong enough to support your planned growth level, or the whole plan will collapse.

Coordinate Costs with Income and Cash Flow

There's always a relationship between your cost and expense budget and your income and cash flow forecasts. Any change in one affects the other two.

A plan that forecasts increases in income but no changes in costs is seldom realistic. Any loan officer reviewing the plan is sure to see the discrepancy — and probably deny the loan. Be sure to write a realistic, balanced plan.

BASE YOUR COST ESTIMATES ON INCOME

Your cost and expense estimates and the success of your budget depend largely on your income forecasts. This is true for a number of reasons:

1) Direct costs change in direct proportion to income levels.

2) Variable expenses are also affected by volume, although not to the same degree as direct costs.

3) Fixed expenses are "fixed" only within certain ranges of volume. Major increases in income will usually require major increases in fixed expenses.

4) Keeping costs and expenses in line isn't easy. There's a tendency to relax controls when you're very busy handling new work.

Costs and Expenses Vary with Income

There's a predictable relationship between income and variable expenses. As income rises, so do the variable expenses — especially travel, telephone, hourly wages, some forms of insurance, licenses, and interest (if the growth in volume is financed with short-term loans).

While variable expenses fluctuate with income, they're not always a predictable percentage of revenues. Say your variable expenses equal 10 percent of gross revenue today. If you double the level of income over the next three years, those same variables should be somewhat less than 10 percent. Higher sales should bring greater efficiency.

For example, your telephone system charges a basic rate, including local calls. Your phone expenses probably won't rise much as your volume increases, unless you take on some out-of-town jobs. In this case, you'll actually have a better margin with higher volume.

Try to fix direct costs and variable expenses at a set percentage of sales volume. If you can, your percentage of profit will increase or decrease with changes in fixed expenses. You may find that within a given range of income, fixed expenses are controllable and truly fixed. As long as controls are enforced, higher volume will mean higher profits.

Fixed expenses include general and administrative commitments like rent, administrative salaries, your own salary, payroll taxes, state and local taxes and assessments, fixed insurance, office supplies, and other overhead. Remember, though, that these expenses aren't written in stone.

There will be a point where increasing volume raises fixed expenses. If you rent a larger office and hire a new office manager, you'll have to accept an increase in fixed expenses. This is one of the danger points in planning. You'd better be sure that a substantial increase in volume is permanent. Most increases in fixed expenses are hard to reverse.

Say you need a larger office and more room in your equipment yard. You sign a five-year lease and move to the new location. But two years later less work is available and sales slip back to lower levels. You're stuck with your higher

the effect of volume

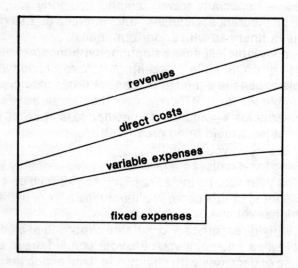

revenues

direct costs

variable expenses

fixed expenses

Figure 11-1

overhead. Profits will go down. There may be no way to recover until volume increases again.

The relationship between increasing income and your direct costs, variable expenses, and fixed expenses, is shown in Figure 11-1.

TRACK YOUR GROSS MARGIN

To help control the level of direct costs, develop a simple procedure for tracking your gross margin. That's the percentage of gross profit compared to total revenues. Let's assume your financial statement for last year shows the following:

Income	$496,300
Direct Costs	297,800
Gross Profit	$198,500

When you divide the gross profit by income, you find that your gross margin is 40 percent. If that seems a reasonable margin to you, then adopt 40 percent as the standard you'll strive for. Any time the margin falls below that level, it indicates that there's a problem. You need to look for the problem, and take steps to correct it.

Here are a few points you should understand about tracking your margin:

Compare apples to apples— Be sure to look at the same items each time you do the comparison. That should include salaries paid to tradesmen (but not office employees), materials purchased for jobs, and other direct expenses only. If you change the components each time you calculate the gross margin, the results will be distorted.

One contractor ran into problems because he'd changed his accounting codes. One year, he included all labor, payroll taxes and union welfare as direct costs. The following year, taxes and welfare were moved down to general expenses. To track margin, he needed consistency from one year to another. He had to refigure the labor portion of payroll taxes and welfare payments as direct costs. That's a lot of work to do every time you calculate margin. Try to be consistent.

Count your inventory— If you keep an inventory of building materials, calculate gross margin based on a physical count of your stock. Otherwise, the calculation won't be dependable. It isn't always practical to count stock every month, especially if you have many different items. You might have to settle for tracking on a quarterly basis.

Inventory is a special problem for those contractors who must calculate gross margin between physical counts. You can reduce this problem by identifying sections of your stock where errors are most likely to occur (due to damage, high volume of replacement, or the chances of spoilage). Count these items and estimate the value of the remainder of your inventory. This may also help reduce any problems you've had with inventory losses and damage in the past.

One builder counts stock every quarter and does a gross margin calculation at the same time. He doesn't bother to calculate gross margin monthly, since it would be based on estimated inventory levels. An accurate margin figure every three months lets him keep his business on track. There's one section of inventory he counts monthly, however, because he's had significant losses in the past. Losses are down now.

Watch for margin changes as volume increases— Be especially aware of changes in the margin when your volume goes up. Watch for that tendency to relax controls when business is good. As a general rule, when you're busier, you just aren't thinking about controls. It's only when business falls off that you begin worrying about margins and profits. But by practicing control regularly, you can improve the profit picture considerably. Well-designed controls don't take much time to put into effect and supervise.

One home builder runs into this issue every summer when his business gets active. But he's disciplined himself to spend a half hour several times a week to review financial information and ensure that controls are being followed. That's all it takes. His foremen report on the daily use of materials, labor efficiency, and scheduling, and he delegated the analysis to his office manager. This frees up his time for site work and for supervising the control process. He still has the time for the work that must be done, while the controls are in place and working.

Allow for fluctuations in income source— When you have two or more different sources of income, the trend of your gross margin won't be as reliable an indicator of how your business is doing. Unless each type of work you handle is equally profitable, your gross margin will vary with changes in the mix of work completed each month.

For example, one contractor splits his time between bidding commercial work and doing home improvements. His profit is much greater on the residential work, and his gross margin changes when the mix of the two kinds of work changes. Several years ago, only 30 percent of all work came from commercial work. Two years later, nearly 80 percent came from that commercial work. His mix changed dramatically: He had higher volume but a lower margin. This didn't indicate a control problem, however. It was due entirely to the change in his business mix.

BASE FUTURE PLANNING ON PAST RESULTS

You can only control the future if you understand what happened in the past. This is especially true in planning. Base your assumptions on what has worked and what hasn't worked in previous years.

For example, I know a contractor who was able to hold his gross margin at about 40 percent of sales in most years — until he won several large military jobs. Then he found that gross margin fell below 35 percent. In looking for the reasons, he found that the major change was in material costs. His tradesmen were wasting too much stock, materials were disappearing off the job site, supplies not needed to complete a job were being discarded, and he wasn't getting competitive bids from some suppliers. With the company handling more and more work, the contractor wasn't able to supervise the buying and use of materials. No one in the company was handling this important task. The result was predictable: higher material cost and lower profit.

To reduce the erosion of his profits, he set standards for the purchase of materials. For example, he stopped buying in large quantities to get 5 percent discounts unless the material was going to be used within three months. He also set up a procedure for counting stock regularly. Some stock was counted monthly and other stock only quarterly. He locked up small tools and parts to reduce the opportunity for theft. And he set up a monthly report procedure that compared the volume of sales to inventory levels.

Try comparing your gross margins from year to year. See Figure 11-2. Note how the gross margin narrows when income

direct cost analysis

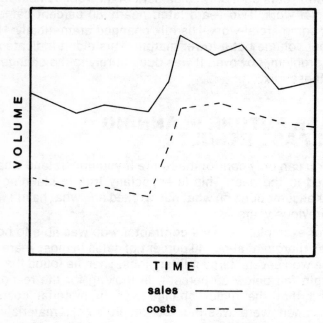

Figure 11-2

increases. This isn't as serious as it might seem. Remember that gross profit in dollars may be increasing even though gross profit in percent may be falling. For example, compare these revenue and cost figures:

Year	Revenue	Costs	Gross	Percent
1	$105,600	$63,400	$42,200	40.0
2	138,100	85,400	52,700	38.2
3	210,000	134,300	75,700	36.0
4	262,700	176,100	86,600	33.0

In this example, the amount of gross profit rises each year. But profit as a percentage of sales is falling. In the final year, it's a full 7 percent lower than the first year's margin. That adds up to over $18,000. If there's a control problem here, it's a costly one.

Always remember the need for controls on spending. In this section of the plan, describe what you're going to do to reduce direct costs as well as variable and fixed expenses.

MAJOR EXPENSE SUMMARIES

On the expense side, you can summarize your forecast for the year by concentrating on major accounts. In your detailed budget, of course, you'll have an analysis of each and every account. For the purposes of your plan, you summarize all expenses for the year, detailing only those accounts where big changes will occur or where a control procedure will be needed.

Your emphasis will probably be on variable expenses. In cases of major expansion (like moving to a new office and hiring a new employee), you'll also need to explain changes in fixed overhead.

You could include a spreadsheet in your plan that shows budgeted monthly expenses for the entire year. But this would require a large page that would have to be folded into the plan. Try to avoid this. Consider these alternatives:

- Show quarterly summaries only.

- Show your monthly budget on two pages, one for each half of the year.

A quarterly summary requires a description and five columns:

Expense budgets
for the year _____

Account	First quarter	Second quarter	Third quarter	Fourth quarter	Total

The only problem with this format is that it probably doesn't show as much detail as you need. Having a monthly listing is more useful, both as a summary for yourself and for outside review. Don't use a quarterly listing just because it's a more convenient size. If you need space for a more complete explanation, use that space. Dividing the budget into two parts makes more sense. On page one, you would include:

Expense budgets
for the year _____

Account	Jan	Feb	Mar	Apr	May	Jun	Sub-total

Page two would look like this:

Expense budgets
for the year _____

Account	Jul	Aug	Sep	Oct	Nov	Dec	Total

In addition to the expense budget summary, include a summary of each account that involves a major change from the previous year. List the monthly amount as well as the assumptions that went into the budget. Use a form like Figure 11-3.

Keep your plan a reasonable size. Include only as many of these expense summaries as are actually needed. If you have less than five, place them all in this section of the plan. If you must include more, refer to them in your explanation and include them at the back of the plan. That keeps the expense section to a readable size. And if you or an outside reviewer needs more information, it's right at the back of the report.

expense summaries

MONTH	BUDGET	MONTH	BUDGET
Jan		Jul	
Feb		Aug	
Mar		Sep	
Apr		Oct	
May		Nov	
Jun		Dec	
		Total	

Assumptions

1 _____

_____

2 _____

_____

3 _____

_____

4 _____

_____

Figure 11-3

coordinating the budget

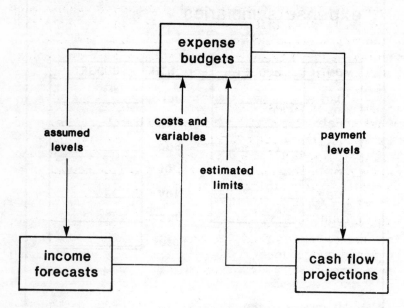

Figure 11-4

OTHER PLAN SECTIONS

Spend some time on the expense summary section. Expect it to receive the most intensive review. Of course, every section of the plan depends on the accuracy of every other section. But in the case of expense budgets, there's a direct relationship between income forecasts and cash flow projections. This is shown in Figure 11-4.

Let's look at each point of this relationship:

Assumed levels— The budget is your prediction of approximate volume for the coming year. Base this estimate on past experience and knowledge of your company and market.

For example, you prepare your budget with the assumption that total expenses will be approximately the same as last year. But you also forecast a large increase in volume. Stop and think. Does that mean you'll need to pay more rent, finance your expansion with a loan, hire more employees, or rent equipment? Chances are that expenses will go up along with income.

Costs and variables— You need to be aware of two points. First, consider the relationship between the cost/expense factor and sales. Second, plan to stay in control. That's the primary purpose of the analysis and planning you go through. Know the historical margins, set a standard for yourself, then monitor your plan to make sure the standard is met.

Payment levels— Planning your cash flow is an important part of the planning process. The commitments projected in your expense budget must be realistic and in line with the cash flow estimates in your income forecast.

Estimated limits— Every business has limited capital, whether that money is invested (equity) or borrowed. The budgets you put in your expense section will be based on the cash you expect to have available.

Your banker will be impressed if you've planned for expansion within the limits of cash available. It's part of a loan officer's job to look for holes in your assumptions. When he finds none, that adds to his confidence in you as a prospective borrower. It demonstrates that you understand your business and your financial limits.

The plan is a guide to growth with the resources you have available. That's the best definition of planning. Anyone with unlimited money and no competition could expand without limits. No plan is needed. But in the construction industry, we all have competition and limited capital. And there's one final limitation: You have only a finite number of hours to generate the income you're after.

Too many business plans are prepared and presented without taking any of these realities into account. And loan officers, potential investors and other reviewers will immediately identify the problem. You're way ahead of the game if you prepare accurate forecasts and budgets, and express them in a complete plan.

THE EXPENSE CONTROL TIME LINE

Include a time line in your plan that shows when changes will be made in expense control procedures. Have a time schedule that shows when each necessary step will be taken: from monitoring expenses to instituting checks and controls.

For example, your time line might include three different issues, broken down into several steps for each:

1) Expense budget reviews
   - monthly comparison report
   - explanation of variances
   - determining required actions
   - six-month budget revision

2) On-going analysis
   - gross ratio report
   - variable expense report
   - controls as needed

3) New controls
   - to reduce excessive expenses
   - to determine problem trends
   - to review procedures

Assign each step a deadline. In the case of recurring procedures, set a monthly deadline. For example, you might prepare a monthly variance report. That's part of the control you need to keep expenses within budget.

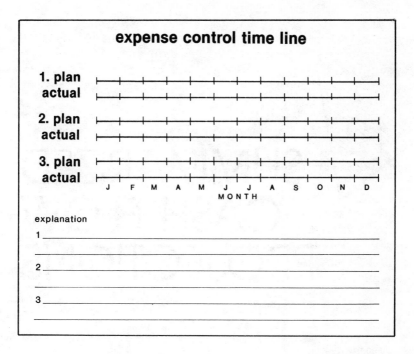

Figure 11-5

An expense control time line is shown in Figure 11-5. Use the explanation section to explain exactly what each division of the time line includes. Write in the plan deadlines at the appropriate month, and show your progress on the "actual" line.

Use the expense control time line to help you keep expenses within budget, increase gross margin, and expand net profit. But even when profits are increasing, you can get in trouble if the cash flow isn't there when needed. In the next chapter, we'll look at cash flow projections.

12 SUMMARIZED CASH FLOW PROJECTIONS

Cash flow is the amount of money coming in, versus the amount going out. Your commitments — salaries, rent, loan payments, and expenses — are constant. But income isn't. During slow periods, cash flow is likely to lag behind expenses.

Planning your cash flow may be the hardest part of business planning. Predicting income, costs, and expenses is relatively easy if you know your market and your business. But anticipating your bank balance six months from now may be much harder.

Because cash flow is harder to predict, it deserves intense and detailed planning. Unfortunately, many business plans don't even consider cash flow. Rather than confront the problem, the planner elects to ignore it.

I don't recommend that, of course. Your business plan won't be complete — or accurate — if you don't face cash flow problems head on, and look for solutions.

DEVELOPING SOLUTIONS TO CASH FLOW PROBLEMS

There are solutions to cash flow problems — *if* you approach the issue logically. The first step is to identify trends in cash flow. The second is to avoid problems by carefully scheduling spending, saving, and borrowing. We'll start with the first step.

Identify Trends in Cash Flow

Begin by analyzing trends in cash flow over the past three years. This is like the analysis of income trends we discussed earlier. Your purpose is to estimate the average cash balance you'll have available at key times during the year. Use this information to identify problem periods, and make plans to anticipate and avoid seasonal difficulties.

You probably know already the months when business will be slow. But that isn't enough. You need to identify predictable trends, and use those trends to make forecasts and develop budgets. You'll find that it's possible to predict and avoid most cash flow problems.

Several sets of records can be used to analyze cash flow trends: the general ledger cash account, the general ledger ending balances, and your monthly bank statements.

The general ledger cash account provides only a rough estimate, but it takes only a few minutes of checking to get the information you need. Refer to your cash account, where total cash increases and decreases are summarized. Subtract the difference between receipts and disbursements. Use that difference to show the change in cash. In a few minutes you can summarize transactions for the last two or three years.

The general ledger ending cash balances will be revealing but may not tell the whole story. You may have a healthy month-end cash balance, but that doesn't reveal payables you have on hand that are due by the 10th of the following month.

cash trend analysis

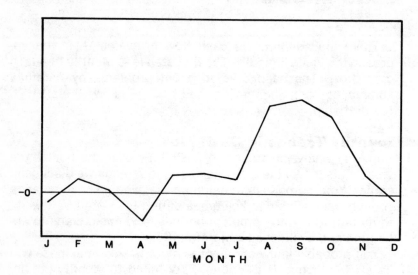

Figure 12-1

Your bank statements— Many banks report the daily and monthly average balance in addition to the ending balance. This is useful information in computing your cash flow over a period of time. Of course, the bank reports only on those transactions that have been completed. There are always a number of checks in transit. Compare the same average balance figure each month to pinpoint cash flow trends.

Once you develop an accurate summary of cash flow, average the totals. If you use information from three years, total the net cash for each month, then divide by three. For example, if your January net cash for the past three years was $5,672, $7,540, and $6,433, your average net cash for January is $6,548. When you have an average for each month, plot the averages on a graph like Figure 12-1. The line labeled -0- is the zero cash balance. If the line goes below the zero, it shows that you'd overdrawn your cash.

In this example, high volume in the summer produces a temporary surplus of cash. But it's quickly used up by the end of the year. It then takes six to eight months of fairly low average balances to rebuild a cash surplus. This is a common pattern for many construction contractors.

Anticipate and Avoid Cash Flow Problems

In this section of the plan, summarize how you'll anticipate cash flow problems. Then describe the steps you'll take to prevent them. These steps might include:

- Timing of capital asset purchases

- Controls over accounts receivable and payable, considering the season

- Control over inventory levels, with both the season and volume of business in mind at each point in the year

- Establishing a cash reserve during high-volume periods

- Using short-term loans during the slow season

Many business plans are put together solely to get loans. If you ask for a loan because you're short on cash, the lender will be concerned that you won't have cash available to repay the loan. In other words, the worse your situation, the greater the lender's risk. But if you have a complete business plan which includes an analysis of your cash flow, your lender will understand that you've thought the problem through and anticipated problems.

PUTTING TOGETHER THE SECTION

This section of the plan, like the income and expense sections, should be as brief as possible. But short doesn't mean incomplete. Include a complete summary of your cash flow projections and your solutions to the problems that will arise during the year. The details are in the budget, available to any reviewer who wants more information.

Show the Major Influences

For this section, concentrate on showing the major influences on cash flow. Provide a summary of the entire year's projection.

Six major factors influence cash flow:

1) Expected net profits on a cash basis (or your budgeted net profit adjusted for non-cash items like depreciation)

2) Major changes in the level of outstanding accounts receivable

3) Planned purchases of fixed assets

4) Planned sales of fixed assets

5) Loan proceeds you expect to request during the year

6) Loan repayments you're required to make

Of course, cash flow for the entire year will be affected if you start the year with a pile of unpaid bills. If that's the case, build a payment schedule into the plan.

For major items affecting cash flow, use a worksheet like Figure 12-2 to report and summarize the information. But don't clutter your plan with a lot of these summaries. If you have more than five, include them at the back of the plan and simply refer to them in this section.

Here's a sample of what might be included in a cash flow summary. Assume you're going to request a $30,000 loan in March, with repayments to begin May 1. The interest rate is 12 percent, and you'll repay the loan over a period of two years. Here's what you'd list on the worksheet:

Jan	-0-	Jul	-1,412
Feb	-0-	Aug	-1,412
Mar	30,000	Sep	-1,412
Apr	-0-	Oct	-1,412
May	-1,412	Nov	-1,412
Jun	-1,412	Dec	-1,412

cash flow summaries

MONTH	PROJECTION	MONTH	PROJECTION
Jan		Jul	
Feb		Aug	
Mar		Sep	
Apr		Oct	
May		Nov	
Jun		Dec	
		Total	

Assumptions

1 _____

_____

2 _____

_____

3 _____

_____

4 _____

_____

Figure 12-2

229

This shows both cash accumulations and cash reductions. Of course, monthly payments include interest. Interest expense actually belongs in the expense budget. If you don't have a breakdown available, I suggest this alternative:

1) Prepare the expense budget without an estimate of interest expense.

2) Consider the total loan repayment as a factor of cash flow (as though it were all interest).

3) Adjust your year-end estimate of profits and tax liabilities for the full year's interest.

Your lender can tell you the interest rate you'll probably have to pay, and the amount of your monthly payments. If you need to estimate these before talking to a lender, get a book of amortization tables from the library. These books show the monthly payment for each rate of interest, and for each repayment term. If your loan will be paid off in full (fully amortized) over a period, these tables will be accurate. If your loan won't be paid down to zero over the period, ask your lender to estimate the monthly payment amount.

Report the Cash Flow for the Year

The cash flow section of your business plan should also include a summary of anticipated cash flow for the year. This means showing the beginning balance, increases to cash, decreases to cash, and ending balance for each month. Divide the year into three- or six-month sections to make the table fit on standard size paper. Figure 12-3 shows this reporting format. The summarized report should show the flow of cash from one month to the next. The ending balance in January will also be the beginning balance in February.

A table showing only one quarter per page will require four pages of tables in the cash flow summary. Details backing up this summary should be left in the budget. Any major ex-

the summary of cash flow

	JANUARY	FEBRUARY	MARCH
Beginning balance			
Plus: Cash profits			
Loan proceeds			
Sale of assets			
Other increases:			
_____			
_____			
Subtotal			
Less: Loan repayments			
Purchase of assets			
Other decreases:			
_____			
_____			
Total decreases			
Ending balance			

Figure 12-3

penses (like the purchase of equipment) would be shown in an attached summary sheet. The report for the first quarter might look like Figure 12-4.

In practice, monthly cash flow can also be affected by many variables. For example, your accounts receivable will grow as your volume grows. Payments don't come in on a predictable schedule. But as your sales volume increases, it's safe to assume that collections will tend to increase in the same proportion.

the summary of cash flow

	JANUARY	FEBRUARY	MARCH
Beginning balance	$24,400	$18,500	$19,100
Plus: Cash profits	2,100	4,600	3,800
Loan proceeds	—	—	30,000
Sale of assets	—	—	—
Other increases:			
Subtotal	$26,500	$23,100	$52,900
Less: Loan repayments	—	—	—
Purchase of assets	8,000	4,000	40,000
Other decreases:			
Total decreases	$ 8,000	$ 4,000	$40,000
Ending balance	$18,500	$19,100	$ 12,900

Figure 12-4

Include an Explanatory Narrative

Besides the summaries of the year's cash flow and of major factors affecting it, this section should include a narrative (preferably of one page or less) explaining several points:

1) What you perceive as problem points, with a description of the solutions you've devised for each

2) An explanation of how loans will be used, and most important, how getting a loan will strengthen your competitive position and increase profitable sales volume

coordinating the projection

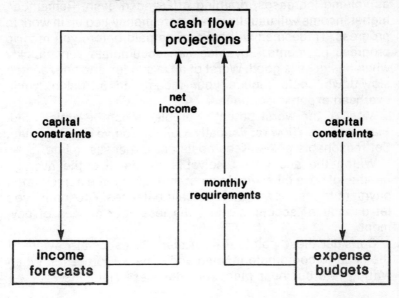

Figure 12-5

3) How receivables will be monitored and controlled, to ensure a regular flow of cash receipts

4) Your plan for keeping accounts payable current

5) Ideas for establishing a reserve, collections of outstanding accounts, and other measures needed to bridge the slow season

COORDINATING OTHER DETAILS

To prepare an accurate cash flow summary, you need to anticipate income, costs and expenses. In theory, the forecast and budget by themselves show how the year will turn out. But they don't guarantee that you'll have cash available in the bank at all times. Figure 12-5 plots cash flow projections, income forecasts, and expense budgets.

233

Consider these possibilities: Receivables will probably rise as volume increases, draining off needed cash. Remember, higher income will usually mean more money tied up in work in progress. Tradesmen will have to be paid before you receive progress payments. Payables can accumulate very quickly when business is good. Worst of all, a sudden and unexpected slow-down could reduce your income to a trickle, while overhead expense continues.

Most of the worst potential problems can be anticipated. Plan your cash flow realistically. Build a reserve into your plan. Set reasonable goals. Keep costs and expenses in line.

Watch the accounts receivable trends, like the average number of days bills remain outstanding. Enforce agreed-upon payment terms. Don't ignore unpaid balances. The longer you let delinquent accounts slide, the less your chance of payment.

Consider these points in your plan. Be especially aware of the need to coordinate income and expense forecasts. When writing your business plan, consider these elements:

Capital constraints (on income)— Your growth is limited by the cash you have available. Keep your income projections realistic, so you're not stuck with less working capital than you anticipated.

I know a contractor who planned to double gross receipts in a year. He had good reason to believe that this was possible. Competition was weak, demand was growing, and he had a good reputation with developers. But he didn't understand that growth would require more equipment, more money for salaries, more office space, and more office staff. He simply didn't have the money to support that much growth.

Net income— The income in your forecast will affect cash flow. First, if your forecast is overly optimistic, the money you expect just won't be there. Second, even the money you've earned won't be in the bank yet if collections are slow. Have a plan to collect what's due *when* it's due.

One remodeler I know had a small operation that had grown slowly but steadily for a year and a half. He had every reason to expect the trend to continue. When he prepared his business plan, he considered control of receivables. He had his book-keeper prepare two reports each month. The first showed the age of outstanding accounts. The second listed the average number of days required to collect money. Whenever a customer was more than 30 days late, the bookkeeper called to request payment. If a progress payment was more than 45 days late, work on the job was suspended. These steps nearly eliminated slow collection problems.

Capital constraints (on expenses)— The cash you have available will limit the expenses you can take on. When your budget is completed, take a close look at the cash flow. And remember that you don't always receive income when it's earned. Be realistic about your ability to match cash with ex-penses.

Most larger construction companies find that it takes from 30 to 45 days to collect money that has been earned. When you prepare the cash flow analysis, don't enter earned income un-til 45 days after it comes due. You'll probably identify several problem periods that will come up during the year. Usually you'll be able to bridge these periods with a series of 90-day loans.

Monthly requirements— Your expense budget should not ex-ceed the cash flow projection for any month. Cash can't be spent until it comes in. This limits the commitments you can make.

To make sure he wouldn't commit money he didn't have, an architect prepared his budget by assuming that expenses would be paid in the month budgeted. But he also assumed that income wouldn't be received until a month after it was earned. To make sure his cash flow stayed in control, his budget showed no receipts for the month of January. The money earned in January wasn't budgeted until February. This set the standard: at least one month's gross income would always be on hand to meet current obligations.

THE CASH FLOW TIME LINE

To avoid a cash flow crisis, anticipate problems. If you identify possible trouble periods, plan ahead to resolve them. A time line can help schedule the steps you're going to have to take. Here are some steps that could be built into your plan:

• Arrange for short-term financing before you need it. It's easier to qualify for a loan when you're in a good cash position. If you wait until the crisis, lenders will be less willing to take the risk.

• Design and install a tracking system that monitors receivables, payables, and work in progress.

• Plan major expenses like the purchase of equipment. Try to arrange for large payments when the most cash is available or when outside financing can be arranged.

• Plan to sell major assets when you'll need the cash most. Of course, tax considerations and the availability of replacements should also be considered.

• Monitor your cash flow projection as well as the forecasts and budgets. Revise projections after six months.

Identify as many cash flow control points as you need. Figure 12-6 shows a three-part time line. This is a schedule with three control phases. For example, you might plan the following:

1) Obtain financing to purchase new equipment, accounting for loan proceeds, a down payment, and continuing monthly loan payments.

2) Tracking procedures for accounts receivable: reporting, monitoring and control of expenses and income.

3) A review process, including monthly status reports of expected and actual results, and a planned six-month revision.

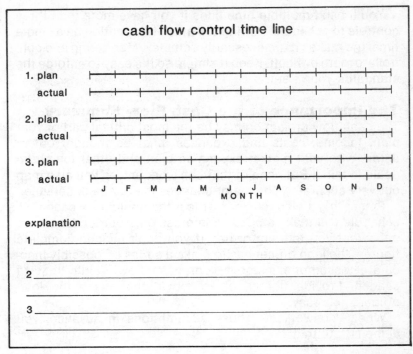

Figure 12-6

The explanation section explains the purpose of each of the three phases, including indicated schedule points. For the loan, you would schedule:

a. the request for financing
b. expected approval date
c. date to receive proceeds
d. date to arrange payment and delivery of your purchase
e. the date and amount that repayments will begin

Schedule each of the steps on the time line. Track it as it actually occurs. The time line for step one might look like this:

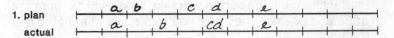

237

You'll need multiple time lines if you have more than three controls to schedule. Putting too much information on a single time line makes it unnecessarily complex. Monitoring and control are more difficult. Keep it simple so it's easy to enforce the standards you've set.

The Importance of the Cash Flow Summary

The cash flow projection may be the most critical part of your plan. Income, costs and expenses must be thought out in detail, with your market expansion plan and other long-term goals in mind. But none of that can work unless you also map out very accurately the major changes in your bank balance.

Presenting a plan to a loan officer that includes a cash flow schedule will make a positive impression. Your lender knows only what you tell him or her. If you don't include complete figures, the loan officer has to make a series of (possibly inaccurate) assumptions about your cash flow. Don't trust to chance. Provide figures of your own that make the loan officer's job easy.

When you work out those assumptions in advance, you demonstrate that:

- You've thought about repayments, and have scheduled them in your plan.

- You're aware of the risk element in lending money, and have taken steps to reduce that risk.

- You're able to plan so that problems are solved in advance.

- Getting that loan will improve your capital structure and financial strength.

In addition, the cash flow summary and time line set up the control mechanism you'll need during the year. They reduce the time required to stay in control, and help you focus on what's really important from one month to another. With an eye on the cash flow demands coming up and an awareness of seasonal changes, the action you take today will be more than an educated guess — because you've already eliminated most of the uncertainty.

13
THE FINANCIAL STATEMENT

Your business plan is a forecast of the future — all except this section. A financial statement is included to summarize the past. Your plan wouldn't be complete without a current financial statement. It confirms that the growth you project is realistic and reasonable, based on the results for the last year or two.

If you have financial statements prepared by your accountant, you can save time by including them just as they are. But if your financials aren't as good and clear as they might be, it's probably better to prepare a set especially for your plan.

But be aware that you need only a summary here, not a detailed explanation of every figure. Your plan is most effective if the financial statement is limited to what's really essential.

TYPES OF STATEMENTS

There are three forms of financial statement to include in your business plan: a balance sheet, income statement, and cash flow statement. Let's take a look at each form.

Balance Sheet

This is a summary of assets, liabilities and net worth as of the end of a certain period. At the end of the year, for example, the statement lists current assets (cash and accounts convertible to cash within one year, like accounts receivable and inventory), long-term assets (equipment, trucks, and real estate, all reduced for accumulated depreciation), and other assets. This balance is equal to the sum of liabilities and net worth. Current liabilities are all debts payable within one year, including the next twelve monthly payments on any notes payable. All your payments beyond twelve months are long-term liabilities. Net worth is what's left, your equity, the difference between assets and liabilities.

Income Statement

Also called the profit and loss statement, this is a summary of your total sales, cost of goods sold, operating expenses, and net profit for a specified period of time. For example, a yearly income statement shows twelve months of activity. The net profit increases your net worth from the beginning of the year to the end of the year, while a net loss will decrease the net worth account.

Cash Flow Statement

This statement shows how your working capital has changed during the year. Working capital is the difference between current assets and current liabilities. The cash flow statement (also called a statement of sources and applications of funds) usually has two sections. The first section breaks down the activities that cause cash to flow in or out. Sources of funds include net profits (adjusted for non-cash expenses like depreciation), proceeds from the sale of assets, loan proceeds, or a reduction in accounts receivable. The application of funds includes loan repayments, assets purchases, and your own withdrawals of cash from the business (or dividends paid, for corporations). In the second section, the net change in working capital is shown in current asset and liability accounts.

You can draw up any of these statements at any time of the year — as long as the ending date is the same for all of them. Your balance sheet reports as of a specific date. The accompanying income statement and cash flow statement should also reflect the status as of that same date.

A growing, prosperous construction company should always have a current set of financial statements available. When you prepare your business plan, you shouldn't have to start from scratch in compiling financial statements. You should be able to excerpt key information from the existing financial statement into a "plan version" of the statements. But even though the plan version is less complete, the content and totals should be the same.

THE COMPARATIVE FORMAT

Because the emphasis in your plan is on income, costs and expenses, and cash flow, it's especially helpful to show the income and cash flow statements on a comparative basis.

Every financial statement is more valuable when you show two years side by side. Simply reporting the results of one year gives a reviewer no basis for comparison. When you prepare the income and cash flow statements for your plan, consider showing two years of actual results. Then show the projected figures in the plan. That way, a reviewer can judge your plan by how it compares with actual results to date.

Figure 13-1 shows a comparative income statement. Figure 13-2 is a comparative cash flow statement.

Comparing the forecast with two years of actual results will show the trends very clearly. Be sure to explain variations in those trends. For example, if you're showing a big increase in gross sales and net profits, include a short statement explaining your expansion plans. Although this change will be well

comparative income statement

	January 1 to December 31:	
	THIS YEAR	LAST YEAR
gross sales		
cost of goods sold		
gross profit		
variable expenses		
fixed expenses		
total expenses		
net operating profit		
less: federal taxes		
net profit		

Figure 13-1

documented in other sections of the plan, a cross-reference and brief summary can prevent a misunderstanding by someone less familiar with how your company operates. You'll see cross-references like these in the sample plan in the appendix.

The comparison of cash flow is less revealing than a similar comparison of profits. If you have a business that has a healthy cash flow in the summer but a slow winter season, a cash flow summary done at the end of the year will seem

comparative cash flow statement

	January 1 to December 31:	
	THIS YEAR	LAST YEAR
sources of funds		
applications of funds		
net increase (decrease)		

	Increase or (decrease)	
	THIS YEAR	LAST YEAR
components of change:		
current assets		
current liabilities		
net increase (decrease)		

Figure 13-2

unrealistically poor. Address the problem of seasonal changes in working capital in the cash flow projection section of the plan. Refer to other financial statements if necessary.

The balance sheet doesn't have to show projected figures because you don't really forecast future assets and liabilities. You could project what the balance sheet will look like a year from now, but a reviewer will be more interested in income and cash flow. Your balance sheet should compare the figures for the past two years. See Figure 13-3.

Comparing figures for two years will show the change in

comparative balance sheet

	THIS YEAR	LAST YEAR
current assets		
long–term assets		
other assets		
total		
current liabilities		
long–term liabilities		
subtotal		
net worth		
total		

Figure 13-3

working capital, the level of liabilities, and the change in equity. If your financial strength has been improving over the period reported, a comparative balance sheet supports your estimates of continued growth in the immediate future.

The latest year is always shown first, with the past year on the far right. It will be assumed that you're showing actual results as of the end of your fiscal year if you don't include dates. But it's a good idea to always include the ending date on the balance sheet.

OTHER REPORTING IDEAS

I recommend including only summarized financial statements in the plan. Complete financial statements should be available if needed. Notice that my sample balance sheet, income statement, and cash flow summary include little detail.

Your business plan is primarily concerned with the future. Including historical information supports the reasonable estimates of growth that you make, but it's not a major portion of the document. Your income statement shows how actual numbers compare to your forecast and budget. But in most cases, this comparison is just as effective if you use a summary rather than the complete statements. For example, if variable and fixed expenses remain approximately the same in each year (and in your budget), there's no need to show every account.

Summarize the Data

There are several ways you can summarize the information in your complete financial statements:

1) Show only the major accounts in comparison, with "all other" lumped together.

2) Include a two-part breakdown between variable and fixed expenses.

3) End with a one-line total. Attach a more complete comparison in an appendix to the plan.

Highlight the Differences

Don't leave the reader wondering what the figures show. Emphasize the comparisons in your plan. There are two methods you can use to do that. First, consider adding a column that shows the difference between years, or between actual and the plan. Or, second, you can add columns that show the changes on a percentage basis.

If you compare the plan to one year, showing the dollar amount of difference is a fairly simple task. It becomes more complicated when you include two years of historical information in the plan. You'll need six columns to do it (three for reported amounts and three for the differences). Your plan will

amount and percentage comparisons

	January 1 to December 31			
	PLAN		THIS YEAR	
	AMOUNT	%	AMOUNT	%
gross sales	$714,000	100	$526,400	100
cost of goods sold	407,000	57	311,600	59
gross profit	$307,000	43	$214,800	41
variable expenses	78,500	11	63,200	12
fixed expenses	156,800	22	129,600	25
total expenses	$235,300	33	$192,800	37
net operating profit	$71,700	10	$22,000	4
less: federal taxes	14,800	2	3,300	1
net profit	$56,900	8	$18,700	3

Figure 13-4

be easier to understand if you show comparisons. That makes judging the plan and the past results easy. For example, you might break down the current year's results and the forecast in the format shown in Figure 13-4. This lets a reviewer make comparisons at a glance.

THE FOOTNOTE SECTION

Most financial statements need additional information to explain unusual changes in accounts, one-time occurrences that affect the numbers, or facts that just don't fit onto the statements themselves. Large corporations nearly always include footnotes in their financial statements to explain these special situations. The financial statements in your plan can and probably should include footnotes.

It's better to put a comment in a footnote than to include extra pages of text that explain the report. If you have a comment to make about accounts receivable, for example, show the ending amount on the balance sheet. Then include a note reference mark. The entry on the statement would look like this:

Accounts receivable (NOTE A) $214,600

Then, in a footnote section, you write the explanation:

Note A   Accounts receivable includes balances totaling $84,683 that are more than 30 days past due. The reserve for bad debts is adequate to allow for the portion of these accounts that may become uncollectible in the future.

Other notes could be included for a variety of reasons. Some examples:

Preparation method: This statement was prepared on the accrual basis. However, taxes are reported on the cash basis.

Unreported value: Real estate includes the building owned by the corporation. The book value of $214,000 does not reflect current market value. Based on an appraisal six months ago, current value is approximately $310,000.

Contingent liability: The company has one contingent liability not shown on the financial statements. The owner of the Ames Project has filed a $30,000 lawsuit against us. However, our attorney believes we will not incur a debt for this claim.

> ***One-time loss:*** The budgeted reduction in cost of goods sold is expected to result from improved inventory and purchasing procedures. A $15,000 write-off of obsolete stock last year is not expected to repeat in the next twelve months.

Footnotes explain unusual situations, large changes in accounts from one year to another, and any facts not reflected on statements. They should anticipate and answer any questions an informed reviewer might raise. Figure 13-5 shows how to cross-reference between your financial statements and the footnotes section.

HOW TO PREPARE YOUR FINANCIAL STATEMENTS

To make your statements accurate and easy to understand, follow these steps in preparing them.

• When you summarize, be sure that the subtotals and totals agree with the more detailed statements. Double-check your math, or have your bookkeeper verify your totals.

• Attach the full statements prepared by your accountant as an appendix to the plan. Although this level of detail doesn't belong in the plan, it should be available to an outside reviewer.

• Include a one-sentence explanation on the bottom of each sheet, telling whether the statement was prepared on a reviewed or compiled basis, or if it was prepared without an accountant's review. Also state that the version you're including is a summarized version of an accountant's report.

• Break down income statements on a percentage basis, using gross sales as 100 percent. This makes it easier for you or anyone else to grasp the significance of comparisons.

footnotes

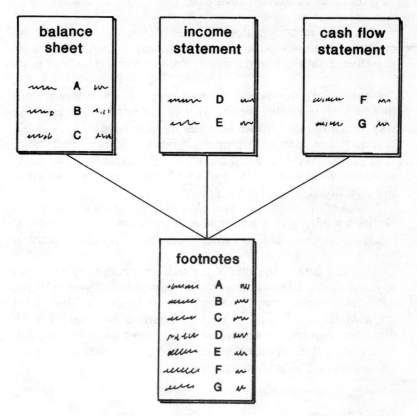

Figure 13-5

• Show the income statement and cash flow statement on a comparative basis between the last two years.

• Note significant points a reviewer should know about your statements, and cross-reference to the line of each statement.

• If you prepare statements on your own as part of your plan, ask your accountant to review them for accuracy and compliance with your books and records. If they're not reviewed, be sure to include a disclosure that lets the reader know they haven't been audited or reviewed.

- On your income statement, summarize expenses and include a more detailed list on an attachment. Don't include insignificant details that have only a minor bearing on your plan.

Depend on your accountant to prepare and analyze your financial statements, especially if you're not familiar with the way that financial information is usually reported. Your accountant can also help prepare other sections of your plan. This professional help will be especially valuable if you know what you want to forecast, but aren't sure how to express it in the traditional financial statement formats.

This section on your current financial situation should show highlights only. Use attachments to show whatever additional information an outside reviewer (such as a lender) will want to see.

Consider what someone outside of your company will need to know. Being unfamiliar with your operation, and most likely, with the industry, they have no point of reference. They don't know whether your estimates are realistic or not. But showing historical results lets them see what you've done in the past. This makes it easier for them to make a judgment about your estimates for the immediate future.

14 OUTSIDE THE PLAN: DETAILED BUDGETS

As explained earlier, your business plan will include a summary of the company budget for the period covered by the plan. But this is only a summary budget. You'll need a detailed budget to support it. This detailed and complete budget won't be a part of the plan itself, but should be available if you're asked for more information.

The appendix shows a complete sample budget. This chapter will describe the *process* to use when preparing this detailed budget.

Should you do your plan first, or start out with the budget? There are two opinions on this question. If budgeting comes first, you can identify income, expenses and cash flow for the year before you really start to plan. The second opinion is that the plan has to define goals for the year. Setting goals must come first. The plan dictates how the budget will be prepared.

Decide for yourself which way you think is most persuasive. I'll show how *I* plan and budget in the following section.

COORDINATE THE PLAN AND THE BUDGET

I believe that the plan and budget are both part of the same process. To be most effective, they must be coordinated and prepared together. Here's the ten-step process I recommend:

1)   Review your records for the last several years.

2)   Identify major goals for the coming year.

3)   Match goals to resources and prepare a preliminary time line and schedule.

4)   Sketch out a preliminary forecast and budget with your goals in mind.

5)   Write assumptions supporting major goals.

6)   Prepare your market expansion plan.

7)   Prepare detailed income forecasts, expense budgets, and cash flow projections.

8)   Review the sections of the plan already prepared. Make adjustments for any flaws discovered while preparing detailed budgets.

9)   Complete the budget.

10) Complete the plan.

Neither the business plan nor the detailed budget can be prepared in isolation. The two processes are related so closely that they must be viewed as parts of the same puzzle. Still, they're designed for different purposes, and each has its own function. The plan is a summary, intended for your review and control throughout the year. The budget is a larger document that you and your employees use to actually control each income, cost, and expense account during the year.

The goals in your plan provide a framework for the budget. No budget can be reasonable if it's not based on what you plan to do. But if your first set of goals won't fit in a budget, revise the goals until they will. You might have to make adjustments several times before a workable plan takes shape.

There's nothing wrong with changing your mind. If you find that something probably won't work, the time to change it is immediately, before the year begins. The more realistic your budget and plan, the better your chances of succeeding. Planning isn't an exact science — it's just your best guess. But the more complete your assumptions, the better. And if you're willing to put the effort into planning at all, you should strive for the most accurate and realistic results possible.

Here are three ideas that will help you coordinate the budget and the plan.

Delegate responsibilities— Concentrate on defining major goals. Delegate to others what can be done best by others. Don't try to do the whole job on your own. Have your bookkeeper or accountant do the detailed analysis of accounts, make comparisons of historical to estimated future expenses, and test your major assumptions. But first, make sure they understand your goals. Concentrate on coordinating the entire process, not on the details of putting the budget together.

Take an active stance— Prepare budgets actively, not passively. That means you should use the budgeting process to take control of expenses. Assume that you can control future costs. *You* decide what your profits will be. Don't just let profits happen.

Let's say that expenses for operating supplies, printing, travel and telephone have increased steadily for the past few years. Should you budget a higher level for the coming year (assuming another increase)? No. This is a chance to control the level of expense. Put effective controls into place to increase your profits.

Communicate with employees— In too many companies, employees are given the task of putting together a "reasonable" budget, often without firm guidelines. Be sure your employees know the goals you've set and plan around them. Challenge them to test your plan. Even if they prove that it has flaws, you win. You can modify the original plan to fit reality and still end up with a solid budget that increases profitability.

I know the owner of a civil engineering firm who has had good results with these budgeting and planning principles. He writes up a list of major goals and assumptions each year, usually with the belief that some expense levels can be held steady even while income rises. Then he presents the major assumptions to the office manager, who prepares a detailed budget. The ground rule is that the budget prepared must achieve one of two things: Either it must support the major goals, given the assumptions he's made; or it must disprove those assumptions and offer realistic alternatives. He then asks the office manager to suggest ways of controlling key expenses that have gone over budget in previous years.

When the budget is being prepared, the owner and office manager meet several times to compare and review the budget and plan. The time required for this is usually no more than an hour or two. These meetings give the office manager a clear idea of what's required.

If the budget challenges the plan, some modifications are needed in the assumptions. But usually the budget supports the market expansion plan. The owner and office manager have come to think of the budgeting process not as part of the planning process, but as a profit center of its own.

DEVELOP BUDGET ASSUMPTIONS

In earlier chapters I described how to develop major assumptions for your plan. When preparing a detailed budget, the process is similar, but more detail is required.

When employees budget for the coming year, the figures will usually be based on the past year's expenses. That's passive budgeting at its worst. Here's why:

• It assumes you can't reduce last year's expense levels. You're conceding that expenses are beyond your control.

• It carries forward any overspending you've had in the past. Your lack of control and the tendency to spend more than necessary are built into your future budget.

• The budget isn't related to your plan. The budget is developed arbitrarily and in complete isolation.

Provide Budget Guidelines

Provide guidelines to employees when they're preparing budgets. If you simply ask that they "do the budget," don't expect to get much that can be used. It's your responsibility to introduce the business planning concept. Show how goals and assumptions become a basis for the budget. In other words, the budget will only be as complete and useful as you make it.

In some cases the budget will be based on last year's expenses plus a small percentage for inflation. But that shouldn't always be true. You don't have to assume that costs and expenses will rise every year. Take control!

One general contractor I've worked with spends about $484 per month on office supplies. In preparing the budget, the bookkeeper assumed a 5 percent increase and budgeted $508 per month for the coming year. At my request, the contractor questioned the need for the increase, and asked what was included in the account. To answer that question, the bookkeeper analyzed the account for the past year, discovering that:

• Some expenses had been miscoded. For example, a printing bill was charged to the supplies account.

• In September, they'd purchased a one-year supply of bond paper at a good discount. So it would be reasonable to expect a lower cost for the coming year.

• The company had converted to a more compact and economical filing system during the last year. They wouldn't have that expense again this year and less would be spent on filing supplies.

After making this analysis, the office supplies account was actually decreased instead of increased for the coming year. This won't happen in every account, of course. But a little analysis will show reasons why expenses don't have to increase every year in every category.

RELATE ASSUMPTIONS TO ACCOUNTS

Detailed budgeting requires that you analyze every account. But the procedure isn't necessarily the same for each account. In the case of supplies, for example, you might need to analyze what expenses go into that account, consider any changes in expense levels, and then make some assumptions about how expenses will change. Some accounts, like rent, can be budgeted fairly easily. You know what the current lease requires and can anticipate the cost of more floor space if that's needed. It's best to budget variable expenses, like travel and entertainment, on the basis of income forecasts.

Test your assumptions, using:

1) **Historical information:** What did you spend last year?

2) **Analysis:** Was the coding correct? Did major one-time expenses inflate the account last year? Do you expect others in the coming year?

3) **Existing contracts:** Are you committed to office or equipment leases, or other obligations that must be met?

4) **Known expansion plans:** Will the plan increase your overhead? Will you need more office space? Will you spend more on promotion, salaries, or other expenses?

Make Your Assumptions Traceable

Your budgeting process should leave a trail — written clues that show the assumptions behind each figure. Many companies have detailed budgets that don't show how a particular account was estimated. That makes any comparison between actual results and the budget meaningless. Keep notes on each line in your detailed budget. When the year is over, compare budgeted and actual figures. If there's a major difference, read through the notes to find the flaw in your assumptions. That should help prevent similar mistakes in the future.

To make your budget traceable, use a summary like the one shown in Figure 14-1. This shows the assumptions behind each account in the budget. Preparing a summary like this for each account will take an hour or two. But it should save both time and money if done conscientiously.

Organize your budget in the same order that it's reported on your income statement. Staple the assumption summary to all attachments related to that account. Keep these attachments in order in a budget file. Then, when an account varies from budget during the year, find the mistake.

In the assumptions summary, there's enough space for as many as six different expense categories for each account. For example, you could break down auto and truck expenses into gas and oil, repairs, auto allowances, tires, and parts. That's five categories. Explain each category in the explanation section. Describe briefly what's included in each column. That provides a complete trail for your budget.

Attach to the summary any worksheets you needed to develop the budget. Use an assumption worksheet like the one

assumptions

Account ______________________ Year ________

MONTH	REFERENCE 1	2	3	4	5	6	TOTAL
January							
February							
March							
April							
May							
June							
July							
August							
September							
October							
November							
December							
Total							

References

1 ______________________

2 ______________________

3 ______________________

4 ______________________

5 ______________________

6 ______________________

Figure 14-1

shown in Figure 14-2 only when you need to analyze an account as part of the assumption. This worksheet is set up to show what goes into the account, usually based on your cost

assumption worksheet						

Account _____ Year _____

Description	Jan	Feb	Mar	Apr	May	Jun

Description	Jul	Aug	Sep	Oct	Nov	Dec

Figure 14-2

experience. But in some cases, an account may be based purely on your plans for the future. If you have a market expansion
plan that includes new categories of expense, there won't be
any historical cost records to help anticipate future expenses.

The assumption worksheet is more detailed than the
assumption summary in Figure 14-1. For example, you might
break your auto expenses into five sections, including repairs.
On the summary sheet, you only fill in the monthly totals. On
the assumption worksheet, you break down the repairs by
truck. Expenses will vary by vehicle, based on age, usage, and
the repair history. In some accounts, you may need several
assumption worksheets to explain each of the sections.

You need this much detail on income, costs, and expenses
in your budget. When you're forecasting income, depend on
the guidelines in the market expansion section of your plan. If
you have several large residential jobs going during the year,

include in your budget estimated income and expenses for each. If you do only a few large jobs in one year, estimate the value of the bids you'll win, and the timing of completion and payment.

USE YOUR BUDGET TO MAINTAIN CONTROL

Although you'll just summarize your budget in the plan, you'll use the actual detailed budget to control costs and expenses during the year. Don't let the budget become the most ignored document in your office. Creating it was a waste of time unless it's used and reviewed throughout the year. And once you've found a problem, take steps to correct potential overruns.

Let's say you discover that telephone expenses are exceeding the budget. Are employees making personal long-distance calls on your company phone? Are you making toll calls not anticipated in the original budget? Something has gone wrong. To get back on track, first identify the problem, then find a way to eliminate it. That might mean using a phone log and reviewing bills more carefully when they come in. It might also mean your budget is flawed and has to be revised.

The Monthly Report

Comparing the budget to actual results is easy if you have a summary sheet like Figure 14-3. It shows on one page actual income, costs, and expenses. With a report like this, it's easy to spot problems. And if you don't recognize the problems, you can't solve them.

Use this report to identify problems and plan your responses. What if you discover that printing expense is 30 percent over budget? How could that have happened? What if:

• The budget omitted a major expense for the year? Maybe the budget has to be revised.

monthly budget report

DATE _____

ACCOUNT	REF.	ACTUAL	BUDGET	VARIANCE	%

Figure 14-3

- An expense budgeted for a future month came in ahead of schedule?

- The cost of printing is running much higher than expected? Maybe you should be using another supplier.

The report shows the dollar amount and the percentage of the variance. That percentage should always be based on the budget figure. To find the percentage, subtract the budget figure from the actual figure. Divide the answer by the budgeted amount. For example, in your repairs account, the following information is shown on the report:

Account	Ref.	Actual	Budget	Variance	Percent
Repairs	A	$1,415	$1,200	($215)	(18%)

The variance is 18 percent of $1200, the budget figure. If the variance is unfavorable (income is under the estimate or expenses are over), put the variance in brackets. If it's a favorable variance (income is higher or expenses are under budget), don't use the brackets. If you're using a spreadsheet program like Lotus 1-2-3 or Quattro, budgeting like this is fast and easy.

Every major variance needs an explanation. Begin by defining the term *major variances*. One general contractor I know defines a major variance as any amount at least $500 above or below budget (and at least 15 percent).

This definition eliminates explanations for variances that are big in percent but small in actual dollars. For example, your telephone account might be budgeted at $80 a month. But one month the bill is $100. That's a 25 percent variance. But it's also only $20. That's not worth the trouble. You have better things to do with your time. Remember that a budget is only an estimate. It will never be exact.

The monthly report should show year-to-year totals. So in March, the report shows three months of actual expenses, compared to the budget total for those months. The June budget shows six months worth of actual and estimated totals. There will be timing problems, even in the most precise budget. If you pay a bill a month before it's budgeted, that account may be well over budget for the month. But in the following month, the variance will disappear. Using year-to-year totals will eliminate many of these timing problems.

Attach the reference sheet to a sheet of explanations. Cross-reference it by placing a letter in the reference column that refers to a line on the reference sheet. That way you can have all the financial results on one page so it's easy to tell how you're doing on the budget.

Explain the Variances

No one likes explaining why an account is over budget. Try asking someone why their costs are running over budget. Usually you'll get a non-explanation such as: "Travel expenses were higher than we thought." Of course, but that's not an explanation. It only repeats what you already know.

Here's another classic: "Travel expenses were higher than budget because we spent 14 percent more than we anticipated." That means we spent too much money because we spent too much money. Yet, even in the largest companies, experienced professionals who should know better write explanations like these. And executives with years of experience in management accept them as valid explanations.

It's impossible to write a meaningful explanation if you don't have your assumptions down on paper. But if you do, you can analyze *why* expenses are running higher. It could be a flaw in the budget, a control problem, or something that came up after the budget was prepared.

Always get the explanations, even if you're the one primarily responsible for the variance. Review the original budget assumption. When you find the problem, devising a solution should be easy.

Let's look at an example. Say your budget for printing expenses will include letterhead and envelopes, internal forms, and some direct mail ads you plan to send out. You prepared the budget with these assumptions:

1) Letterhead will be reordered and paid for in the month of May. You base the amount on last year's bill, adding 3 percent because your printer raised their prices.

2) On average, you spend $33 per month reprinting office forms. You continue this level in your new budget.

3) Your plan calls for promotional mailings in April, May and July. So you budget printing expenses during those months.

In June, your monthly budget report shows a 19 percent unfavorable variance. To find the causes, you compare the budgeted amounts to the actual expenses. Here's what you discover.

1) There are timing differences. The mailing campaign scheduled in July actually went out a month earlier than expected. This discrepancy will disappear next month.

2) Cost estimates were too low. Your printer didn't have enough of the low-cost paper and had to use a more expensive grade. This raised the price more than 3 percent.

3) This year, you're spending an average of $42 per month reprinting office forms. The budget allowed $33 per month. Checking figures for last year, you discover that the price increased steadily during the year. The original budget was flawed because it didn't consider these increases. You can still review the forms to see if money can be saved, but the budget assumption was wrong.

Ask your employees to explain variances in terms that help solve the problem, not just restate it. Good explanations help. Non-explanations are a waste of time. A good explanation helps you identify how to correct the problem and will save money during the year. The time required to prepare the report, analyze it, and make the changes needed should yield big dividends over the course of a year.

REVISE THE BUDGET AS NEEDED

What can you do to correct a budget when you discover it's flawed? Some companies have a policy of revising the annual budget after six months. But if you find a flaw after two months, there's no reason for waiting. Correct it at once. There are two strong arguments, however, against changing the budget too often. First, it takes valuable time. Second, a budget can't be used as a guide for your business if it's revised constantly.

Make Revisions on Change Forms

Budget revisions shouldn't be confusing. They shouldn't leave any doubt about which figure you're using. It's best to leave your original budget intact. Make changes by memo only. Figure 14-4 shows the budget revision form I recommend. Note that there's room for the entire year on this form, showing both the original budget and the proposed change for each particular account.

If necessary, you can do a major revision each six months. But you may not need it. If the budget is generally accurate from the beginning, consider incorporating changes by memo instead of redoing the whole thing.

Here's how memo changes are made. Suppose you find that the printing budget is too low. Average monthly expenses are running much higher and can be expected to stay higher. Take these steps:

1) Make a budget revision on a change form.

2) When the monthly report is prepared, report the printing expense budget according to the revised amount, not the amount on the original budget.

3) After six months, revise the entire budget and incorporate the changes into it if necessary.

You can stay in control of the revision process by requiring that you approve all the changes before they're made. That will help you avoid these potential problems in the budget revision process:

• Employees making changes without your knowledge and prior approval.

265

budget revision

Account _____ Date _____

MONTH	EXISTING BUDGET	PROPOSED CHANGE
January		
February		
March		
April		
May		
June		
July		
August		
September		
October		
November		
December		

reason for change _____

_____

_____

_____

Approved _____ Date _____

Figure 14-4

- Changes being made merely because more money is being spent than expected. Allow a change only when a flaw in the budget is proven.

- A large volume of minor changes that becomes unmanageable. Be sure that changes are proposed only for major flaws that are discovered during the six-month period.

Revise Only for Major Flaws

In many companies, there are so many revisions and amendments that the budget becomes a patchwork quilt held together by a thread. It becomes a paperwork nightmare. That's a mistake. Reduce time and effort spent on budgeting by insisting that only major flaws in the budget be corrected. And be sure that a paper trail is left for each change that's made. You should be able to trace all changes back to the original budget figure. Every change should include an assumption note, so that you know what went wrong with the original plan and budget.

This trail of changes will be very useful when preparing the next budget. Finding the problems will make the budgeting process much easier in future years. Don't repeat the same mistakes year after year — learn from them. Of course, you'll never be perfect. That's not the purpose. You only need good assumptions that support your goals. Look at each variance as an opportunity to improve future budgets.

BUDGET CONTROL ACTIONS

The entire planning process is designed to keep you in control. You want to not only predict the future, but to *mold* it. This is possible only if you respond to changes as they occur.

You already know that variances can't be adequately explained when the budget is arbitrary. And arbitrary budgets are a common flaw. There's another flaw that's just as common, and just as damaging: the failure to follow up on what you discover.

Let's say that expenses are exceeding the budget every month in a particular account. How do you respond? What can and should you do? Here are some examples:

Outside providers— Expenses like postage and delivery, dues and subscriptions, and printing can be controlled with a simple approval system. When employees order supplies without oversight and with no regard for the budget, you can expect higher costs. But if you require approval, either from you or from a responsible manager, you can expect lower costs.

For example, in one firm an employee was sending plans and specifications by overnight delivery service. A review showed that most could have been sent by regular mail, or by the less expensive second-day service. To control costs, the owner started requiring prior approval before using an overnight service. Sometimes the requests were turned down. The employee learned to mail packages a day to two earlier by regular mail or U.P.S. rather than waiting until the last day and then using overnight express. Savings came to more than $120 per month or $1,440 in a year.

Supplies and inventory— The same type of abuse can occur with goods that are ordered and consumed by employees, like office supplies. A good requisitioning and approval system adds little expense but can reduce costs significantly.

Be aware that minor pilferage can become a major loss over a period of months. Have a system for storage of tools, equipment and materials that makes them available when and where needed, but reduces the chance of loss. One electrical contractor had to lock up small parts because they kept disappearing. When only foremen had keys, losses dropped considerably.

In the largest construction companies, ordering may be done through a requisitions office. One department is responsible for collecting internal requisitions and for purchasing and safeguarding supplies. Most smaller construction companies give several departments authority to order the supplies they need. A simple requisitioning and authorization system will save money and minimize abuse.

If you keep supplies on an open shelf, the shelf should be where several responsible people can keep an eye on it. That will discourage pilferage. If the pilferage problem is chronic, you might have to lock up key supplies and give one employee authority to make distributions from stock. This might seem too regimented for a small company, but think about the money you can save with a simple change in procedures.

Transportation and telephone— Some forms of expense are difficult to control because they can't be approved in advance. You can't expect employees to ask permission to make long distance phone calls or to fill up a truck gas tank. But you can control these expenses in other ways.

Require employees to keep a telephone log and compare log entries to spot improper calls. Require a truck mileage log to reduce unnecessary truck mileage. If employees have to account for their calls and mileage, they'll reduce the amount of personal business handled with company assets.

Direct labor— Every good supervisor knows how easy it is to waste manhours on any job. One morning of idle time, waiting for a material delivery or completion of work by a tardy subcontractor, can wipe out your profit on the entire job.

Schedule carefully and coordinate with suppliers and other contractors to reduce the chance of labor overruns. You have to deal with this every day. Break projects down into logical phases and control the labor cost at each phase. If labor cost is running higher than you estimated, find out why and fix the problem promptly — even if personal supervision is necessary.

Salaries and wages— Office help may be paid either a flat salary or an hourly wage. Hourly employees should keep time cards for the hours they work. Avoid overtime. It costs more and shows a lack of effective scheduling. Of course, there are busy periods when overtime is needed. But regular overtime shows a lack of planning.

There are many other ways to reduce costs and expenses. I've mentioned only a few of the more common areas where problems come up in most companies. The important point is this: You must respond to problems as they're discovered, and solve them. Otherwise the budget is useless. It doesn't matter how accurate it is, or what insights you gain, if you don't take the time to correct problems as they're uncovered, the time you spent preparing the budget was a waste.

15 MEASURING THE RESULTS

*I*f you've followed the suggestions in the book so far, you've finished a complete business plan and a detailed budget. Together, they're the standard you'll try to meet throughout the next year. But it's too soon to breath a sigh of relief over a job well done. Your job has only begun.

All of this work is a waste of time unless you now use the plan and budget to *measure results.* The plan outlines your goals and proves that your assumptions are sound and realistic. But that's not enough. Now you've got to design procedures to keep your business on track throughout the year.

THE IMPORTANCE OF TRACKING

A plan that isn't tracked is no plan at all. It's just more paper cluttering your office. Your plan is only valid if you monitor results and compare them to the plan. If it's done right, this monitoring process won't take much time. But it will keep your operation on the right track.

Remember that the plan **anticipates potential problems.** For example, the cash flow projection is designed to prepare you in advance for low volume periods. You can avoid problems during those months — **if** you take the steps outlined in the plan. You can expand your market **if** you follow through on the steps you've identified in the plan. And expenses can be kept in line **if** you monitor them and enforce controls. Every step of your plan needs direct management.

Many of these steps can be delegated to your office manager or bookkeeper. To keep track of your plan, you'll compare and analyze figures from your records — but don't **you** spend your time gathering that information. Your time is too valuable for that. Just review the information gathered by your bookkeeper or office manager. But be sure your employees understand what you want to see, when you need to see it, and the form the information should be in.

Here's a practical example: Assume you've developed a plan that calls for a 20 percent increase in gross income for the year. You've also included ideas in your plan to control fixed overhead. This has been a problem in the past. If you don't take time to monitor expenses, you may meet your income goal but find that profits are actually down. Why? Because fixed expenses continued to increase faster than sales.

You're not in control if you don't pay attention to all parts of the plan. If overhead is a problem, set up a monthly report that concentrates on the problem accounts. Have your bookkeeper complete it each month. Whenever one of those accounts goes over budget, ask the bookkeeper and others who may be involved to identify the cause. This entire procedure shouldn't take more than three hours a month, mostly the bookkeeper's time. Your investment in time may be only a half hour a month

— six hours during the entire year. That should be time well spent. Keeping problem accounts in line can save thousands of dollars a year.

Simple controls do pay off. That's the whole point of planning and budgeting. And most of the time it takes will be spent by your bookkeeper or office manager. Your only participation will be to set up the system, review the results, and take action when needed. Of course, getting adequate information from employees can be a problem. I've found that it's easier to get employees involved in the planning process if you:

1) Give employees copies of the complete plan.

2) Ask for their ideas on major assumptions in the plan.

3) Whenever an employee presents a problem, ask him or her to help find the solution that helps meet the major goals.

4) Set up systems that require little participation on your part. You should do the monitoring and others should do the clerical work.

5) Invite employee suggestions and listen to them carefully. They're experts on their own jobs. They'll have practical solutions to many of the routine problems.

MEASURING METHODS

Suppose you have a report that shows a major discrepancy between budget and actual expense. What then? What can you do to change those numbers?

The answer should be in the plan. First, review the assumptions that went into the plan. Break the problem account down into its components. Check the assumptions behind each budgeted figure. What assumption or assumptions aren't being met? That question should lead you to the solution.

One plumbing contractor estimated a gradual increase in gross income for the year. By the fourth month, it was apparent that income was slipping below the forecast amount. His bookkeeper reported this on the monthly budget report. But he didn't know how to explain the problem. The contractor referred the bookkeeper to the assumptions in the plan. Income was based on the number of jobs anticipated and projected from historical records of average job size. It turned out that average income per job was accurate. But there just weren't enough new jobs coming in to meet the income forecast. Once the contractor saw these results, he could ask the appropriate questions:

- Was the forecast reasonable? Can I build the forecast number of new accounts?

- Why aren't we meeting the estimate?

- What steps can I take today to reverse the trend and get back on track?

In answering the first question, he decided the forecast was reasonable. It was developed with the understanding that additional help would be needed, and one extra plumber had already been hired. There was enough demand to support the higher volume of accounts.

Second, he found that the sales forecast wasn't being met because they hadn't done as much promotion as the plan required. He had planned to send out a bulk mailing, make calls to a hundred previous customers, and bid on at least 12 jobs each month. Unfortunately, he hadn't found time to do most of this promotion.

Third, he decided it was time to follow the original plan. He began work on the promotional mailing and collected the phone numbers of 100 previous customers. This brought in about 45 new jobs in the following four months, putting the company back on track toward the plan goals.

Whether you use direct mail, newspaper advertising, word of mouth, or some other method of promotion, *you have to do the*

income range tracking

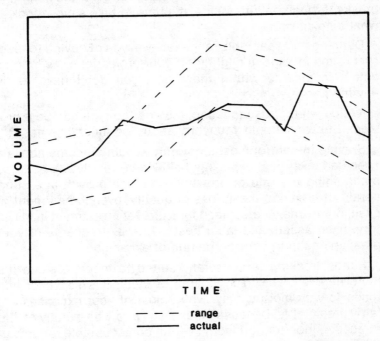

Figure 15-1

promotion outlined in your market expansion plan. If you don't, you won't meet your goals. It's that simple.

Following the plan isn't a guarantee of success. But ignoring it can guarantee failure.

Range Tracking for Income

One effective way to measure income is to track within a range, rather than by the exact figures in your plan. For example, you might define an *acceptable range* of income as being within 5 percent below your target and 20 percent above it. You can put these limits on a chart which you use to track income.

Figure 15-1 shows an income range tracking chart. The solid line is the actual income. As long as the solid line stays within the broken lines, it's in the acceptable range. If the solid line breaks through on either side, it's time to take a close look at what's going on.

Defining an acceptable range relieves you of having to react every time income is slightly off your projections. As long as actual income is within the range, you don't have to do anything.

Notice what I'm suggesting: Income too high can be a problem. But why should you worry about too much business?

Staying in control means not only keeping income above a specified level (and expenses below a certain level), but also maintaining the rate of growth. Too much growth in a short period of time can mean loss of quality, over-commitment of cash, or the unexpected need for a greater investment in inventory, fixed assets and labor costs. To stay in charge of your plan, you need to control the rate of expansion.

Range tracking is especially suited to income, since it's more unpredictable. The volume of income is seasonal and tends to vary more widely, while most of your expenses are fairly predictable. Because income will rarely be exactly on the forecasts, monitoring income within an acceptable range can save you a lot of time. Don't worry about small variances.

Tracking for Costs, Expenses and Cash Flow
Range tracking is less appropriate for costs, expenses or cash flow. Here's the procedure I recommend for each category:

Direct costs— Costs are best controlled by comparing them to gross volume — so track them on a percentage basis. Your bookkeeper should prepare a two-part monthly report that shows direct costs as a percentage of sales, and compares them to previous cost levels. Your analysis should include the following:

• The current month and year-to-date percentage of direct costs

- Direct costs for the previous two years (and, if direct costs vary by season, a comparison to the same month in the past two years)

- A breakdown between direct labor, materials, inventory levels, and other direct costs

Expenses— These are best controlled by analyzing individual accounts. Your bookkeeper doesn't need to review every account — just those that are over budget. It might also be a good idea to follow certain problem accounts every month, even when they're within budget. Here's why:

- Problem accounts often have a large volume of transactions. If several months pass before an unfavorable variance shows up, the analysis will be time-consuming. By completing the task every month, you cut down on work later.

- In high-volume accounts, you're more likely to find coding errors each month. A monthly analysis enables your employees to identify and correct these problems as they arise, so errors aren't carried forward.

- Regular analysis helps spot trends as they occur, so you may be able to head off serious problems.

Cash flow— Tracking cash flow is essential to most contractors, especially since the business is often seasonal. You need to anticipate potential problems and take steps to keep them from affecting your business.

Have some system for monitoring your cash flow. Set aside a few minutes each day or week to check your company's working capital position. Review developing problems. If necessary, arrange a line of credit, plan to sell an asset, or delay unnecessary expenses for a while. Have your bookkeeper prepare regular status reports, in the same format as your projections:

	Actual	Projection	Variance
Beginning balance			
Plus: additions			
Less: applications			
Ending balance			

The bookkeepers's report should show details of additions and applications of cash, and identify any variances. Study the variances. Find out where you've strayed from the plan. Do what's needed to get back on track. That could mean calling past-due accounts to request payment, setting up better controls over payment of bills, or simply taking the steps originally outlined in the plan.

Planning Your Profits

You hope to meet both income and expense goals. Of course, if you fall short in either area, your profits probably won't be as high as estimated in the plan. What can you do if performance is falling short of the plan?

The usual reason for failure to meet plan goals is failure to follow the market expansion plan. Break that plan down into phases, with completion dates scheduled throughout the year. Then carefully monitor progress — just as you would monitor progress on a construction project.

On a major job, you have to schedule subcontractors, material deliveries, and your own crews. You have to stay on schedule and within budget — and you're probably working on a thin margin. Your involvement is vital, though you delegate many tasks to foremen or supervisors. It's the same with the market expansion plan.

First, schedule the steps you'll take. Be careful not to overextend your resources: employees, equipment, capital. Then follow the schedule closely. Your office manager should be helping with this.

Set up a market expansion tracking schedule like the one shown in Figure 15-2. Schedule the specific phases that you defined in the plan. Pencil in actual results as they occur. If the

market expansion tracking

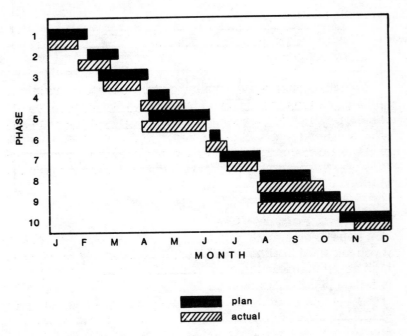

Figure 15-2

plan schedule is a solid black line, chart actual results as a series of diagonals or a lighter penciled line. Then you'll be able to tell at a glance when you're off schedule, and where problems might occur. If you don't track market expansion and monitor costs and expenses, you're probably not going to meet income goals.

And, of course, you must also be aware of limits on the cash available. You can't judge the success of your plan solely by the profit and loss statement. The plan fails the day you can't pay bills that are due — even if sales are growing and profits are up.

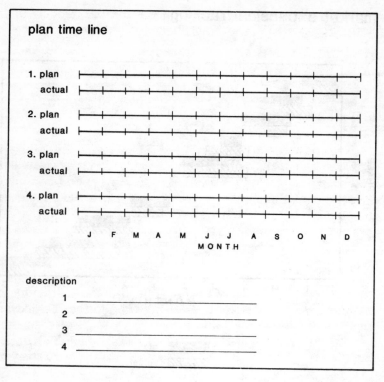

Figure 15-3

THE PLAN TIME LINE

I suggest that you draw a time line that plots all the major steps in your business plan. Be sure to include all key dates in the market expansion plan. If you have other major changes in your plan, like moving to a larger office, hiring new employees or beginning a new service, include those in the time line.

Set up your time line as shown in Figure 15-3. In this example, four major phases are included. Some items listed may be financial control milestones. Others may be steps you intend to take during the year to carry out the plan. Bring all important dates together like this to see at a glance what has to be done and when.

Briefly explain each phase on the bottom section of the form. For example, your four phases might be:

1) Budget tracking and review
2) Market expansion
3) Review and revision of plan and budget
4) Facilities and labor

Break down each phase into a series of steps. Enter them on the *plan* line for that phase. Also summarize these steps in an attached list, so that you can refer to it when you update your tracking system. Then, on the *actual* line, write in the corresponding number when it's completed. This shows how closely you're following your plan and where the problems are.

You might, for example, find that you've fallen a month behind in several of the steps. And the time line may show that there are many more steps scheduled in the next couple of months. You're facing a choice: put in some extra time on planning now, to catch up — or fall even farther behind and risk losing the whole plan. When you can clearly see that choice, you're more likely to do what's needed to catch up. Doing that should mean money in the bank at the end of the year.

Every single phase of your plan requires continued overseeing. If your attention wanders, your plan simply won't succeed. There are a number of reasons for this:

1) When there's no direct supervision from the top, goals usually aren't met.

2) Employees relax controls if they're not reminded about them from time to time.

3) Employees won't meet your priorities unless you remind them what those priorities are.

4) There's a tendency to relax controls when volume increases, even if profits are off and cash flow is suffering.

5) Trends aren't always obvious. More often than not, you'll only recognize them by interpreting the information you gather by tracking your results.

6) Most employees will report in the format you give them, but very few will take the extra step of interpreting information for you. That's your responsibility.

These are realities. No one will care as much about your plan — not to mention your goals — as you do. So be prepared to become involved and stay involved. Monitor what your employees present to you. You can't build insight into a reporting format. That's something you, the owner, have to provide on your own.

MINIMIZE YOUR OWN TIME COMMITMENT

Much of the detail work in your plan can and should be delegated to your bookkeeper or office manager. Of course, you can't delegate responsibility for the whole plan, but you can minimize the time spent each month without losing control.

Face the time issue right from the start. Business planning takes time, both to do the planning and to reach the goals you've set. If you aren't willing or able to make that time, postpone what I'm suggesting until you are. Your bookkeeper or office manager also has ongoing commitments and responsibilities. Little time may be available to prepare extra monthly reports. If collecting information for these reports becomes a burden rather than an opportunity, the whole plan is in jeopardy.

It's the owner's responsibility to set priorities for employees. How important is this work, compared to other tasks? Obviously, tasks like meeting payroll and paying taxes on time have a higher priority. But what about closing the books each month or posting the week's receipts? If the work required to monitor the plan can be reduced to two hours a month (less than six minutes a day) you should be able to find that much time. Select a time each week when you can isolate yourself from the phones and from your business routine. Devote a few minutes to reviewing plan progress exclusively.

Here are some guidelines to follow in setting up your planning time:

1)   Allow yourself at least one-half hour per week just for planning.

2)   Spend that time comparing actual results to your plan and budget, looking for trends, making sure you're on the right track, and reviewing your goals.

3)   At the end of each planning session, make a list of what you need to do and what you're going to ask employees to do.

That brings us to the end of the last chapter of this manual. But I've included some forms and a model business plan on the pages that follow. These samples are intended as models for the forms and the plan you'll develop. Of course, every business plan is unique. It has to be. Every business is unique. But whether you're a carpentry contractor or an HVAC installer, the documents on the following pages should help you develop an effective, practical business plan for your company.

A commitment to planning should yield financial dividends for both you personally and for your company. But there's an even more important benefit to getting in the habit of planning for success. The planning habit will increase your self-confidence and enthusiasm for taking on even more ambitious goals, and keep you alert to business opportunities that exist in your community.

Many of the benefits of planning can't be measured in dollars and cents. You'll find that being in control of your company and its future is much more satisfying than drifting with the current wherever it takes you. The personal satisfaction from turning dreams into reality can be the most gratifying reward of all.

Finally, let me add some encouragement. It's possible that you're still unconvinced about the need for business planning — even after reading 15 chapters on the subject. If that's true, I'll make a point and then offer a suggestion.

Here's the point: There's no magic in the planning process I've described. Most larger companies do it, of course. And lenders have come to expect it from their applicants. But just preparing a plan and following through on that plan aren't, by themselves, a magic formula for success.

But here's what the planning process does. It tends to bring out the best in *you,* the planner, the boss, the person making the decisions and running the company. If you have the capacity to develop a thriving, successful, profitable construction contracting business, that ability will be obvious when you start planning for success. It's possible that you have business skills you never knew you had — and never would have discovered if you didn't try your hand at creating and following a plan.

Here's my suggestion: Try it! You'll never know if business planning is right for you until you try it for yourself. Even if there's only a 10 percent chance that business planning fits your style and can yield major financial dividends, take that chance. It's worked for thousands of companies. It's worked for my company. Chances are it will work for you too. Planning is the only way to make sure that your personal expectations will become realities in the future.

APPENDIX
A

THE COMPLETE BUSINESS PLAN

*T*his is a typical business plan for a contractor who works in both residential and commercial areas. This plan isn't the only format you can use, and the details may not represent your own experience. In different parts of the country, salaries, rents, and other overhead expenses will vary from the range shown in this plan. And the gross revenues from operations will also vary by region.

There is no one plan suitable for everyone. You should design and write your plan to fit the details of your operation. Just use this one as a guide.

SMITH CONSTRUCTION COMPANY

Business Plan for the Year 1989

INTRODUCTION—

This business plan demonstrates that we can reasonably expect substantial growth in revenues for the coming year, that general expenses can be held to a reasonable level, and that net profits can be improved.

Each major goal is supported by assumptions about the market, the competition, and our ability to directly control the level of costs and expenses.

Smith Construction began operations in 1982, when John Smith left his position as chief estimator with a large national construction and engineering firm. The operation was capitalized with funds received through inheritance, and the company was incorporated in 1984. Work is performed within the tri-county area, so that no job site is more than 45 minutes from the headquarters office.

The predominant work is residential improvement, with a minor involvement in commercial contracts. The firm will not pursue commercial work in the future, due to increasing competition by larger, better-financed firms, and a lower rate of return on that type of work.

We currently employ six field personnel, the president, one estimator, a bookkeeper, and one clerical employee. No staff increases are budgeted during the coming year, and we expect to add only one field employee (seasonal).

All books and records are maintained manually. In looking into automation, we determined that the cost of hardware, software and training would exceed the likely benefits we would derive. Automation may be justified in the future, however, and the option is still open.

We are the largest remodeling contractor in the area, with a great deal of experience in the residential market. Two competitors view residential work as a minor portion of their total income, and do not control a major share of the market. Our firm is strongly capitalized and cash flow controls are working.

In the future, we hope to expand our residential services to an even greater level than today. This year's expected substantial growth is in response to a 10-year high in both new construction and remodeling activity among present owners. More than 80% of residential housing is owner-occupied in the tri-county area, with the average family owning their home for more than eight years. In the last two years, several large employers have relocated in the area, creating an expanding population, more demand for housing, and a reduction of unemployment and families moving from the area.

MAJOR GOALS

During the coming year, we will achieve the following goals:

1) Gross revenues will increase by 15% over last year's level.

2) Direct costs will be held to 58% of gross revenues.

3) General expenses will be kept at approximately the same level as last year.

4) Net profit after taxes will be produced at 12% of gross revenues.

5) New controls over general expenses will be developed and put into place.

6) We will purchase new equipment valued at $50,000 without obtaining an outside loan. No new debts will be incurred this year.

Goal time line:

```
              1           2           3        4
1 /.../.../.../.../.../.../.../.../.../.../.../

          5      6      7      8        9
2 /.../.../.../.../.../.../.../.../.../.../.../

        10     11     12     13     14     15
3 /.../.../.../.../.../.../.../.../.../.../.../

          16        17        18        19
4 /.../.../.../.../.../.../.../.../.../.../.../

  20 21 22      23 24     25     26     27
5 /.../.../.../.../.../.../.../.../.../.../.../

                        28     29 30
6 /.../.../.../.../.../.../.../.../.../.../.../

  J  F  M  A  M  J  J  A  S  O  N  D
```

MONTH

Explanations:

1) Check first quarter, actual versus forecast
2) Check second quarter, revise as needed
3) Check third quarter, evaluate forecast success
4) Check final quarter, prepare next year's forecast
5) Monitor direct cost relationship to revenues
6) Check inventory controls, direct costs

7) Revise budget as necessary
8) Review year-to-date costs to sales
9) Prepare next year's direct cost budget
10) Review two-month variances, take action as needed
11) Review four-month history, take action as needed
12) Review six months, revise if necessary
13) Review eight-month results, take corrective action
14) Review ten months, enforce controls
15) Prepare next year's budget
16) Review quarterly profits, take action as needed
17) Review six months, revise if necessary
18) Review nine month profits, make changes as needed
19) Prepare next year's forecast of profits, set goals
20) Design inventory control system
21) Design office supply control system
22) Install new control systems, train staff
23) Review inventory control system's success
24) Make inventory control system changes if needed
25) Review office supply control system's success
26) Review all expenses, look for negative trends
27) Prepare next year's analysis procedure
28) Compare prices for new equipment, place order
29) Down payment (50%) on new equipment
30) Take delivery of equipment, pay remaining balance

ASSUMPTIONS

The business plan is based on the following major assumptions:

1) With the current influence we have in the residential market, our revenue forecast is conservative.

2) We can achieve the forecast level of volume without expanding the permanent staff or facilities.

3) The budget for general expenses assumes that past expenses in many accounts were unnecessarily high. Direct controls over expenses will enable us to operate with a higher volume, but without a corresponding increase in expenses.

4) Our capital resources are adequate for the level of growth we project.

5) We can control the level of overhead with specific control measures.

6) We will raise enough net income this year to enable us to purchase capital assets without borrowing.

MARKET EXPANSION PLAN

We plan to bring about a growth of 15% in gross revenues. This, combined with cost and expense monitoring procedures, is expected to create an after-tax profit of 12%.

The potential for expansion is good. The local economy is growing, as the population and demand for housing increases. Several new companies have moved their offices to the area, and the unemployment rate is only 4%. Apartment vacancies average 3%. Homes for sale are purchased on average within 30 days after being placed on the market. The average homeowners (living in a home constructed 10 years ago or more) have lived in their home for eight years.

These local statistics indicate that there will be an increasing demand for improvement and remodeling services. Our two competitors hold only a small portion of the market, as they specialize in new construction activities. We intend to concentrate on improvement work, which historically has yielded a higher rate of return than either new construction or commercial work.

This work is seasonal, with a higher level of activity expected from June to September. The following table shows the number of residential contracts we have contracted per month for the last three years:

Month	1988	1987	1986
Jan	2	3	1
Feb	4	3	4
Mar	1	4	1
Apr	4	2	2
May	5	5	2
Jun	7	6	4
Jul	8	5	6
Aug	14	10	8
Sep	10	7	8
Oct	9	10	4
Nov	6	8	3
Dec	3	4	4
Total	73	67	47

During these years, we have also experienced an increase in the average revenue per contract:

Year	Average
1988	$9,403
1987	$9,112
1986	$8,994

We plan to increase the number of contracts, in line with seasonal averages, to 88. The forecast is compared to prior years' contracts in Figure 1.

We expect the coming year's work to average $9,500 per contract during the first six months, and $9,600 during the second half. The average home improvement job takes three weeks or less to complete. Our forecast assumes we will complete 88 contracts during the year. We consider both the number of contracts and the average revenue to be reasonable. Our residential contract forecast is summarized in the table below and in Figure 2.

residential contracts

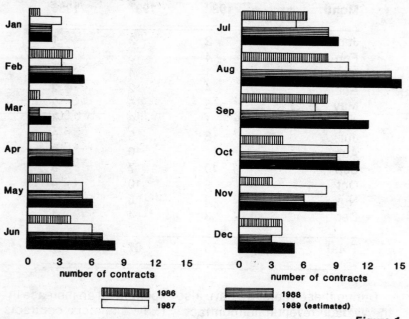

Figure 1

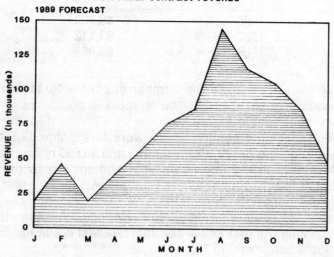

Figure 2

Month	Contracts	Average	Revenue
Jan	2	$9,500	$19,000
Feb	5	9,500	47,500
Mar	2	9,500	19,000
Apr	4	9,500	38,000
May	6	9,500	57,000
Jun	8	9,500	76,000
Jul	9	9,600	86,400
Aug	15	9,600	144,000
Sep	12	9,600	115,200
Oct	11	9,600	105,600
Nov	9	9,600	86,400
Dec	5	9,600	48,000
Total	88		$842,100

We also expect to complete only two commercial contracts this year, both during the month of June. The average revenue from this is estimated at $34,000, for a total of $68,000. In previous years, we had a higher volume of commercial work (three in 1988; five in 1987; and eight in 1986), with two to three contracts won in June. But from this year forward, we will no longer attempt to win a large volume of commercial work.

Our estimated level of growth will not require the addition of permanent new employees. We do expect to hire one additional person between the months of May and October.

We will resist allowing growth to exceed the estimated 15% in our forecast. From past experience, we know that too much growth during a single year can result in loss of quality, lower gross and net profit margins, and the inability to manage growth. We do, however, expect to forecast higher levels of growth in future years.

Our increase will come partially from an obvious increase in demand for our services. However, we will also track our progress on the basis of (a) the number of contracts, and (b) average revenues per contract. We also intend to use direct mail to previous customers to solicit additional business, if needed.

Market expansion time line:

```
      1   2   3           4           5           6
A /.../.../.../.../.../.../.../.../.../.../.../.../.../.../


          1       2       3       4
B /.../.../.../.../.../.../.../.../.../.../.../.../.../.../
   J   F   M   A   M   J   J   A   S   O   N   D
```

MONTH

Explanation:

A Monitoring controls:

   1) Establish internal monitoring system
   2) Train employees
   3) Report on first quarter
   4) Report on second quarter, identify trends
   5) Report on third quarter
   6) Revise monitoring system for coming year

B Additional promotions:

   1) Design direct mail literature
   2) Mail to previous customers
   3) Review results; second mailing
   4) Review direct mail program; spot trends

Market tracking system:

```
     1          2          3          4
/.../.../.../.../.../.../.../.../.../.../.../.../
 J   F   M   A   M   J   J   A   S   O   N   D
```

MONTH

Explanations:

1) Check first quarter forecast to actual
2) Check second quarter, revise if necessary
3) Check third quarter forecast to actual
4) Check fourth quarter, prepare next year's forecast

SUMMARIZED INCOME FORECASTS

Month	Residential #	Residential Amount	Commercial #	Commercial Amount	Total
Jan	2	$ 19,000	-	-	$ 19,000
Feb	5	47,500	-	-	47,500
Mar	2	19,000	-	-	19,000
Apr	4	38,000	-	-	38,000
May	6	57,000	-	-	57,000
Jun	8	76,000	2	$68,000	144,000
Jul	9	86,400	-	-	86,400
Aug	15	144,000	-	-	144,000
Sep	12	115,200	-	-	115,200
Oct	11	105,600	-	-	105,600
Nov	9	86,400	-	-	86,400
Dec	5	48,000	-	-	48,000
Total	88	$842,100	2	$68,000	$910,100

Forecast explanation:

Estimated gross receipts for the year will total $910,000. This is an increase of 15% over last year's level. Residential work accounts for 92.5% of this total.

Residential:

We will emphasize new residential work this year, and are forecasting increases both in the number of new contracts and in the average income per contract. The forecast tracks seasonal variances along the same trend established during the past three years. Average revenue is estimated at $9,500 (first half) and $9,600 (second half). This is reasonable in comparison to last year's average of $9,043, based on recent economic trends.

Commercial:

We estimate two contracts this year, both in June. This reduction from prior years reflects our desire not to pursue commercial work in the future. This decision is based on competition, capitalization, and the historical rate of net profit. The yield on commercial contracts is not satisfactory compared to residential work.

SUMMARIZED EXPENSE BUDGETS

Direct costs can be controlled at 58% of revenues, based on historical information. Following is a summary of the last three years:

Year	PERCENT OF SALES			
	Labor	Materials	Other	Total
1988	27	28	3	58
1987	29	28	3	60
1986	30	28	3	61
Budget:				
1989	27	28	3	58

Here is a summary of the budget for direct costs by month:

Month	Labor	Materials	Other	Total
Jan	$ 5,130	$ 5,320	$ 570	$11,020
Feb	12,825	13,300	1,425	27,550
Mar	5,130	5,320	570	11,020
Apr	10,260	10,640	1,140	22,040
May	15,390	15,960	1,710	33,060
Jun	38,880	40,320	4,320	83,520
Jul	23,328	24,192	2,592	50,112
Aug	38,880	40,320	4,320	83,520
Sep	31,104	32,256	3,456	66,816
Oct	28,512	29,568	3,168	61,248
Nov	23,328	24,192	2,592	50,112
Dec	12,960	13,440	1,440	27,840
Total	**$245,727**	**$254,828**	**$27,303**	**$527,858**

Note: We intend to increase our average inventory on hand by $30,000 during the year. As a result, actual expenditures for materials will exceed this budget by $30,000.

Major expenses:
Following are summaries of our budget for major general expenses, including explanations:

Salaries and wages:

Jan	$11,383	
Feb	11,383	
Mar	11,383	No increases are
Apr	11,450	planned in the number
May	11,680	of administrative
Jun	11,680	employees.
Jul	12,380	Expense increases are
Aug	12,380	for scheduled pay
Sep	12,418	raises during the
Oct	12,418	year.
Nov	12,418	
Dec	12,418	
Total	$143,391	

Payroll taxes:

Jan	$1,286	
Feb	1,286	
Mar	1,286	Calculated at the
Apr	1,294	average rate of
May	1,320	11.3% of salaries.
Jun	1,320	(Note: payroll
Jul	1,399	taxes for direct
Aug	1,399	labor are included
Sep	1,403	as a direct cost.)
Oct	1,403	
Nov	1,403	
Dec	1,403	
Total	$16,202	

Rent:
$900 per month, according to the terms of the current lease. This lease extends for another 2½ years.

Depreciation:
Based on declining balance allowed on existing assets and estimated new acquisitions this year, the expense will be $16,000 for the year. Depreciation expense is booked during March, June, September and December, with a final adjustment at year-end.

Insurance:
Our annual bill for insurance is due in the month of June. We estimate that bill at $9,300, so we're allowing $775 per month.

Federal income taxes:

Jan	$(1,507)	
Feb	188	
Mar	(2,130)	Based on estimates
Apr	(471)	of monthly net income
May	694	or loss. Actual
Jun	5,076	deposits will be made
Jul	2,335	in April, June,
Aug	5,784	September and the
Sep	3,655	following January,
Oct	3,645	in equal installments
Nov	2,487	of$4,118.
Dec	(378)	
Total	$19,378	

Summary, complete forecast and budget:

Gross revenues:
Residential	$842,100	
Commercial	68,000	
Total		$910,100

Direct costs:
Beginning inventory	$101,680	
Materials purchased	284,828	
Direct labor	245,727	
Other direct costs	27,303	
Subtotal	$659,538	
Less: Ending inventory	131,680	
Cost of goods sold		$527,858
Gross profit		$382,242
Operating expenses		253,048
Net operating profit		129,194
Federal income taxes		19,378
Net profit		$109,816

SUMMARIZED CASH FLOW PROJECTIONS

We will control cash flow throughout the year with a combination of controls over outstanding receivables, tight monitoring of costs and expenses, and careful timing of decisions that affect working capital.

Major points:

1. Accounts receivable are expected to decrease during the first and fourth quarters, and to increase during the high volume season.

2. Accounts payable will increase in the first five months. They will be substantially reduced during the high volume season.

3. Inventory levels will be gradually increased during the year by $30,000, which will be needed if we are to achieve expected future higher volume of revenues.

4. We will purchase new equipment during the year, estimated to cost $50,000.

Summary:

Beginning cash balance	$16,403
Plus: Pre-tax profits	129,194
Depreciation (non-cash)	16,000
Insurance prepayment	9,300
Decrease in receivables	44,000
Increase in payables	24,000
Total funds available	$238,897
Less: Federal tax deposits	$14,897
Insurance payment	9,300
Loan principal	808
Increase in inventory	30,000
Increase in receivables	55,000
Purchase of assets	50,000
Decrease in payables	60,000
Total decreases	$220,005
Ending cash balance	$18,892

Balance Sheet

	December 31:	
	1988	1987
Current assets:		
Cash	$ 16,403	$ 20,914
Accounts receivable	109,386	119,382
Inventory	101,680	84,355
Total current assets	$227,469	$224,651
Long-term assets:		
Autos and trucks	$236,346	$236,346
Equipment	192,000	152,000
Office furnishings	51,509	51,509
Small tools	5,000	5,000
Subtotal	$484,855	$444,855
Depreciation reserve	104,990	86,340
Net long-term assets	$379,865	$358,515
Total assets	$607,334	$583,166
Current liabilities:		
Accounts payable	$105,510	$147,583
Taxes payable	1,684	1,115
Notes payable, current	3,408	3,408
Total current liabilities	$110,602	$152,106
Long-term liabilities:		
Notes payable, long-term	$26,418	$28,550
Total liabilities	$137,020	$180,656
Net worth:		
Capital stock	$100,000	$100,000
Retained earnings	370,314	302,510
Total net worth	$470,314	$402,510
Total liabilities and net worth	$607,334	$583,166

Income Statement

	12 months ending 12-31:	
	1988	1987
Total gross revenue	$791,191	$774,848
Cost of goods sold	456,416	462,203
Gross profit	$334,775	$312,645
Total operating expenses	255,006	247,202
Net operating profit	79,769	65,443
Less: Federal income taxes	11,965	29,816
Net profit	$ 67,804	$ 55,627

Cash Flow Statement

	December 31:	
	1988	1987
Total sources of funds	$86,454	$78,127
Total application of funds	42,132	20,860
Net increase (decrease)	$44,322	$57,267

Changes in working capital:

	1988	1987
Components of change:		
Current assets	$ 2,818	$34,417
Current liabilities	41,504	22,850
Net increase	$44,322	$57,267

APPENDIX
B

THE COMPLETE BUDGET

*T*he following is a complete budget for Smith Construction Company. In addition to the summaries and explanations shown in this example, you will also need to complete a number of analysis worksheets when you prepare your own budget. These support the budget but should not necessarily end up as part of the report itself.

A budget should be prepared no less than once per year and reviewed after six months. The revisions should be made to correct assumptions made in error, and to update your estimates based on new information.

The summarized report is cross-referenced to the assumptions that follow.

Budget and Forecast

Description	Ref	January	February
Gross revenue			
Residential		$19,000	$47,500
Commercial		--	--
Total	A	$19,000	$47,500
Cost of goods sold:			
Beginning inventory		$101,680	$106,680
Materials purchased		10,320	18,300
Direct labor		5,130	12,825
Other direct costs		570	1,425
Subtotal		$117,700	$139,230
Less: ending inventory		106,680	111,680
Cost of goods sold	B	$ 11,020	$ 27,550
Gross profit		$ 7,980	$ 19,950
Operating expenses:			
Salaries and wages	C	$ 11,383	$ 11,383
Payroll taxes	D	1,286	1,286
Travel and entertainment	E	--	--
Transportation	F	85	210
Auto and truck expenses	G	95	235
Repairs and maintenance	H	600	600
Rent	I	900	900
Depreciation	J	--	--
Insurance	K	775	775
Interest	L	228	226
Dues and subscriptions	M	360	25
Office supplies	N	400	400
Telephone	O	110	277
Utilities	P	205	205
Postage and delivery	Q	185	185
Licenses and fees	R	300	1,080
State and local taxes	S	490	85
Professional fees	T	300	500
Miscellaneous	U	325	325
Total operating expenses		$ 18,027	$ 18,697
Net operating profit (loss)		$(10,047)	$ 1,253
Less: federal income taxes	V	(1,507)	188
Net profit		$(8,540)	$ 1,065

March	April	May	June	Subtotal
$ 19,000	$ 38,000	$ 57,000	$ 76,000	$256,500
--	--	--	68,000	68,000
$ 19,000	$ 38,000	$ 57,000	$144,000	$324,500
$111,680	$111,680	$111,680	$116,680	$101,680
5,320	10,640	20,960	45,320	110,860
5,130	10,260	15,390	38,880	87,615
570	1,140	1,710	4,320	9,735
$122,700	$133,720	$149,740	$205,200	$309,890
111,680	111,680	116,680	121,680	121,680
$ 11,020	$ 22,040	$ 33,060	$ 83,520	$188,210
$ 7,980	$ 15,960	$ 23,940	$ 60,480	$136,290
$ 11,383	$ 11,450	$ 11,680	$ 11,680	$ 68,959
1,286	1,294	1,320	1,320	7,790
--	1,000	1,000	1,500	3,500
85	165	250	630	1,425
95	190	280	710	1,605
600	620	620	620	3,660
900	900	900	900	5,400
4,000	--	--	4,000	8,000
775	775	775	775	4,650
224	222	220	218	1,338
48	325	--	1,516	2,274
400	400	400	400	2,400
110	221	332	839	1,889
180	145	140	135	1,010
185	185	185	185	1,110
300	300	300	300	2,580
85	585	85	585	1,915
1,200	--	500	--	2,500
325	325	325	325	1,950
$ 22,181	$ 19,102	$ 19,312	$ 26,638	$123,957
$(14,201)	$(3,142)	$ 4,628	$ 33,842	$ 12,333
(2,130)	(471)	694	5,076	1,850
$(12,071)	$(2,671)	$ 3,934	$ 28,766	$ 10,483

Description	Ref	July	August
Gross revenue			
Residential		$86,400	$144,000
Commercial		--	--
Total	A	$86,400	$144,000
Cost of goods sold:			
Beginning inventory		$121,680	$126,680
Materials purchased		29,192	45,320
Direct labor		23,328	38,880
Other direct costs		2,592	4,320
Subtotal		$176,792	$215,200
Less: ending inventory		126,680	131,680
Cost of goods sold	B	$ 50,112	$ 83,520
Gross profit		$ 36,288	$ 60,480
Operating expenses:			
Salaries and wages	C	$ 12,380	$ 12,380
Payroll taxes	D	1,399	1,399
Travel and entertainment	E	1,000	500
Transportation	F	380	630
Auto and truck expenses	G	430	710
Repairs and maintenance	H	640	640
Rent	I	900	900
Depreciation	J	--	--
Insurance	K	775	775
Interest	L	216	214
Dues and subscriptions	M	370	--
Office supplies	N	400	400
Telephone	O	503	839
Utilities	P	135	135
Postage and delivery	Q	185	185
Licenses and fees	R	300	300
State and local taxes	S	85	85
Professional fees	T	300	1,500
Miscellaneous	U	325	325
Total operating expenses		$ 20,723	$ 21,917
Net operating profit (loss)		$(15,565)	$ 38,563
Less: federal income taxes	V	2,335	5,784
Net profit		$ 13,230	$ 32,779

September	October	November	December	Total
$115,200	$105,600	$ 86,400	$ 48,000	$842,100
--	--	--	--	68,000
$115,200	$105,600	$ 86,400	$ 48,000	$910,100
$131,680	$131,680	$131,680	$131,680	$101,680
32,256	29,568	24,192	13,440	284,828
31,104	28,512	23,328	12,960	245,727
3,456	3,168	2,592	1,440	27,303
$198,496	$192,928	$181,792	$159,520	$659,538
131,680	131,680	131,680	131,680	131,680
$ 66,816	$ 61,248	$ 50,112	$ 27,840	$527,858
$ 48,384	$ 44,352	$ 36,288	$ 20,160	$382,242
$ 12,418	$ 12,418	$ 12,418	$ 12,418	$143,391
1,403	1,403	1,403	1,403	16,202
--	--	--	--	5,000
505	465	380	210	3,995
570	520	430	235	4,500
640	660	660	660	7,560
900	900	900	900	10,800
4,000	--	--	4,000	16,000
775	775	775	775	9,300
211	209	207	205	2,600
--	325	55	106	3,130
400	400	400	400	4,800
671	615	503	280	5,300
130	165	180	190	1,945
185	185	185	185	2,220
300	300	300	300	4,380
585	85	85	85	2,925
--	300	500	--	5,100
325	325	325	325	3,900
$ 24,018	$ 20,050	$ 19,706	$ 22,677	$253,048
$ 24,366	$ 24,302	$ 16,582	$(2,517)	$129,194
3,655	3,645	2,487	(378)	19,378
$ 20,711	$ 20,657	$ 14,095	$(2,139)	$109,816

Cash Flow Projection (January through June)

Description	January	February	March	April	May	June	Subtotal
Beginning cash balance	$ 16,403	$ 9,532	$ 8,502	$ 13,016	$ 9,469	$ 11,808	$ 16,403
Plus:							
Pre-tax profit	$(10,047)	$ 1,253	$(14,201)	$(3,142)	$ 4,628	$ 33,842	$ 12,333
Depreciation (non-cash)	--	--	4,000	--	--	4,000	8,000
Insurance prepayment	775	775	775	775	775	775	4,650
Decrease in receivables	6,000	--	10,000	--	--	--	16,000
Increase in payables	4,000	4,000	4,000	4,000	4,000	--	20,000
Subtotal	$ 17,131	$ 15,560	$ 13,076	$ 14,649	$ 18,872	$ 50,425	$ 77,386
Less:							
Federal tax deposits	$ 2,543	$ --	$ --	$ 4,118	$ --	$ 4,118	$ 10,779
Insurance payment	--	--	--	--	--	9,300	9,300
Principal note payments	56	58	60	62	64	66	366
Increase in inventory	5,000	5,000	--	--	5,000	5,000	20,000
Increase in receivables	--	2,000	--	1,000	2,000	10,000	15,000
Purchase of assets	--	--	--	--	--	--	--
Decrease in payables	--	--	--	--	--	10,000	10,000
Total payments	$ 7,599	$ 7,058	$ 60	$ 5,180	$ 7,064	$ 38,484	$ 65,445
Ending cash balance	$ 9,532	$ 8,502	$ 13,016	$ 9,469	$ 11,808	$ 11,941	$ 11,941

Cash Flow Projection (July through December)

Description	July	August	September	October	November	December	Total
Beginning cash balance	$ 11,941	$ 3,213	$ 12,481	$ 12,431	$ 10,433	$ 2,713	$ 16,403
Plus:							
Pre-tax profit	$ 15,565	$ 38,563	$ 24,366	$ 24,302	$ 16,582	$(2,517)	$129,194
Depreciation (non-cash)	--	--	4,000	--	--	4,000	16,000
Insurance prepayment	775	775	775	775	775	775	9,300
Decrease in receivables	--	--	--	8,000	10,000	10,000	44,000
Increase in payables	--	--	--	--	--	--	4,000
Subtotal	$ 28,281	$ 42,551	$ 41,622	$ 45,501	$ 37,790	$ 18,971	$238,897
Less:							
Federal tax deposits	$ --	$ --	$ 4,118	$ --	$ --	$ --	$ 14,897
Insurance payment	--	--	--	--	--	--	9,300
Principal note payments	68	70	73	75	77	79	808
Increase in inventory	5,000	5,000	--	--	--	--	30,000
Increase in receivables	10,000	15,000	15,000	--	--	--	55,000
Purchase of assets	--	--	--	25,000	25,000	--	50,000
Decrease in payables	10,000	10,000	10,000	10,000	10,000	--	60,000
Total payments	$ 25,068	$ 30,070	$29,191	$ 35,075	$ 35,077	$ 79	$220,005
Ending cash balance	$ 3,213	$ 12,481	$ 12,431	$ 10,433	$ 2,713	$ 18,892	$ 18,892

Assumptions

A: Revenues

I - Residential

Assumptions:

The number of contracts completed in one year can be increased by 20%, without a corresponding increase in the number of field or administrative employees.

This estimate of growth will not be restricted by competition as no other firms in the area have the means or interest in this business as of this date.

Demand in the market will continue to grow, based on employment, housing and population statistics.

Historical return on residential work has been greater than on commercial contracts. The firm will emphasize residential from this year forward.

Historical number of contracts per month:

Month	1988	1987	1986	Month	1988	1987	1986
Jan	2	3	1	Jul	8	5	6
Feb	4	3	4	Aug	14	10	8
Mar	1	4	1	Sep	10	7	8
Apr	4	2	2	Oct	9	10	4
May	5	5	2	Nov	6	8	3
Jun	7	6	4	Dec	3	4	4
				Total	**73**	**67**	**47**

Average revenues per contract:

1988	$9,403
1987	9,112
1986	8,994

Forecast:

Month	Contracts	Average	Total
Jan	2	$9,500	$ 19,000
Feb	5	9,500	47,500
Mar	2	9,500	19,000
Apr	4	9,500	38,000
May	6	9,500	57,000
Jun	8	9,500	76,000
Jul	9	9,600	86,400
Aug	15	9,600	144,000
Sep	12	9,600	115,200
Oct	11	9,600	105,600
Nov	9	9,600	86,400
Dec	5	9,600	48,000
Total	**88**		**$842,100**

II - Commercial

Assumptions:

Our firm has not successfully won enough commercial contracts in the past to justify the risks, costs of estimating, and investment. We will, therefore, not actively seek a large number of these contracts.

The rate of return on commercial work does not justify pursuing it for a firm of our size in this community.

Competition is better suited to the winning and profitable completion of these jobs.

Month	1988	1987	1986	Month	1988	1987	1986
Jan	0	0	0	Jul	0	0	2
Feb	0	0	0	Aug	1	0	0
Mar	0	0	1	Sep	0	1	1
Apr	0	0	0	Oct	0	0	1
May	0	1	0	Nov	0	0	0
Jun	2	3	3	Dec	0	0	0
				Total	3	5	8

Average revenues per contract:

1988	$34,933
1987	32,872
1986	33,107

Forecast:

Month	Contracts	Average	Total
Jan	0	$ --	$ 0
Feb	0	--	0
Mar	0	--	0
Apr	0	--	0
May	0	--	0
Jun	2	34,000	68,000
Jul	0	--	0
Aug	0	--	0
Sep	0	--	0
Oct	0	--	0
Nov	0	--	0
Dec	0	--	0
Total	**2**		**$68,000**

III - Combined forecast

Month	Revenue	Month	Revenue
Jan	$19,000	Jul	$ 86,400
Feb	47,500	Aug	144,000
Mar	19,000	Sep	115,200
Apr	38,000	Oct	105,600
May	57,000	Nov	86,400
Jun	144,000	Dec	48,000
		Total	**$910,100**

B: Direct Costs

Assumptions:

We have been able to reduce the percentage of direct costs through improved scheduling and control of direct labor. We believe the current level of 58% is reasonable, and can be maintained with increased volume.

Higher labor costs are associated with commercial work. As we will be emphasizing residential contracts in the future, we believe our budget for direct costs is realistic and attainable.

Historical summary:

Year	Labor	Percent of sales Materials	Other	Total
1988	27%	28%	3%	58%
1987	29	28	3	60
1986	30	28	3	61
Budget:				
1989	27%	28%	3%	58%

Monthly dollar amounts:

Month	Labor	Materials	Other	Total
Jan	$ 5,130	$ 5,320	$ 570	$ 11,020
Feb	12,825	13,300	1,425	27,550
Mar	5,130	5,320	570	11,020
Apr	10,260	10,640	1,140	22,040
May	15,390	15,960	1,710	33,060
Jun	38,880	40,320	4,320	83,520
Jul	23,328	24,192	2,592	50,112
Aug	38,880	40,320	4,320	83,520
Sep	31,104	32,256	3,456	66,816
Oct	28,512	29,568	3,168	61,248
Nov	23,328	24,192	2,592	50,112
Dec	12,960	13,440	1,440	27,840
Total	$245,727	$254,828	$27,303	$527,858

C: Salaries and Wages

Assumptions:

It will not be necessary to add additional administrative personnel during the coming year.
Increases in salaries will occur on employment anniversary dates, as follows:

10% increase for the owner in July

10% increase for the estimator in May

5% increase for the bookkeeper in April

5% increase for clerical employee in September

1988 salary levels:

Owner	(1)	$ 84,000
Bookkeeper	(2)	16,000
Clerical (hourly)	(3)	9,540
Estimator	(4)	27,625
Total		**$137,165**

Budget:

Month	1	2	3	4	Total
Jan	$ 7,000	$ 1,333	$ 750	$ 2,300	$ 11,383
Feb	7,000	1,333	750	2,300	11,383
Mar	7,000	1,333	750	2,300	11,383
Apr	7,000	1,400	750	2,300	11,450
May	7,000	1,400	750	2,530	11,680
Jun	7,000	1,400	750	2,530	11,680
Jul	7,700	1,400	750	2,530	12,380
Aug	7,700	1,400	750	2,530	12,380
Sep	7,700	1,400	788	2,530	12,418
Oct	7,700	1,400	788	2,530	12,418
Nov	7,700	1,400	788	2,530	12,418
Dec	7,700	1,400	788	2,530	12,418
Total	**$88,200**	**$16,599**	**$9,152**	**$29,440**	**$143,391**

D: Payroll Taxes

Assumption:

Payroll taxes will average 11.3% of salaries and wages. (Note: payroll taxes for direct labor is included in cost of goods sold.)

Budget:

Month	Amount	Month	Amount
Jan	$ 1,286	Jul	$ 1,399
Feb	1,286	Aug	1,399
Mar	1,286	Sep	1,403
Apr	1,294	Oct	1,403
May	1,320	Nov	1,403
Jun	1,320	Dec	1,403
		Total	**$16,202**

E: Travel and Entertainment

Assumption:

There is no recurring need for extensive travel and entertainment expenses year-round. Between the months of April and August, the owner promotes for our high volume season, with local entertainment expenses and limited travel.

Budget:

Month	Amount	Month	Amount
Jan	$ 0	Jul	$1,000
Feb	0	Aug	500
Mar	0	Sep	0
Apr	1,000	Oct	0
May	1,000	Nov	0
Jun	1,500	Dec	0
		Total	**$5,000**

F: Transportation

Assumption:

We assume that approximately $4,000 will be spent this year on local transportation expenses. The budget is divided throughout the year on the same relative percentage as gross revenues.

Budget:

Month	Amount	Month	Amount
Jan	$ 85	Jul	$ 380
Feb	210	Aug	630
Mar	85	Sep	505
Apr	165	Oct	465
May	250	Nov	380
Jun	630	Dec	210
		Total	$3,995

G: Auto and Truck Expenses:

Assumption:

We believe that the year's total gas and oil expenses will total $4,500. The budget is broken down on the percentage basis of gross revenues.

Budget:

Month	Amount	Month	Amount
Jan	$ 95	Jul	$ 430
Feb	235	Aug	710
Mar	95	Sep	570
Apr	190	Oct	520
May	280	Nov	430
Jun	710	Dec	235
		Total	$4,500

H: Repairs and Maintenance:

Assumption:

This account is budgeted based on past levels of expenses, with an increase due to higher repair bills and expected increased usage.

Budget:

Month	Amount	Month	Amount
Jan	$ 600	Jul	$ 640
Feb	600	Aug	640
Mar	600	Sep	640
Apr	620	Oct	660
May	620	Nov	660
Jun	620	Dec	660
		Total	**$7,560**

I: Rent

Assumption:

Our present facility is adequate for the support staff, storage and other space needed for the next two to three years. The current lease continues beyond the year, and the budget is based upon that agreement.

Budget:

Month	Amount	Month	Amount
Jan	$ 900	Jul	$ 900
Feb	900	Aug	900
Mar	900	Sep	900
Apr	900	Oct	900
May	900	Nov	900
Jun	900	Dec	900
		Total	**$10,800**

J: Depreciation

Assumption:

This account is budgeted based on levels written off in prior years, and reduced to reflect the declining balance of allowable depreciation.

Depreciation expenses are booked in the last month of each quarter.

Budget:

Month	Amount	Month	Amount
Jan	$ 0	Jul	$ 0
Feb	0	Aug	0
Mar	4,000	Sep	4,000
Apr	0	Oct	0
May	0	Nov	0
Jun	4,000	Dec	4,000
		Total	$16,000

K: Insurance

Assumption:

We believe our annual insurance bill will total $9,300, and is due in June. However, we will budget for a monthly average cost, to reflect the approximate expense applicable to each period.

Budget:

Month	Amount	Month	Amount
Jan	$775	Jul	$775
Feb	775	Aug	775
Mar	775	Sep	775
Apr	775	Oct	775
May	775	Nov	775
Jun	775	Dec	775
		Total	$9,300

L: Interest

Assumption:

The current long-term note will continue amortization at the rate established by terms of our contract.
We believe no additional outside financing will be needed this year.

Budget:

Month	Amount	Month	Amount
Jan	$228	Jul	$216
Feb	226	Aug	214
Mar	224	Sep	211
Apr	222	Oct	209
May	220	Nov	207
Jun	218	Dec	205
		Total	$2,600

M: Dues and Subscriptions

Assumption:

This year's expense will consist of known commitments, to a trade association ($1,500), magazines, and one quarterly bill for a local association.

Budget:

Month	1	2	3	Total
Jan	$ 0	$ 35	$ 325	$ 360
Feb	0	25	0	25
Mar	0	48	0	48
Apr	0	0	325	325
May	0	0	0	0
Jun	1,500	16	0	1,516
Jul	0	45	325	370
Aug	0	0	0	0
Sep	0	0	0	0
Oct	0	0	320	325
Nov	0	55	0	55
Dec	0	106	0	106
Total	$1,500	$ 330	$1,300	$3,130

1 - annual membership
2 - magazine subscriptions
3 - quarterly membership

N: Office Supplies

Assumption:

This account includes printing, stationery and other related expenses. We assume that it can be held to no more than $400 per month.

Control problems in the past have been corrected by establishing an approval system for purchasing supplies and printing.

Budget:

Month	Amount	Month	Amount
Jan	$400	Jul	$400
Feb	400	Aug	400
Mar	400	Sep	400
Apr	400	Oct	400
May	400	Nov	400
Jun	400	Dec	400
		Total	**$4,800**

O: Telephone

Assumption:

Telephone usage has historically varied with the volume of gross income. The budget is divided on the percentage basis of revenue forecasts.

With the establishment of a phone log and monthly review, we believe total telephone expenses can be held to $5,300 for the year.

Budget:

Month	Amount	Month	Amount
Jan	$110	Jul	$503
Feb	277	Aug	839
Mar	110	Sep	671
Apr	221	Oct	615
May	332	Nov	503
Jun	839	Dec	280
		Total	**$5,300**

P: Utilities

Assumption:

Utilities have varied in the past by season. We expect higher billings during winter months, and have prepared the budget based on levels in past years.

Budget:

Month	Amount	Month	Amount
Jan	$205	Jul	$135
Feb	205	Aug	135
Mar	180	Sep	130
Apr	145	Oct	165
May	140	Nov	180
Jun	135	Dec	190
		Total	**$1,945**

Q: Postage and Delivery

Assumption:

Expenses have been reduced by establishing restrictions on the use of messenger and overnight delivery services without prior approval.

We believe this expense can be held down to $185 per month for the entire year.

Budget:

Month	Amount	Month	Amount
Jan	$185	Jul	$185
Feb	185	Aug	185
Mar	185	Sep	185
Apr	185	Oct	185
May	185	Nov	185
Jun	185	Dec	185
		Total	**$2,220**

R: Licenses and Fees

Assumption:

Our annual business license will cost $780 (due in February). Other licenses and fees will average $300 per month, based on historical records.

Budget:

Month	Amount	Month	Amount
Jan	$300	Jul	$300
Feb	1,080	Aug	300
Mar	300	Sep	300
Apr	300	Oct	300
May	300	Nov	300
Jun	300	Dec	300
		Total	$4,380

S: State and Local Taxes

Assumption:

State income tax estimates are due in January (previous year's liability), April, June and September. In addition other taxes average $85 per month (based on historical records.)

Budget:

Month	1	2	Total
Jan	$ 405	$ 85	$ 490
Feb	0	85	85
Mar	0	85	85
Apr	500	85	585
May	0	85	85
Jun	500	85	585
Jul	0	85	85
Aug	0	85	85
Sep	500	85	585
Oct	0	85	85
Nov	0	85	85
Dec	0	85	85
Total	$1,905	$1,020	$2,925

1 - state income tax deposits
2 - other taxes

T: Professional Fees
Assumption:

Accounting fees will involve tax preparation in March, and quarterly consulting that will average $300.

Legal fees will average $500 per quarter, with an additional $1,000 budgeted during our high volume season.

Budget:

Month	1	2	Total
Jan	$ 300	$ 0	$ 300
Feb	0	500	500
Mar	1,200	0	1,200
Apr	0	0	0
May	0	500	500
Jun	0	0	0
Jul	300	0	300
Aug	0	1,500	1,500
Sep	0	0	0
Oct	300	0	300
Nov	0	500	500
Dec	0	0	0
Total	**$2,100**	**$3,000**	**$5,100**

1 - accounting fees
2 - legal fees

U: Miscellaneous
Assumption:

Expenses below $1,000 for the year, or a non-recurring nature, average $325 per month.

Budget:

Month	Amount	Month	Amount
Jan	$325	Jul	$325
Feb	325	Aug	325
Mar	325	Sep	325
Apr	325	Oct	325
May	325	Nov	325
Jun	325	Dec	325
		Total	**$3,900**

V: Federal Income Taxes

Assumption:

The budget reflects 15% of net profits budgeted for the month. In months where a loss is budgeted, the provision for federal taxes is a negative.

Deposits are made based on estimated total net profits for the year, with one-fourth due in April, June, September and the following January. In January of this year, a final tax deposit will be made for the fourth portion of the past year's estimated liability.

Budget:

Month	Budget	Payments
Jan	$(1,507)	$ 2,543
Feb	188	0
Mar	(2,130)	0
Apr	(471)	4,118
May	694	0
Jun	5,076	4,118
Jul	2,335	0
Aug	5,784	0
Sep	3,655	4,118
Oct	3,645	0
Nov	2,487	0
Dec	(378)	0
Total	**$19,378**	

INDEX

OTHER PRACTICAL REFERENCES

Builder's Guide to Accounting Revised
Step-by-step, easy to follow guidelines for setting up and maintaining an efficient record keeping system for your building business. Not a book of theory, this practical, newly-revised guide to all accounting methods shows how to meet state and federal accounting requirements, including new depreciation rules, and explains what the tax reform act of 1986 can mean to your business. Full of charts, diagrams, blank forms, simple directions and examples. **304 pages, 8½ x 11, $17.25**

Builder's Office Manual Revised
Explains how to create routine ways of doing all the things that must be done in every construction office — in the minimum time, at the lowest cost, and with the least supervision possible: Organizing the office space, establishing effective procedures and forms, setting priorities and goals, finding and keeping an effective staff, getting the most from your record-keeping system (whether manual or computerized). Loaded with practical tips, charts and sample forms for your use. **192 pages, 8½ x 11, $15.50**

Contractor's Year-Round Tax Guide
How to set up and run your construction business to minimize taxes: corporate tax strategy and how to use it to your advantage, and what you should be aware of in contracts with others. Covers tax shelters for builders, write-offs and investments that will reduce your taxes, accounting methods that are best for contractors, and what the I.R.S. allows and what it often questions. **192 pages, 8½ x 11, $16.50**

Contractor's Survival Manual
How to survive hard times in construction and take full advantage of the profitable cycles. Shows what to do when the bills can't be paid, finding money and buying time, transferring debt, and all the alternatives to bankruptcy. Explains how to build profits, avoid problems in zoning and permits, taxes, time-keeping, and payroll. Unconventional advice includes how to invest in inflation, get high appraisals, trade and postpone income, and how to stay hip-deep in profitable work. **160 pages, 8½ x 11, $16.75**

Builder's Guide to Construction Financing
Explains how and where to borrow the money to buy land and build homes and apartments: conventional loan sources, loan brokers, private lenders, purchase money loans, and federally insured loans. How to shop for financing, get the valuation you need, comply with lending requirements, and handle liens. **304 pages, 5½ x 8½, $11.00**

Computers: The Builder's New Tool
Shows how to avoid costly mistakes and find the right computer system for your needs. Takes you step-by-step through each important decision, from selecting the software to getting your equipment set up and operating. Filled with examples, checklists and illustrations, including case histories describing experiences other contractors have had. If you're thinking about putting a computer in your construction office, you should read this book before buying anything. **192 pages, 8½ x 11, $17.75**

Cost Records for Construction Estimating

How to organize and use cost information from jobs just completed to make more accurate estimates in the future. Explains how to keep the cost records you need to reflect the time spent on each part of the job. Shows the best way to track costs for sitework, footing, foundations, framing, interior finish, siding and trim, masonry, and subcontract expense. Provides sample forms. **208 pages, 8½ x 11, $15.75**

Construction Estimating Reference Data

Collected in this single volume are the building estimator's 300 most useful estimating reference tables. Labor requirements for nearly every type of construction are included: site work, concrete work, masonry, steel, carpentry, thermal & moisture protection, doors and windows, finishes, mechanical and electrical. Each section explains in detail the work being estimated and gives the appropriate crew size and equipment needed. **368 pages, 11 x 8½, $20.00**

National Construction Estimator

Current building costs in dollars and cents for residential, commercial and industrial construction. Prices for every commonly used building material, and the proper labor cost associated with installation of the material. Everything figured out to give you the "in place" cost in seconds. Many time-saving rules of thumb, waste and coverage factors and estimating tables are included. **528 pages, 8½ x 11, $18.50. Revised annually**

Building Cost Manual

Square foot costs for residential, commercial, industrial, and farm buildings. In a few minutes you work up a reliable budget estimate based on the actual materials and design features, area, shape, wall height, number of floors and support requirements. Most important, you include all the important variables that can make any building unique from a cost standpoint. **240 pages, 8½ x 11, $14.00. Revised annually**

Berger Building Cost File

Labor and material costs needed to estimate major projects: shopping centers and stores, hospitals, educational facilities, office complexes, industrial and institutional buildings, and housing projects. All cost estimates show both the manhours required and the typical crew needed so you can figure the price and schedule the work quickly and easily. **288 pages, 8½ x 11, $30.00. Revised annually**

Estimating Tables for Home Building

Produce accurate estimates in minutes for nearly any home or multi-family dwelling. This handy manual has the tables you need to find the quantity of materials and labor for most residential construction. Includes overhead and profit, how to develop unit costs for labor and materials and how to be sure you've considered every cost in the job. **336 pages, 8½ x 11, $21.50**

Electrical Construction Estimator

If you estimate electrical jobs, this is your guide to current material costs, reliable manhour estimates per unit, and the total installed cost for all common electrical work: conduit, wire, boxes, fixtures, switches, outlets, loadcenters, panelboards, raceway, duct, signal systems, and more. Explains what every estimator should know before estimating each part of an electrical system. **416 pages, 8½ x 11, $25.00. Revised annually**

Estimating Home Building Costs

Estimate every phase of residential construction from site costs to the profit margin you should include in your bid. Shows how to keep track of manhours and make accurate labor cost estimates for footings, foundations, framing and sheathing finishes, electrical, plumbing and more. Explains the work being estimated and provides sample cost estimate worksheets with complete instructions for each job phase. **320 pages, 5½ x 8½, $17.00**

Remodeler's Handbook

The complete manual of home improvement contracting: Planning the job, estimating costs, doing the work, running your company and making profits. Pages of sample forms, contracts, documents, clear illustrations and examples. Chapters on evaluating the work, rehabilitation, kitchens, bathrooms, adding living area, re-flooring, re-siding, re-roofing, replacing windows and doors, installing new wall and ceiling cover, re-painting, upgrading insulation, combating moisture damage, estimating, selling your services, and bookkeeping for remodelers. **416 pages, 8½ x 11, $18.50**

Manual of Professional Remodeling

This is the practical manual of professional remodeling written by an experienced and successful remodeling contractor. Shows how to evaluate a job and avoid 30-minute jobs that take all day, what to fix and what to leave alone, and what to watch for in dealing with subcontractors. Includes chapters on calculating space requirements, repairing structural defects, remodeling kitchens, baths, walls and ceilings, doors and windows, floors, roofs, installing fireplaces and chimneys (including built-ins), skylights, and exterior siding. Includes blank forms, checklists, sample contracts, and proposals you can copy and use. **400 pages, 8½ x 11, $18.75**

How to Sell Remodeling

Proven, effective sales methods for repair and remodeling contractors: finding qualified leads, making the sales call, identifying what your prospects really need, pricing the job, arranging financing, and closing the sale. Explains how to organize and staff a sales team, how to bring in the work to keep your crews busy and your business growing, and much more. Includes blank forms, tables, and charts. **240 pages, 8½ x 11, $17.50**

Paint Contractor's Manual

How to start and run a profitable paint contracting company: getting set up and organized to handle volume work, avoiding the mistakes most painters make, getting top production from your crews and the most value from your advertising dollar. Shows how to estimate all prep and painting. Loaded with manhour estimates, sample forms, contracts, charts, tables and examples you can use. **224 pages, 8½ x 11, $19.25**

Painter's Handbook

Loaded with "how-to" information you'll use every day to get professional results on any job: The best way to prepare a surface for painting or repainting. Selecting and using the right materials and tools (including airless spray). Tips for repainting kitchens, bathrooms, cabinets, eaves and porches. How to match and blend colors. Why coatings fail and what to do about it. Thirty profitable specialties that could be your gravy train in the painting business. Every professional painter needs this practical handbook. **320 pages, 8½ x 11, $21.25**

Carpentry Estimating

Simple, clear instructions show you how to take off quantities and figure costs for all rough and finish carpentry. Shows how much overhead and profit to include, how to convert piece prices to MBF prices or linear foot prices, and how to use the tables included to quickly estimate manhours. All carpentry is covered: floor joists, exterior and interior walls and finishes, ceiling joists and rafters, stairs, trim, windows, doors, and much more. Includes sample forms, checklists,and the author's factor worksheets to save you time and help prevent errors. **320 pages, 8½ x 11, $25.50**

Carpentry for Residential Construction

How to do professional quality carpentry work in homes and apartments. Illustrated instructions show you everything from setting batter boards to framing floors and walls, installing floor, wall and roof sheathing, and applying roofing. Covers finish carpentry, also: How to install each type of cornice, frieze, lookout, ledger, fascia and soffit; how to hang windows and doors; how to install siding, drywall and trim. Each job description includes the tools and materials needed, the estimated manhours required, and a step-by-step guide to each part of the task. **400 pages, 5½ x 8½, $19.75**

Drywall Contracting

How to do professional quality drywall work, how to plan and estimate each job, and how to start and keep your drywall business thriving. Covers the eight essential steps in making any drywall estimate, how to achieve the six most commonly-used surface treatments, how to work with metal studs, and how to solve and prevent most common drywall problems. **288 pages, 5½ x 8½, $18.25**

Carpentry in Commercial Construction

Covers forming, framing, exteriors, interior finish and cabinet installation in commercial buildings: designing and building concrete forms, selecting lumber dimensions, grades and species for the design load, what you should know when installing materials selected for their fire rating or sound transmission characteristics, and how to plan and organize the job to improve production. Loaded with illustrations, tables, charts and diagrams. **272 pages, 5½ x 8½, $19.00**

Roof Framing

Frame any type of roof in common use today, even if you've never framed a roof before. Shows how to use a pocket calculator to figure any common, hip, valley, and jack rafter length in seconds. Over 400 illustrations take you through every measurement and every cut on each type of roof: gable, hip, Dutch, Tudor, gambrel, shed, gazebo and more. **480 pages, 5½ x 8½, $22.00**

Video: Roof Framing 1

A complete step-by step training video on the basics of roof cutting by Marshall Gross, the author of the book **Roof Framing**. Shows and explains calculating rise, run, and pitch, and laying out and cutting common rafters. **90 minutes, VHS, $80.00**

Video: Roof Framing 2

A complete training video on the more advanced techniques of roof framing by Marshall Gross, the author of **Roof Framing,** shows and explains layout and framing an irregular roof, and making tie-ins to an existing roof. **90 minutes, VHS, $80.00**

Spec Builder's Guide

Explains how to plan and build a home, control your construction costs, and then sell the house at a price that earns a decent return on the time and money you've invested. Includes professional tips to ensure success as a spec builder: how government statistics help you judge the housing market, cutting costs at every opportunity without sacrificing quality, and taking advantage of construction cycles. Every chapter includes checklists, diagrams, charts, figures, and estimating tables. **448 pages, 8½ x 11, $24.00**

Contractor's Guide to the Building Code

Explains in plain English exactly what the Uniform Building Code requires and shows how to design and construct residential and light commercial buildings that will pass inspection the first time. Suggests how to work with the inspector to minimize construction costs, what common building short cuts are likely to be cited, and where exceptions are granted. **312 pages, 5½ x 8½, $16.25**

Easy-To-Use 10 Day Examination Cards

 Mail This No Risk Card Today

☐ Please send me the books checked for 10 days free examination. At the end of that time I will pay in full plus postage (& 6% tax in Calif.) or return the books postpaid and owe nothing.

☐ Enclosed is my full payment or Visa/MasterCard/American Express number. Please rush me the books without charging for postage.

☐ 17.25 Builder's Guide to Accounting Revised
☐ 11.00 Builder's Guide to Const. Financing
☐ 15.50 Builder's Office Manual Revised
☐ 17.75 Computers: The Builder's New Tool
☐ 16.75 Contractor's Survival Manual
☐ 16.50 Contractor's Year-Round Tax Guide
☐ 15.75 Cost Records for Const. Estimating
☐ 17.00 Estimating Home Building Costs
☐ 17.50 How to Sell Remodeling
☐ 18.50 National Construction Estimator

In a hurry?
We accept phone orders charged to your MasterCard, Visa or American Express.
Call (619) 438-7828

☐ Visa ☐ MasterCard ☐ American Express

Exp. date _____

Name (Please print clearly)

Company

Address

Card no.

City/State/Zip

cg&pg card

 Mail This No Risk Card Today

☐ Please send me the books checked for 10 days free examination. At the end of that time I will pay in full plus postage (& 6% tax in Calif.) or return the books postpaid and owe nothing.

☐ Enclosed is my full payment or Visa/MasterCard/American Express number. Please rush me the books without charging for postage.

☐ 17.25 Builder's Guide to Accounting Revised
☐ 11.00 Builder's Guide to Const. Financing
☐ 15.50 Builder's Office Manual Revised
☐ 17.75 Computers: The Builder's New Tool
☐ 16.75 Contractor's Survival Manual
☐ 16.50 Contractor's Year-Round Tax Guide
☐ 15.75 Cost Records for Const. Estimating
☐ 17.00 Estimating Home Building Costs
☐ 17.50 How to Sell Remodeling
☐ 18.50 National Construction Estimator

In a hurry?
We accept phone orders charged to your MasterCard, Visa or American Express.
Call (619) 438-7828

☐ Visa ☐ MasterCard ☐ American Express

Exp. date _____

Name (Please print clearly)

Company

Address

Card no.

City/State/Zip

cg&pg card

BUSINESS REPLY MAIL

FIRST CLASS MAIL   PERMIT NO.271   CARLSBAD, CA

POSTAGE WILL BE PAID BY ADDRESSEE

Craftsman Book Company
6058 Corte Del Cedro
P. O. Box 6500
Carlsbad, CA 92008—0992

NO POSTAGE
NECESSARY
IF MAILED
IN THE
UNITED STATES

BUSINESS REPLY MAIL

FIRST CLASS MAIL   PERMIT NO.271   CARLSBAD, CA

POSTAGE WILL BE PAID BY ADDRESSEE

Craftsman Book Company
6058 Corte Del Cedro
P. O. Box 6500
Carlsbad, CA 92008—0992